Goo(

Jonathan Clatworthy is an Anglican priest with parish experience in Manchester, Sheffield, and now Staffordshire. His academic qualifications include a first degree from the University of Cardiff, and a Diploma in Social Administration and an M Phil in Theology from Manchester University.

He has been a council member of the Modern Churchpeople's Union since 1991, when he also founded the journal *Theology in Green* (now published as *Ecotheology* by Sheffield Academic Press).

Good God

Green Theology and the Value of Creation

Jonathan Clatworthy

Jon Carpenter

First published 1997 by Jon Carpenter Publishing,
The Spendlove Centre, Charlbury OX7 3PQ
☎ 01608 811969
Please write or phone for our catalogue

ISBN 1 897766 37 8

Printed and bound in England by J W Arrowsmith Ltd., Bristol

Contents

Acknowledgements

There are many people I would like to thank for their help. Tony Dyson, John Barton, Bruce Chilton, John Muddiman, Gerald Downing, Tim Belben, Russell Hand, Arthur Peacocke, Robin Attfield, Mary Grey, Ed Echlin and Dave Leal have all read part or all of it and offered helpful advice and encouragement. My wife Marguerite and Barry Mills did the proof reading. I would especially like to thank Tony Dyson for the training, advice and encouragement without which I would not have been able to embark on this project.

The biblical quotations are from the NRSV translation unless otherwise specified. I have aimed to use gender inclusive language, and for this reason I have often resorted to plurals where a gender inclusive singular would have been more accurate, if the English language had supplied one. I have used male pronouns of God only when referring to a specifically male God. I have used the capitalized 'God' when referring to a single supreme deity and the uncapitalized 'god' when referring to one of many gods.

Introduction

ONCE UPON A time there was an island where it rained every day. Everybody was so used to the rain that they considered it extreme bad manners to be seen in public without an umbrella.

But one day the Prime Minister caught a cold. Something had to be done, so the Government erected a glass shelter over the whole island to keep the rain off.

It was a momentous success. Within days everybody could see the advantages. Nobody got their shoes wet in the grass. People could plan outdoor parties and barbecues without fear of being rained off. The Prime Minister got better. But soon they noticed the disadvantages. Plants died. Rivers dried up. To offset the problems, the Government embarked on an even more ambitious project, to provide water pumps and desalination plants all over the island so that there would be enough water for everyone.

It was hard work and cost a huge amount of money. As time went by, the water table got lower and water technology needed to improve in step with it. Every year's new technology improved on the previous year, and the prospects of future development were the commonest subject of conversation. As the Government trumpeted its achievements, everybody agreed that the erection of the shelter was the most important event in the island's history. The calendar was changed to make New Year's Day, in Year 1, the day the shelter was completed. It was a worthy tribute. All the centuries before that time had been one long dark age, with virtually no water technology at all. Since then, the onward march of progress had gone from strength to strength.

After some years, the project was completed. Every part of the island had a desalination plant and provided that the water table did not get any lower, there would always be enough water for everybody.

But the island's rejoicing was brought to a sudden end. A group of disrespectful desalination workers turned up for work without their umbrellas. The incident made front page news. Umbrella manufacturers and church leaders sprang into action, campaigning against the decline in moral standards.

At the same time a leak appeared in the shelter. Water poured onto the ground. The Archbishop preached a sermon declaring that it was an act of God and warned the people against going out without their umbrellas. Those who lived near the leak were split into two camps. Some anarchists argued that water was just what the people needed. Others were horrified at the prospect of more colds. Some weeds grew. The views of the anarchists could not be allowed to prevail: if they were to spread, more people might ask for holes in the shelter and in no time the island would be plunged back into the Dark Ages. They were put to death. The Archbishop declared that their execution was a triumph for decency and moderation.

This story illustrates the theme of this book. It is about value judgements, how we justify them and which actions they lead us to perform. It is motivated by a conviction that the value judgements which dominate our society today are the wrong ones and are leading us to do the wrong things.

This is why I begin with an absurd story. Because we do not think that building a shelter over a whole island is a sensible response to a prime minister's cold, we remain unconvinced that it was a good idea. When the water shortages demand desalination plants, we can suggest an easier solution. When the days before desalination technology are despised as a dark age, we can point out that before the shelter was built there was no need for it. Because we do not share their value judgements, we can laugh at their actions.

When our own society does equally absurd things, we fail to notice the absurdities because we are caught up in its value judgements. Like the islanders, we work harder and harder to achieve the wrong objectives. When we fail, we try again. When we succeed, our success brings more problems and we apply the same mistaken methods to them too. The harder we work for them, the more committed we become to them and the more we have to convince ourselves that past ages must have been dreadful. Even when we are shown that our ideas cannot work, we keep believing that a solution will turn up.

There is no shortage of examples. We take pride in our modern technology, as it produces far more labour-saving devices than the world has ever known before. On the other hand we are as busy as ever. We take pride in our advances in farming methods, which mean more food is being produced than ever before and transported all round the world. On the other hand, as many as ever are starving. We take pride in our medical technology, as we cure more and more diseases. On the other hand, as many as ever are ill. We take pride in our information technology, which spreads news round the world in seconds. On the other hand, there are as many as ever who feel that their lives are empty and there is nothing to live for.

Our values, like the values of the islanders, are full of contradictions. But we do not laugh at them, because they are our own. Instead we live with the contradictions and accept them as normal. With our public values we applaud the new motorway; it will save travelling time and help the economy. With our private values we lament the new road widening; it will mean more pollution and noise and the neighbours' children will not be able to cross it on their own. With our public values we are pleased that the price of components is going down because of new technology; with our private values we feel sorry for our friend whose business is closing down because it cannot compete. With our public values we are pleased to hear that people are spending more money, because it helps get the country out of recession; with our private values we do not intend to waste our own money on things we do not need.

We are proud of our modern civilization because, it has been drummed into us, we have advanced much further than any previous age. On the other hand the crime rate, the suicide rate, drug addiction and alcoholism, homelessness and poverty, keep telling us that we have got our priorities very wrong. To add to all these, scientists now warn us that the world is finite and we cannot carry on demanding more and more from it. A whole range of crises loom, caused not by our failures but by our successes. Global warming, the ozone hole, acid rain, destruction of habitats and many others are shouting at us to stop doing all this damage. Most of us know that we are getting it wrong. But we are too lazy, or too self-interested, or too afraid, or too confused to face up to it. There are always ways to avoid the issue. Most of the time we respond just like the islanders, willing to discuss the technical details but unwilling to question our value judgements.

A great deal of public debate runs along the lines of a heated argument my son had with a friend at a young age. They were walking along the pavement with their mothers, pointing emphatically at different buildings, and the argument ran: 'That's where my Dad works', 'No, *that's* where *my* Dad works', 'No, *that's* where *my* Dad works' — and so on. Both were right! All too often, this is how our society responds to its crises. You point out that global warming is a serious threat; if present trends continue, the concentration of carbon dioxide in the atmosphere is expected to double every 50 years. I reply that experts often make mistakes: the 1990 Review of the Intergovernmental Panel on Climate Change estimated that carbon dioxide would double by 2025, but the 1992 Report estimated that doubling would not take place until 2050.[1] You point out that the thinning of the ozone layer is expected to increase sunburn, allergic reactions and skin cancer, and may even damage basic foundations of life, like DNA molecules and some proteins. I reply that we do not know how long is the time-lag between emitting CFCs and the thinning of the ozone layer, and the world is so complicated that scientists cannot possibly take every variable into account.[2]

So what are we disagreeing about? You accept my facts, I accept yours. Clearly, the real disagreement is about how to *respond*. The statistics on their own do not tell us, but our value judgements do. In this example, there is a disagreement about the value of the world's natural order and how it compares with the value of human technology. As long as we disagree about our value judgements, statistics are of little help.

Our value judgements do not appear from nowhere. Every society provides its members with methods for evaluating their lives and the world around them. Its methods are generally based on its traditions of *philosophy* and *theology*. These are the traditions, then, which this book will explore in order to analyse value judgements.

To suggest that philosophy, or even theology, might help us solve our disagreements about the crises of our age may seem absurd. We are used to thinking of them as irrelevant to ordinary life. But both philosophy and theology, at their best, aim to answer the deepest and most important questions of their age. I believe that the most pressing issues which confront us will not be resolved until we take a fresh look at them. I claim no expertise in philosophy, and in theology I confine myself to what is called the Judaeo-Christian tradition. This is my own, and although I hope my arguments are not exclusive to Christianity, I am not qualified to apply them elsewhere.

Evaluations of the world

Every society puzzles over the deepest questions of life. What is the purpose of life? Does it have any real value? Why is the world around us the way it is? The questions usually impose themselves on us as we try to make sense of our experience. Each of us feels the deepest emotions: pain when we are wounded, delight when we achieve a goal we have longed for. When we take part in a sexual relationship, or give birth to a baby, or lose somebody we love, our emotions are so strong that we cannot control them. The pleasure and pain, the joy and terror, make us feel our experiences have *significance* and *value* beyond anything we can describe. Yet, on the other hand, when they happen to somebody else and not to us, it is easy to dismiss them as unimportant. When we are old, we can look back on the passions of youth and wonder what all the fuss was about. When death comes, it may seem that all the meaning, all the significance, all the value which had once been so intense has come to nothing. So is the meaning of life, with all its richness, variety and excitement, just a mistake, a creation of the self-interested imagination? Or is there more to it?

These questions cannot be answered by science. Science relates the things we observe to laws of nature, through sequences of cause and effect. Most people, most of the time, need *evaluative* explanations more than scientific ones: that is, explanations which help us decide how to interpret, and respond to, the ups and downs of life. When our husband or wife dies, or has an affair with somebody else, or is murdered, we are not helped by medical or psychological text books which analyse the process of dying, or being sexually aroused, or killing. What does help us is the process of evaluation. We discuss our feelings with friends, argue about moral principles, read novels or watch soap operas. These activities help us to reflect on our experiences and evaluate them, so that in time we may conclude that 'God must have needed her in heaven', or 'Everybody is wife-swapping these days, so I should just accept it as normal', or 'I am not going to rest until the murderers have been brought to justice'.

We *feel* our experiences have value. What is this 'value'? When we reflect on the idea and try to justify it, we do not find it easy. Characteristically, when we say 'I value the car because it means I can visit my friends', or 'The doctor tells me that I shall never live without pain, but I must keep going because the family needs me', or 'My work is important because it helps the firm to be successful', in each case we are justifying the value of one thing by putting it within the context of something else, which we also value. In these examples we are justifying the value of car, life and work by appealing to the value of visits, the family and the firm.

But are *they* valuable? And if we justify *their* value by appealing to something else again, how far back do we go? The car is valuable because I can visit friends. Visiting friends is valuable because I enjoy their company and they enjoy mine. Enjoying other people's company is valuable because... how far back do we go? Do our *lives* have value? Does the *universe* have value? Or are they completely valueless, and are all our valuings mistakes, attempts to imagine that our actions have a quality which is not there?

Most of us, most of the time, do not think of these questions. Even so, we depend on them. When we make our day-to-day decisions, we all presuppose that what we are doing has some kind of value, and this in turn presupposes some kind of value judgement about our lives and the world. We inherit most of our evaluations from our society, often without noticing that we have them, but whether we notice them or not they are essential to our lives.

This is why, throughout history, humanity has puzzled over the value of life and the world. Most individuals, most of the time, deal in more immediate matters; but every *society* reflects on the deeper questions as a way of justifying the more day-to-day evaluations of its members.

I shall concentrate, then, on evaluation of 'the world', as the overarching value question which sets the framework for other evaluations. By 'the world' I do not necessarily mean planet Earth. As I discuss the theories of different societies, I shall refer to 'the world' as the total context within which each society understands itself to be living. For some, 'the world' consisted of a flood plain and not much else. For some, it meant a flat earth surrounded by layers of heavens, full of angels and demons. For many today, it means the physical universe together with a potentially infinite number of eternal laws of nature. For some, the most significant feature of life's context is the twin possibility of eternal bliss or damnation after death; I shall include this as well. In each case, what I am concerned to evaluate is the total context within which a society understands human life to be lived. Although 'the world' is not an accurate label for this total context, I cannot think of a better one.

I shall concentrate on judgements about the value of the world *for humans*, because this is how humans normally evaluate it. I am also concerned about the value of the world for animals, God and any other beings there may be; but where these evaluations differ from human ones, they raise specific questions which will be considered in their turn.

My basic categorization divides evaluations of the world into three types: we believe the world is either *good* or *evil* or *neutral*. The first two make strong, objective claims, that there is a truth about the world's value, over and above any use which we make of it, or any decision by a human community to count it as valuable. In the third type, there are no given answers. What we experience, in our bodies and the world around us, is just *there*, a valueless given, and if there are to be any values we must create our own.

How do we justify our value judgements? Characteristically, by *cosmologies*; that is, by theories of how and why the world was made. If we evaluate the world as good, we may believe that it was made as an act of love, by a God who also evaluates it as good. Most cosmologies of this type add that God deliberately intended to make it good. If we evaluate it as evil, we may believe that it was made by spiteful gods, or accidentally as the result of a quarrel between the gods. If we evaluate it as neutral, we may believe either that it was made by a god who does not care about it, or that it came about as a result of impersonal processes.

Evaluations, in turn, lead to practical implications. If we believe the world around us is evil, we shall feel led to have as little as possible to do with it. We shall seek out whatever is not evil and aspire to it: intellectual contemplation, perhaps, or the inner self, or life after death. Alternatively, if we believe the world around us is good, we shall give ourselves permission to enjoy it with a clear conscience. Or if we believe it is neutral, we shall feel that the onus is more squarely on us to make what we will of it.

Thus evaluations of the world are characteristically justified by cosmologies, and in turn justify agendas for human living. It is their links with cosmologies and agendas which gives them their importance: it is only when we can say 'The world is a good (or evil, or neutral) place *because it came about like this and has these characteristics*' that we can then go on to say 'Therefore I think we should do *this*'. Without these links, the evaluations cannot tell us what to do.

My analysis, then, is based on my three evaluations of the world: as good, evil or neutral. I shall refer to these respectively as 'optimistic', 'pessimistic' and 'neutralistic' theologies or philosophies. Part 1 will examine 'objective' evaluations, beliefs that the world is good or evil. Part 2 will explore the belief that it has no objective value. Part 3 will develop my own proposals. By opting for one particular type of evaluation, and explaining why I consider it a true account of the world's value, I hope to explain reality in a way which is more coherent than alternative theories and makes useful recommendations about what the human race today ought to do and refrain from doing.

1   K T Pickering and L A Owen, *An Introduction to Global Environmental Issues*, pp. 72, 80-81.
2   D D Kemp, *Global Environmental Issues: A Climatological Approach*, pp. 130-6.

PART 1

Chapter 1

The value of the world: myths and explanations

W E ALL MAKE value judgements. Without them, we would not know what to do. Life would have no sense of direction, no purpose, no distinction between right and wrong, between what is worth doing and what is not worth doing. Are these values simply expressions of the way we feel? Do we 'create our own values', and do they mean no more than we make them mean? Or is there a deeper truth behind them? In Part 1, I shall explore the theory that there is a truth about the value of the world, independently of the way we evaluate it. If there is such a truth, value is objective: it exists over and above our own opinions and provides a standard for judging whether our value judgements are right or wrong.

The value judgements which dominate our own society are often the hardest to notice, because we take them for granted as 'obvious' or 'common sense', and so do most people we meet. It is easier to spot them when we disagree with them. For this reason I shall begin, not with our own ideas, but far away with the myths of ancient and traditional societies, societies very different from our own. They will need some explanation, but once we have clarified how other people have made value judgements, it should be possible, later in the book, to compare our own ideas with theirs.

To go back in time to the people of ancient history and to study, of all things, their myths, may seem an odd way to shed light on the problems of modern society. But I believe it will. This chapter will show how myths evaluate the world and then look more closely at one particular tradition to see what evaluations it makes. I shall use the word 'myth' in its technical sense, not its popular sense. By describing a story as a myth I do not mean that it is untrue: I mean, rather, that it is a story about the gods. Whether it is true or not is another matter.

The evaluative power of myths

When the nineteenth century European explorers set out to study the religious stories of traditional tribes, they took with them their own presuppositions. Most archaeologists and anthropologists thought they knew what religion was about. Just as humanity had evolved, step by step, from the most primitive to the most advanced, they believed that religions had too. They treated the myths of traditional societies as earlier stages of evolution, the errors of those who had not yet progressed beyond the 'mythical' stage of development.

The evidence now shows that these myths had a practical importance which the nineteenth century researchers did not notice because they were too influenced by modern theories. Like modern science, myths attempt to *explain* the way things are. In addition, and unlike modern science, they attempt to answer those deeper questions, about meaning and value, which have always haunted human societies.

All over the world, researchers find the same questions cropping up in myths. Where do I come from? Where does my family, or tribe, come from? Why do people die? Are animals the same as us, or different? Why is childbirth so painful? Why do we find some things funny? Why do we get so much pleasure from the opposite sex? Why do people kill each other?[1] Often surprisingly similar stories appear in places so far distant that neither can have borrowed from the other; because human living throws up the same questions all over the world, different societies find the same answers independently.

Among myths, evaluations vary. Mortality, for example, is often described as a misfortune. In the ancient Sumerian *Epic of Gilgamesh*, the hero Gilgamesh goes on a long journey to ask about the secret of immortality. He is told to get a plant from the bottom of the sea. He succeeds, but on his way home he goes for a swim, leaving it unguarded, and a snake steals it. One is left with a despondent sense of regret — *if only* he had not gone for that swim, or the snake had not been there, things might have been so different![2]

We might compare this with an Indonesian myth. In the beginning, God hung his gifts on a cord for the first couple to take. One day he hung a stone on it, but the couple were surprised and indignant, and refused it. Some days later, God let the cord down again, this time with a banana. They immediately accepted the banana. Then they heard God's voice: 'Since you have chosen the banana, your life shall be like the life of that fruit. If you had chosen the stone, your life would have been like the existence of stone, unchangeable and immortal'.[3] Again, if they had acted differently they would have become immortal, but this time it is possible to evaluate mortality differently. By retelling the story, Indonesians cannot help but reflect that they still enjoy bananas more than stones! We value the things which live and die more than permanent and unchanging things. Who would really wish to be more like a stone than a banana? Perhaps mortality is not such a tragedy: it is a necessary part of a life which grows, develops and changes.

In this way, myths served a purpose which has little or no parallel in modern western religion. That purpose was all the more meaningful because they did not make a sharp distinction, as we do, between 'religious' matters and other matters. Because we make this distinction, whenever we come across stories which include gods or spirits, we tend to label them as 'religious' stories and do not expect them to say anything about what the world is like. That, to us, would be science, not religion.

Thus there are important differences between ancient mythological religions and modern western religion. In our society, we think of 'religion' as one part of our culture, separate from the other parts. This is unusual. True, our society has spread over all the world, taking its values to every community; but compared with other cultures, ancient and modern, we are the exceptions. To most people, throughout most of history, God or the gods related to the whole of life. Whatever theories they had about how the world began and what it is like, they expressed them in stories which, in our terms, would count as religious. Moreover, they were the only stories: there was no alternative, non-religious, description of the way things are.

Today religion is treated as a personal matter, mainly to do with the individual's private life and beliefs. Scientific hypotheses, on the other hand, are treated as public questions which can be debated openly. We have developed a sharp distinction between the 'public' sphere and the 'individual' or 'private' sphere. Most people, throughout most of history, have not treated their religious beliefs as being any more private, or personal, than their beliefs about the natural world.

Today, religious doctrines often have no practical purpose. For example, people may claim to be firm believers in the Virgin Birth, without ever considering what difference it makes, to the life of the world today, whether or not Mary was a virgin all that time ago. To this extent religious belief-statements have become ends in themselves — conversation pieces, or, like football scarves, labels of tribal loyalty. Traditional religions were clearer about the purpose of their beliefs; they explained the way things were, so as to help people understand how to relate to real life and cope with it.

Once we recognize these differences, we can see that ancient religion had the kind of explanatory value which is more akin to what we today expect from science, than to what we expect from religion. But the way it explained things was different.

Modern scientists tend to adopt the stance of independent, detached observers, looking away from themselves at something different from themselves. There is a sharp distinction between the observer and the observed. Quantum theory challenges it, but it is still very much with us. The ancients were more aware of themselves as part of the world they were exploring. To explain how the world functioned was to explain how they themselves functioned within it. The questions asked were the great questions about which people felt strongly. Characteristically, myths were the response not of curious speculation by comfortable and leisured people, but of societies which knew only too well that their survival depended on forces beyond their control. Faced with the reality of human life on earth with all its terror, fragility, beauty, joy and uncertainty, they asked: 'Why is life like *this*?'

Modern scientific studies are primarily concerned to ask *how* processes take place, in order to manipulate them. The ancients did that to some extent, but were far more concerned to ask *why* they take place, in order to evaluate them and cope with them. Once we recognize this difference, we can see that they were just as concerned to understand reality as we are, but their concerns covered a wider range than modern science does.

Modern scientific explanations exclude, as a matter of principle, all discussion of gods. To say that the universe was caused by an original big bang is, for us, a scientific explanation: to say it was created by God is not. More traditional societies, being more concerned to evaluate than to manipulate, have found that the best explanations are ones which relate to other evaluating beings, rather than to impersonal processes. Their stories and rituals therefore express the character of the gods and how we relate to them.[4]

Babylon

Let us now relate these generalizations to a particular culture. A good example is the religion of ancient Babylon. For a while the Babylonians controlled a vast empire centred on the Tigris and Euphrates valleys, now in Iraq. Early in the sixth century BC, they conquered Jerusalem and deported many leading Israelites to Babylon. While there, the exiles will have attended the New Year Festival and heard the Babylonian creation epic, the *Enuma Elis*, being publicly recited. They will have compared it with their own stories about the creation of the world, and they will have reflected on the differences.

In the beginning was chaos. Chaos had two principles, Apsu the fresh water ocean and Tiamat the salt water ocean, male and female respectively. The description reflects the flood plain, where fresh and salt water meet. According to the story, when the waters met other gods were born. In time conflict arose between the children and their parents. Eventually the children won. Ea, one of them, had a son, Marduk. The story continues with Tiamat, seeking her revenge, creating seven monsters to attack her children. The children did not dare to fight the monsters; instead they appealed to Marduk, who agreed to defend them — but on condition that he was appointed leader of the gods, with unlimited authority. They assented.

Marduk killed Tiamat and cut her in two. One half he placed in heaven as a protection against 'her water'; the other half was the ocean below. He then created the stars and humans, and perhaps the rest of creation as well — there is a gap in the text here. The leader of Tiamat's monsters was put to death, and humanity was created from his blood. The reason for creating humanity was quite instrumental: our task is to provide food and shelter for the gods in the form of sacrifices and a temple.

> Blood I will mass and cause bones to be.
> I will establish a savage, 'man' shall be his name.
> Verily, savage-man I will create.
> He shall be charged with the service of the gods
> That they might be at ease![5]

This account speaks volumes about how the Babylonians understood their relationship to the gods and the world. Humanity has been created to provide for the gods. There is no sense in which the world is intended to be an ideal habitat for us. Provided we survive, and can offer sacrifices, that is all the gods care about. Apart from our religious duty, we can make what we like of our lives.

Babylonian literature confirms this attitude often enough. In worship, the gods are often highly praised. But there is self-interest behind it: they have power and need to be kept sweet. Demons abound, performing acts of spite and causing illness. It is the skill of the priest to know which demon causes which illness and heal the patient by incantation or prayer. An incantation against toothache has survived: it contains a mythical introduction about the worm which caused the pain, a command to pull out the tooth and a prayer to the god Ea to smite the worm.[6]

If we ask why the gods permit so much human suffering, the answer is that they do not care much about us. The story of the flood, in the *Epic of Gilgamesh,* is a good illustration. Utnapishtim, the Babylonian equivalent of Noah, describes it:

> In those days the world teemed, the people multiplied, the world bellowed like a wild bull, and the great god was aroused by the clamour. Enlil heard the clamour and he said to the gods in council, 'The uproar of mankind is intolerable and sleep is no longer possible by reason of the babel'. So the gods in their hearts were moved to let loose the deluge; but my lord Ea warned me in a dream. He whispered their words to my house of reeds, 'Reed-house, reed-house! Wall, O Wall, hearken reed-house, wall reflect; O man of Shurrapak, son of Ubara-Tutu; tear down your house and build a boat...'[7]

When the rain came the gods themselves panicked. On the seventh day the storm died down and the ship stuck on Mount Niris, in Urartu, the biblical Ararat. After a few days Utnapishtim sent out a dove and a swallow, each of which returned, and then a raven which did not. Utnapishtim left the ship and made a sacrifice. The gods, recognizing the smell, 'gathered like flies' around him![8]

Thus the gods were quite willing to wipe out the human race because of the noise; but one of them enabled us to survive. In the end the gods were pleased, but only out of self-interest.

If our present life is unsatisfactory, life after death is worse. Not much is said about the fate of the dead, but the descriptions we have are all gloomy.[9] In an incomplete tablet of the *Epic of Gilgamesh*, Gilgamesh calls up the spirit of his dead friend and asks him about the land of the dead. The friend replies 'I do not want to tell, for if I do so, you will sit down and weep'. From the text we have, it seems that the worst fate awaits those who were not properly buried, or whose graves are not properly tended, but nobody's fate was a happy one.[10]

Evaluative stance

This was one society's account of reality. Let us now consider what it says about the value of the world.

The story begins on an impersonal note. In the beginning there was just chaos, represented by the waters. There was no initial, or overriding, purpose. One thing led to another, and the result was the creation of the gods, and eventually our world. As far as we know, the Babylonians did not speculate about the laws of nature: what happened was *chance*. The objective truth about the value of the world, then, is that it has no objective value or disvalue: it just happens to have developed this way. In terms of my categories, it is a neutralistic theory.

The gods do evaluate. They have purposes, ideas and values. But they evaluate *within the context of an objectively valueless world*. The gods disagree with each other: most praise Marduk for his creation, but there is no sense in which Tiamat is wrong to despise it. Even if the gods had been unanimous about the goodness of the world, it would be their evaluation, from their point of view, not an objective truth.

There is a parallel here with modern moral philosophy. Theologians have often appealed to God as the final judge of right and wrong. If God says a particular act is wrong, wrong it is. Many philosophers reply that even if we knew with certainty what God's moral rules are, they would only be *God's* moral rules. We would still have to decide on other grounds whether God was right. I shall return to this argument later; here, clearly, it is justified. For both modern secularism and ancient Babylon, the world has no objective value. Even gods, if they evaluate the world as good or evil, are making no more than a personal assessment from their own point of view.

To the gods, the world has *instrumental* value. Philosophers distinguish between two kinds of value, 'intrinsic' and 'instrumental'. Something with intrinsic value has value in and for itself. Something with instrumental value helps us achieve some other value. If music has intrinsic value, the piano has instrumental value. Similarly, for the Babylonian gods, the world has instrumental value in that humans provide them with food and shelter, but that is all.

This leaves humans free to make our own value judgements about the world, without any obligation to agree with the gods. But on this point ancient Babylon differs from modern neutralism. Whereas modern neutralists usually argue that *individual* humans are free to make their own evaluations, in ancient Babylon it was humanity as a whole which responded in its own characteristic way. Everybody dislikes floods and droughts, but enjoys a big harvest. On this basis, it was possible to make judgements about what the world is like for humanity as a whole. We may describe the main points as follows.

The created order has been designed to provide for the gods. Human life depends on it and would be impossible without it. In this sense we have no option but to welcome it. At the same time much of it, like illness and flooding, is unpleasant. There is nothing we can do about these things: this is the way the gods have made the world, and it suits *their* purposes well enough. We cannot change the way things are; we have to accept the tragedies of life fatalistically.

The world order is the work, not of all the gods working in harmony, but of one particular god. Politically, this justifies the domination of Babylon over other cities. Since order is the result of conflict, there remain other gods, awaiting their opportunity to wreak their revenge. In theory the created order could be swept away at any stage, either by a power struggle between the gods or by Marduk's decree. We today, brought up to think that the created order depends on unchanging laws of nature, do not share their sense of insecurity. To appreciate it, we might imagine what it would be like if scientists discovered that the sun was burning out, and life on earth could easily end any day!

As for our relationship with the gods, we have been created with a specific task: to provide them with food and accommodation. That the purpose of human life should be presented in such blunt and material terms leaves the situation clear. Within the insecure, threatened world governed by self-interested scheming gods, humanity has negotiating leverage. Because the gods want their sacrifices and temples, they depend to some extent on humans. This gives us some self-respect and a reason for supposing that, other things being equal, the gods will maintain order. But the balance of power remains one-sided. They can wreak massive destruction if offended. The system is also a tool of political oppression: the farmers, however poor they are, must keep bringing their sacrificial gifts to the priests at the temple, or the entire created order may revert to chaos.

Apart from maintaining the temple and offering sacrifices, the gods do not provide purposes for human life. Particular gods may develop an interest in particular people for particular reasons, but the well-being of humanity in general does not concern them. As long as we keep burning the sacrifices, what we do the rest of the time is our own affair. They sanction neither moral theory nor political programme: if we develop them, we do so for our own reasons.

Perhaps the most gloomy part of the picture was the belief about life after death. After all, what could they expect? Once they were dead, the gods had no more use for them. It may have been pure mischance which deprived us of immortality, but there was no reason to suppose that anything would be done about it. There was simply no alternative to accepting our tragic lot.

To summarize, then, in the Babylonian system the fundamental evaluation of the world is neutralistic. Objectively, the world as a whole is neither good nor evil. Within this neutralistic framework, gods and humans interact and develop their own evaluations. Humanity experiences the world in its own characteristic way, and on this basis we can say that *from the human perspective* the created order can be evaluated as partly good and partly evil. The gloomy features of the world order tend to dominate over the better ones. Both good and evil features are imposed by the gods for their own purposes; humanity cannot do anything to change them.

We can see in this example how the cosmology — the account of how and why the world was made — leads to the evaluation. The world was created as the result of self-interested gods interacting with each other. There is no overriding purpose, or even an overall authority on the way things ought to be. This cosmology produces a variety of conflicting evaluations. Gods and humans alike respond to situations which are not of their own making, each in his or her self-interested way. Nobody expects them to do otherwise, because there is no supreme standard of right and wrong: each evaluation is just as legitimate as any other. As a result there cannot be any way of resolving the conflicts. There is a characteristic way in which humans evaluate the world — overall, a gloomy one, though with redeeming features — but this evaluation is in no sense objectively true. It simply expresses the normal human experience of life.

We can also see how the evaluation leads in turn to the agenda. The task of human life is to provide for the gods. That done, we live a directionless life in a static environment, enjoying the good things when they come and fatalistically accepting the bad things.

We need not assume that every Babylonian accepted every detail of this account, any more than every British person today agrees with the dominant value systems of our society. But this was the establishment's picture of reality and it will no doubt have influenced every area of Babylonian society with its gloomy and fatalistic mood.

It did not suit everyone, as we shall see in the next chapter.

1   C Westermann, *Genesis 1-11*, pp. 4-6, 22.
2   N K Sandars trans., *The Epic of Gilgamesh*, p. 114.
3   M Eliade, *A History of Religious Ideas, Volume 1: From the Stone Age to the Eleusinian Mysteries*, pp. 115-6.
4   C Westermann, *Genesis 1-11*, pp. 20f.
5   *Enuma Elis* 6.5-8, J O'Brien and W Major, *In the Beginning: Creation Myths from Ancient Mesopotamia, Israel and Greece*, p. 25.
6   H Ringgren, *Religions of the Ancient Near East*, pp. 89-99.
7   N K Sandars trans., *The Epic of Gilgamesh*, p. 105.
8   N K Sandars trans., *The Epic of Gilgamesh*, pp. 105-8.
9   H Ringgren, *Religions of the Ancient Near East*, pp. 121-3.
10   H Ringgren, *Religions of the Ancient Near East*, p. 122.

Chapter 2

A good world created by a good God

IF THE BABYLONIANS had a gloomy attitude to life, the exiles from Jerusalem were very different. We can imagine them attending the New Year Festival at Babylon, hearing the priests recite the *Enuma Elis* with its story of creation, and disapproving of what they heard. They — or, at least, those we know about — stood out against it, became a minority ghetto in a foreign land and set about preserving and editing the scriptures of their own tradition.

Scholars believe that a large part of what we now call the Old Testament was written or edited by these people. Since we do not know their names, they are called 'the Priestly source', or 'P'. As we would expect, they emphasized the parts of Israelite religion which were different from Babylonian.

In this way the nearest Hebrew equivalent to the Babylonian Creation Epic, the first eleven chapters of Genesis, were set in their present form. In this chapter I shall describe what I mean by 'optimistic theology' and these chapters from Genesis will provide a basis.

There are so many different theories about how to interpret the bible that I ought to state my position at the beginning. I believe it has been created by human reflection on the nature of reality, not by a divine intervention which by-passed it. To understand what the authors meant, it helps if we know something about the context within which they were writing. In the case of Genesis 1-11 an important part of the context was the reaction against Babylon. When the text disagrees with Babylonian texts, it is likely that the authors meant to disagree and meant it strongly. When it does not, they may well have been passing on ideas which they had not questioned, or were not important to them. The task facing their successors today is to build on their insights by contributing our own, while recognizing that they were capable of error just as we are. In order to draw out the significance of the text, I have aimed to follow the consensus of modern scholarship,[1] though the way I apply it to the purpose of this book is, of course, mine.

Genesis and creation

The first section, Genesis 1:1-2:4a, describes how God created the world. Its style suggests that it was used in worship. If so, it will have been not merely committed to writing, but regularly affirmed in public worship at the second Jerusalem temple.

Creation as intended

> In the beginning when God created the heavens and the earth, the earth was a formless void and darkness covered the face of the deep, while a wind from God swept over the face of the waters. Then God said, 'Let there be light'; and there was light (Genesis 1:1-3).

The Babylonian version took a long time to get to this point. The first half of the *Enuma Elis* describes all the interactions between the gods before anything at all is created. Here in Genesis, the very first thing that happens is that God creates. Before then, there is nothing to report.[2] There is no hint of an alternative outcome if God had been less powerful, or if different gods had had their way. God is *omnipotent*. Nor is there any possibility that God could have made a mistake, or acted out of ignorance. God is *omniscient*. The text emphasizes the point: on each of the six days of creation, at least once — sometimes twice — God decrees an act of creation, and it gets done. The usual refrain is 'God said… And it was so.'

The contrast with the *Enuma Elis* could not have been sharper. The quarrels between the gods, their fickleness, their lack of interest in humanity, or at best their use of humanity purely for their own ends — all these traditional beliefs, which taught the human mind to treat life as fragile and uncertain, were edited out by one of the longest red pens of history. There is only one God, and the way things are is the way God *intended*. God accepts absolute responsibility for creation.

The key theological point is divine *harmony* rather than the existence of only one God. Other divine creatures appear in some later Old Testament texts, but with one exception[3] they do not threaten the monotheist character of Hebrew religion, because they have been robbed of their independence. There is no possibility of God's plans ever going wrong. The created order is *secure*.

Modern Christians have often interpreted the text as a scientific account of *how* God made the world. Was it really made in six days? How could there have been light before the sun and stars had been created? Questions like this have had a long innings and many have concluded that Genesis is simply wrong. We can now appreciate what it is really saying. Of course, the authors of Genesis 1 will have believed that the world is flat and the sky sits over it like an inverted basin. On these points they agreed with the Babylonians. In their day there was little reason to question them. What they positively taught was not that God made *a flat world* but that the flat world was made *by this God*.

Creation as good

And God saw that it was good (Gen 1:10, 12, 18, 25; cf. 1.4 & 31).

God's creating was not only successful, but good. The statement in effect occurs six times in Genesis 1. We can imagine the worshippers in the temple at Jerusalem, using words which repeat the main message over and over again, like the chorus of a hymn: God made the world *good*. It is another contrast with Babylonian religion. To the characteristics of the created order we can add *value*.

What does it mean to describe the world as good? Modern philosophy challenges value judgements of this type on a number of counts.

(a) Good for what purpose? Many philosophers today, like the ancient Babylonians, deny that there is any absolute truth about value judgements. They argue that the goodness of a thing can only be meaningful when related to a particular purpose.

(b) Good for whom? From whose point of view? Again like the Babylonians, many philosophers today argue that goodness is relative to a particular point of view; for example, high prices are good for sellers but bad for buyers.

(c) What is the status of the value judgement? Philosophers often argue that it is never possible to derive a value from a fact. It follows that all theories about who made the world, and for what purpose, are irrelevant: it is open to us to evaluate it in whatever way we will.

Being a response to Babylonian religion, Genesis 1 replies to these questions. The reply has been the foundation stone of the massive theological structures of Judaism, Christianity and Islam through the centuries. Usually it is summarized in the claim that there is one God who is *omnipotent*, *omniscient* and *good*.

On this basis, the answer to (a) is that God's purposes are supreme and are the standard by which all other purposes are judged. Other purposes are legitimate if they reflect God's purposes. The answer to (b) is that true goodness does not benefit one person at the expense of another. God the good creator has seen to it that true harmony, to the benefit of all, is possible. The answer to (c) is that God's evaluative judgement is so far superior to ours that, even though we have the freedom to make different value judgements, it makes no sense to do so. If we disagree with God we are certain to be wrong.

Because God intended the world to be good for humanity, people who find fault with it are criticizing God. We might compare a group of children playing in a forest or a playgroup. In the forest, they find much to enjoy, but the owners did not plant the trees specifically for that purpose. If the children decide that the forest is less fun than the forest they played in last Saturday, the owner will not feel disappointed. But it is different at the playgroup, where everything has been designed to be a good experience for the children. If they go home from the playgroup saying it was not as good as the one they were at last Saturday, the organizers may well feel disappointed. Similarly the Hebrew God, unlike Marduk, intends the world to be a good one; if we disagree, we are criticizing God.[4]

Thus P tells us not only that the world is good, but that its goodness is *objectively* true. This objective nature of the evaluation is only possible within P's tightly defined theory of God. If we deny God's omnipotence, perhaps God would have preferred to create a different world but was unable to. If we deny God's omniscience, perhaps there are mistakes. If we deny God's goodness, perhaps the order of creation is not intended to be in our interests. By affirming that God is completely omnipotent, omniscient and good, P closes all the loopholes. The world really is good and anybody who denies its goodness is simply wrong.

Genesis and the problem of evil

The first chapter of Genesis, then, is a ringing declaration that God is omnipotent, omniscient and good and has created a good world. It was a matter of debate even then, and has been ever since. The biggest problem is: where does evil come from?

It is an obvious question. We should not be surprised that P immediately sets out to answer it. Given the starting point, three types of answer are theoretically possible. One is to deny God's omnipotence or omniscience or goodness, and conclude that evil has been created by evil gods, or by mistake, or by God's evil intention. These possibilities are still debated today.[5] I shall return to them in the next chapter. Genesis rejects them, because they undermine its distinctive account of reality.

The second possible answer is that evil does not really exist: everything in the world, and every event, is good and should be welcomed without reserve. This view is usually associated with pantheists. Others find it counter-productive. It leads us to question our own experience of life. When we endure great tragedy or suffering, to be told that it is 'good, really' only helps us if the reason why it is good shows us how to overcome it. If pain is caused because we ate too much, the answer is to stop eating. But if *everything* is good, not for any purpose but in itself, then pain must be welcomed for its own sake. This does not help us cope. Rather, it sets us against the way things are and leads us to conclude that our personal interests are opposed to the universal good. As long as our bodies are telling us that pain is *not* welcome, 'the good' comes to be 'that to which I am opposed'. This position turns out, in practical effect, to be much the same as the Babylonian position: we are obliged to accept, fatalistically, whatever unpleasant experiences befall us.

The third possibility is P's. Evil is real. The possibility of evil, though not its actuality, is part of God's good provision and humanity has the power to overcome it. This theory affirms the goodness of life more strongly than the alternatives: it takes our unpleasant experiences seriously but affirms that we can do something to overcome them.

For P, evil is caused by human sin. However, Christians have interpreted this doctrine in different ways and we need to avoid confusing them. *Sin* depends on *free will* to choose between good and evil, and P tells us that the gift of freedom is *part of* creation's goodness. The doctrine of the *fall*, which has so often been read into Genesis, is based on a quite different theory — that the world was originally perfect but it lost its perfection at a particular point in time. Modern Christians often fail to distinguish between the two, and even refer to humanity as 'fallen' when all they mean is that we are 'sinful'. In fact the doctrine of the fall occurs neither in Genesis nor anywhere in the Old Testament. To justify it, one has to believe either that God is not omnipotent and the plans went wrong, or that God deliberately caused evil by permitting Satan to lead Adam and Eve astray. P will have none of it. By putting the goodness of creation at the beginning of the story, P asserts that everything takes place within the context of God's good creation.[6]

If the world has been made good, and if this includes being good for humans, why should we ever sin? It will not do to say that God deliberately created us in such a way that we are bound to sin: if so, God would have deliberately created evil as well as good, and this divinely created evil would be inescapable. On the other hand, to say that we promote our own interests by sinning would imply that the means to human fulfilment are in conflict with God's intentions for our lives. We would have to conclude that God did not want us to be fulfilled, and this would make God less than good.

The answer must be that we misuse features of life which are themselves good. What are these features and why do we misuse them? In the second chapter of Genesis, P describes four: freedom, law, creativity and desire. Without law, the exercise of freedom never becomes sinful; without freedom, we cannot disobey; and without creativity and desire, there is no motivation to disobey.

Freedom

> The Lord God commanded the man, 'You may freely eat of every tree in the garden...' (Gen 2:16).

On its own, divine omnipotence suffocates. One of the commonest criticisms of the omnipotent God of 'classical' Christian doctrine is that it seems to leave no space for human freedom. If God controls everything, there is no room for us to develop in our own ways. P, however, affirms first that God has total control and then that God deliberately withdraws from it in order to provide us with genuine freedom. This withdrawal is an act of goodness because our freedom is a blessing. However it means there are two poles to God's omnipotence. In the first instance, it is absolute. It is not limited in the sense that God might have created a completely different world but was unable to do so. Such an absolute limitation was affirmed by Plato, as I shall note in Chapter 3, and is affirmed today, among others, by process theologians.[7] In the second instance, God's power is shared with humanity. This means it is only limited to the extent that God has chosen to withdraw from total control. There is no sense in which God and humanity are joint victims of 'the way things are': God lacks power only to the extent that it is good for us that we should share it.

Law

> ...but of the tree of the knowledge of good and evil you shall not eat (Gen 2:17).

A different criticism of 'classical' Christian theology is that God is so self-sufficient as to need nothing from us. The view was most clearly expressed by Aristotle who believed that God, being perfect, does not think about anything imperfect and therefore spends eternity contemplating himself.[8] P says no such thing. Whereas for Aristotle divine perfection had a static quality about it, for P God's goodness involves relating to others.

Does this mean God 'needs' humans? If so, Aristotelians can argue that such a God is neither self-sufficient nor omnipotent. However I do not think we need to go this far. Love, which is a positive, desirable experience, involves relating to other people. Just as God is absolutely omnipotent in the first instance but withdraws from absolute omnipotence, we can also understand the idea that God is self-sufficient in the first instance but, as an act of goodness, chooses to relate to us in such a way that the relationship matters to God as well as to us. An obvious analogy is the relationship of a mother and baby. The mother can live without the baby and does not need anything the baby gives her. On the other hand, it is characteristic of the good, self-sufficient mother that she desires to pour herself out in love to a baby of her own.

Law, then, expresses the fact that God cares about us. We have been given freedom and it matters what we do with it.

This does not mean that God stacks the odds against us using our freedom well. Public debates on morality are often oppressive. All too often people invoke an angry God who presents us with long lists of things we should not do and commands us to walk in the narrow way. We end up feeling that every time we have the opportunity to choose between different actions, all except one are immoral. To please God, it would seem, we must sacrifice our freedom. This passage is quite different. It is not that the garden is full of forbidden trees but there is one from which

Adam may eat; rather, all the trees except one are permitted. The world is full of possibilities, but there are limits to what we ought to do.

Creativity

> Out of the ground the Lord God formed every animal of the field and every bird of the air, and brought them to the man to see what he would call them; and whatever the man called every living creature, that was its name (Gen 2:19).

Like every parent of a young child, God takes a piece of mud, makes it into the shape of an animal and asks 'What shall we call this one?' When Adam offers a suggestion, that is its name. Good parents withhold their own ideas and encourage their child's creativity. So also God withdraws from total control and gives humanity space to express itself in freedom.

Desire

> The rib that the Lord God had taken from the man he made into a woman and brought her to the man. Then the man said, 'This at last is bone of my bones and flesh of my flesh; this one shall be called Woman, for out of Man this one was taken' (Gen 2:22f).

Western Christianity is so full of negative attitudes to sexuality that it is difficult to read this text without expecting something to be wrong. There is nothing wrong. The Hebrew text uses words of intense excitement. The strength of delight in the opposite sex, the bonds of passion, the joy of sexual activity and even the shameless enjoyment of the other person's naked body, are all parts of the good creation.

Now, the necessary ingredients for sin are all in place: freedom, law, creativity and desire. Each of them has been given by God and in itself is a good, enriching element of life. Between them they make it possible to sin, but they do not oblige us to sin. Why, in God's good world, do people turn these good gifts to evil?

Temptation

> Now the serpent was more crafty than any other wild animal that the Lord God had made. He said to the woman, 'Did God say, "You shall not eat from any tree in the garden"?' The woman said to the serpent, 'We may eat of the fruit of the trees in the garden; but God

said, "You shall not eat of the fruit of the tree that is in the middle of the garden, nor shall you touch it, or you shall die."' But the serpent said to the woman, 'You will not die; for God knows that when you eat of it your eyes will be opened, and you will be like God, knowing good and evil' (Gen 3:1-5).

The story knows of no devil. In such a fiercely monotheistic text, how could it? Temptation comes from a serpent, nothing more.[9] This story, like the others, is describing what life is like. The serpent represents the created order. All over the world it is ordinary, God-given, good parts of creation which tempt people to exceed the limits God has set. There is no unforeseen trickery, no conspiracy against the human race. Temptation and sin are to do with ordinary people with their ordinary desires in ordinary circumstances faced with choices. The dice are not loaded against us. Human responsibility is for real.

Sin

So when the woman saw that the tree was good for food, and that it was a delight to the eyes, and that the tree was to be desired to make one wise, she took of its fruit and ate (Gen 3:6).

Eve has been denounced through the ages, but the text itself has every sympathy for her. She saw that it was good for food *and* a delight to the eyes *and* to be desired for wisdom... the narrative savours the growing desire in Eve's mind, almost urging the reader to ask for a bite.[10]

In the same way, every mother has had occasion to lay down quite firmly that her child is not to have even one more biscuit, and has watched, half with amusement and half with concern, while the expression on the child's face changes, first to tears, then to a guilty look and then to a furtive glance to see whether mother is still watching. As they develop, children learn that they can disobey their parents and, by doing so, get what they desire. A person who never developed this awareness would not be a good person, but a person stuck in the immaturity of early childhood. If we are to become morally mature, we must learn that sometimes our desires fall out of step with the true fulfilment for which God has made us and tempt us to do what we should not do.

So, then, the answer to the question 'In a world made altogether good, how does anybody come to do anything evil?' is that tension develops between our faculties, each of which is good in itself. People respond to it in ways which satisfy part of themselves at the expense of other parts. It is not that sin *entered* the world, once upon a time, and then grew. Rather, this is how it characteristically arises. God respects us so much as to give us the power to mess things up.

We are all torn between two responses to wrongdoing. Our own misdeeds, and those of our friends, we easily understand and excuse. When it comes to other people's misdeeds we notice the dreadful results which follow and build up feelings of indignation. It takes spiritual maturity to recognize that when a person does something wrong, it is both very understandable and very disastrous. Yet this is what Genesis does. At this point it stresses how easy sin was for Eve; soon it will reflect on the serious consequences.

Complicity

And she also gave some to her husband (Gen 3.6).

Although any satisfactory theory must explain how sin originates, most sin arises from, and responds to, other sins. Eve was positively tempted; we were invited to share the workings of her mind, looking at the tree longingly and coming round to the idea of trying the fruit. Adam simply follows her lead. Yet at the end of the story his sin is condemned just as much as hers. Later generations, using the text as an excuse for treating women as more sinful than men, have missed the point: simple complicity is just as wrong as taking the lead.

Changing relationships

Then the eyes of both were opened, and they knew that they were naked; and they sewed fig leaves together and made loincloths for themselves. And they heard the sound of the Lord God walking in the garden at the time of the evening breeze, and the man and his wife hid themselves from the presence of the Lord God among the trees of the garden (Gen 3:7-8).

After doing what was forbidden, they feel guilty. They can no longer meet God face to face with confidence. The awareness of sin puts a barrier between them. They hide. They also feel a sense of self-loathing; but instead of admitting the real reason, they project it onto their nakedness and set about hiding that too. Actually, there is nothing wrong with their nakedness.

This, then, is what happens when we sin. We do something we know is wrong. We feel a desire to avoid the person we have offended. At the same time we justify our self-loathing by projecting it onto something else.

The social dimensions of sin

Some theories of evil claim it only causes suffering to people when they freely choose it or at least accept it. For example we become ill because we smoke, or eat too much. If all evil can be explained like this, it follows that *each individual person* has the power to overcome all the evils in his or her life. The view is common in the New Age movement and some theories of reincarnation. What makes it attractive is that everybody gets what they deserve. We do not need to feel obliged to help those in need. But this is also its main weakness. Morality comes to mean nothing more than enlightened self-interest.

P describes evil in more social terms. The story of Adam and Eve focuses on the relationship between humanity and God. The next story, about Cain and Abel, explores what happens when people sin against each other within the family. Then comes the story of the flood, where the whole of human society is described as sinful.

To P, then, some people suffer because of evil acts by others. Even in a world governed by God's harmonious goodness, there can be a difference between doing what is of immediate benefit to ourselves and doing what is for the greater good. We are often faced with a choice between the two, and it is up to us to decide what to do.

Punishment

Therefore the Lord sent him forth from the garden of Eden (Gen 3.23).

'Very well,' asks the sceptic, 'but not all suffering is caused by sin. How do you explain pain in childbirth, or the arduous nature of work, or floods?'

The answer we get is punishment. God punishes Adam and Eve, then Cain, and eventually the whole human race except Noah and his family.

Now the earth was corrupt in God's sight, and the earth was filled with violence. And God saw that the earth was corrupt; for all flesh had corrupted its ways upon the earth. And God said to Noah, 'I have determined to make an end of all flesh, for the earth is filled with violence because of them; now I am going to destroy them along with the earth. Make yourself an ark...' (Gen 6:11-14).

In P's time, every theology had to explain floods. When we compare this explanation with the one in the *Epic of Gilgamesh*, we can see that it fits a world which is intended, secure and good. God has given us free will and we have misused it. God is still in control of the world and is still doing everything for the best.[11] I suspect that most people would rather live in P's world, where everything is controlled by a single all-seeing and all-punishing supreme deity, than in the Babylonian world where nobody knows what will happen next because everything depends on the changing moods of quarrelling gods. But P's is still not a convincing picture, and we must question whether we can accept it. There are two main difficulties.

The first is practical. If the unpleasant features of life are all divine punishments for human sin, people who sin less should suffer less. Many people came to believe that they do; the theory is often expressed in the Psalms and debated at length in Job. It is still common today. But there is a lot of evidence that they do not.

The other difficulty is theoretical. If the whole point of giving us free will is so that we have the opportunity to become holy by freely choosing to do good instead of evil, is not divine punishment counter-productive? If it really were the case that morally upright people did not suffer, people would become morally upright to avoid the suffering. Obedience to the laws would become a matter of pure self-interest and this would make it harder to become good for the sake of being good.

Modern penal theory has the same problem. If we ask 'Why is the state morally justified in punishing criminals?' there are three main answers: to *reform* the individual offender, to *deter* potential offenders and to impose a deserved *retribution*. Retribution theory dominates the bible, virtually to the exclusion of other theories.[12] In modern legislation, deterrence plays an important part, but it does not replace retribution altogether. Deterrence theory knows no limits: if a given punishment does not deter enough people, the answer is to increase it. Retribution theory, being based on the idea that the offender 'deserves' a punishment, limits the sentence according to the crime. The problem is that nobody has adequately explained what we mean when we say an offender 'deserves' a given punishment. This leads to a dilemma: in practice, penal systems cannot manage without a theory of retribution, but nobody has provided a satis-factory account of it. Modern theorists continue to puzzle over it.[13]

In Babylonian theology, the purpose of punishment was much clearer. If people displeased the gods, the gods would retaliate. Divine retaliation could easily threaten the entire cosmic order. They did not expect the gods to act justly. The reason why the state punished criminals, then, was to appease the gods and thereby preserve or restore the cosmic order.

P seems to have faced a dilemma. On the one hand, the cosmic order is intended, secure and good. We have been created not merely to provide sacrifices, but for our own sakes, so failure to offer sacrifices does not provoke God to abandon the cosmic order. On the other hand, natural disasters do happen, and the only way of accounting for them was by divine punishment. God, therefore, must be angry when we disobey the law.

Has P transferred an explanation from a context in which it made sense to a context in which it does not? By replacing a set of quarrelling, bad-tempered and demanding gods, who retaliate when their interests are threatened, with a single, omnipotent and benign God who needs nothing from us, the reason for punishment — whether divine or human — collapses.

What function, then, does punishment have in P's account? If we look outside Genesis to the laws of Exodus and Leviticus, we are told that God commands the Hebrews to impose punishments for a wide range of offences. When we ask *why* God demands these punishments, we find a strange silence. Other ancient near eastern texts tend to be far more forth-coming. They usually tell us that punishment appeases the gods and restores the cosmic order. In the Old Testament, we find occasional refer-ences to the idea,[14] but they are very few: elsewhere, punishments are to be imposed for no other reason than that God so commands. It seems that the Hebrews, with their optimistic theology, could not make sense of the traditional justifications for divine and human punishment. They edited them out of their scriptures but did not find a satisfactory alternative.

It seems to me, then, that P lets us down at this point. At one stage we are introduced to the loving, painstaking Creator who thinks up countless animal shapes to amuse Adam and makes clothes for the couple after they have ruined their beautiful nakedness, just like a mother who patiently provides clean clothes when her daughter tears a hole in her expensive new dress. To move from there to the God who is so shocked by human wickedness as to wipe out all but one family, is, surely, to reintroduce polytheism under the guise of God-as-loving-creator and God-as-righteous-punisher.

This weakness in the system was to cause problems for Jews. Some held on to the theory that all suffering is divine punishment. When people are ill, they must have sinned. The solution is not to call a doctor but to try all the harder to obey the law. The idea is often expressed in the Psalms and is debated at length in the book of Job. The result was a self-righteous sense of superiority. Even today, people who display it are often accused of 'Pharisaism'. The alternative was to abandon the doctrine that God is in complete control, and open the door to pessimistic theology.

Genesis and the value of the world

Although I have argued that P's account of punishment does not fit the overall theory, once we leave it out what is left is a coherent account of reality which is quite different from the Babylonian one. First, the universe is created good. What it means to call the world good is that it was created by God with a benign intention, to be a fulfilling experience for created beings. Although we are able to evaluate the world differently, or seek fulfilment in some other way, to do so is to set ourselves against God. Within this context, human life is given freedom and the opportunity to choose between good and evil. For this reason, sin is a perennial fact of life.

This positive evaluation of the world depends on a specific cosmology: the world was created by a God who is omnipotent, omniscient and good. God fully intended the creation to be as it is and fully understands the implications of this creative work. God's evaluations, unlike ours, are absolute. To say 'The world is a good place' is objectively true, not merely one particular point of view. To judge the world as good is not only to be on God's side, but to be right.

The positive evaluation leads in turn to a positive agenda for human life: what we have been given is to be welcomed, explored and enjoyed, for the good of all. Together with this positive agenda is an emphasis on ethics: it is within our power to make our experience of life better still. What we experience as evil is the result of human sin. God does not want us to sin, and we *ought* to overcome our sinfulness by living the way God intends for us.

Optimism in the Christian tradition

Christians today will ask 'But is the theory Christian?' Over the course of nearly two thousand years, the Christian tradition has been far too varied to allow for a simple answer. One could find many examples from past and present which are *predominantly* optimistic. Recently many theologians have celebrated parts of the tradition for affirming the goodness of the world — the Benedictines, the Orthodox Church, the Celtic Church, some medieval mystics, Francis of Assisi, the early Anglican theologians; but to most Christians today the key questions will be: is this what Jesus taught, and is it what the bible teaches?

P's theology, hammered out by a cultural ghetto in opposition to foreigners, set the scene for the Jewish religion established by Ezra and his successors. On the whole, contrary theologies have been edited out of the Old Testament. We can find exceptions. God's enthusiasm to win wars for Israel, for example, does not impress us today, even though at the time it seemed to reinforce the conviction that their God was in control of the world. Overwhelmingly, the writers of the Old Testament *intended* to affirm P's benign monotheism, even if we do not always think they succeeded. By comparison with other ancient near eastern texts, it is remarkable how systematically other gods have been removed from the scene, or at least turned into God's obedient servants.

The New Testament varies much more widely. We find within it a range of different theories, some of which are optimistic but many of which are very different. When we ask 'Did Jesus agree with P?', scholars do not know the answer. Most today believe his message was centred on the Kingdom of God, but there is no consensus on what he meant by it. Of the wide variety of current theories, many present a Jesus who was far removed from optimism. Of those who interpret his teaching more along optimistic lines, the best example I know of is B Chilton and J I H McDonald, *Jesus and the Ethics of the Kingdom*. To Chilton and McDonald, Jesus taught not about when the Kingdom will come, but about what it is like, and challenged people to respond to it immediately. In this case, Jesus will not have understood the Kingdom as a future state and speculated about when it would come; God's rule, rather, was a present reality, expressed when people did what they ought to do. Jesus will not have believed that he was bringing in a new age, since there was nothing wrong with the old one.[15]

If we accept this interpretation of Jesus, he seems to have drawn out the implications of optimism even further than P did. There are two developments. One is his teaching about forgiveness. Despite the punitive views sometimes expressed in Matthew's Gospel, the evidence as a whole indicates that Jesus taught divine forgiveness rather than punishment. The best known examples are the parables of the Lost Sheep, the Lost Coin and the Prodigal Son in Luke 15.

The other is life after death. P, like most of the Old Testament, does not mention it. Most scholars believe that, whatever else Jesus said about the Kingdom of God, *some* of the references will have pointed to life after death. By his time, Jews were influenced by a variety of theories: Egypt, Greece and Persia each had distinctive traditions about it, and it would not be surprising if Jesus believed in it.

To believe in life after death is not necessarily optimistic; after all, some doctrines encourage us to spend our lives cringing in fear of the next world! However, if a good God has created us for good purposes, it seems odd that our lives come to an end without anything of lasting significance surviving. It makes more sense to believe that God's purposes for our lives continue in some way, even if we do not know how.

Elsewhere in the New Testament, despite the influence of alternative theologies, we find many affirmations that the created order is as God intended, and is secure and good.[16]

Equally relevant is the manner in which the New Testament canon of scripture was closed. Towards the end of the second century AD, many alternative versions of Christianity were being taught and the Church's leaders deemed it necessary to establish which scriptures were to be considered authoritative. One of the leading figures in this movement was Irenaeus, Bishop of Lyons and author of a five-volume work *Against the Heresies*. Scholars wonder whether his descriptions of the heresies are exaggerations; but whether they are or not, they tell us about the issues which were considered important in his day. Time after time Irenaeus defends God's omnipotence, omniscience and goodness. When his opponents argued that the world was made by an evil god, or angels, contrary to the will of the one good God, he replied:

This would imply that angels were more powerful than God; or if not so, that he was either careless, or inferior, or paid no regard to those things which took place among his own possessions... But if one would not ascribe such conduct even to a man of any ability, how much less to God![17]

Others argued that God's power to create a good world was limited by the way things are: destiny or necessity limit God's freedom of manoeuvre. Irenaeus replied:

It is not seemly... to say of him who is God over all, since he is free and independent, that he was a slave to necessity, or that anything takes place with his permission, yet against his desire, otherwise they will make necessity greater and more kingly than God... And he ought at the very beginning to have cut off the causes of the necessity, and not to have allowed himself to be shut up to yielding to that necessity, by permitting anything besides that which became him. For it would have been much better, more consistent, and more God-like, to have cut off at the beginning the principle of this kind of necessity, than afterwards, as if moved by repentance, to endeavour to extirpate the results of necessity when they had reached such a development.[18]

Irenaeus was not always consistent in his arguments and it is easy enough to pick holes in them. Nevertheless, his intention was quite clear: to defend God's omnipotence, omniscience and goodness, and the goodness of the world as God's creation.

Not only does Irenaeus defend optimistic theology: he also extends it. P affirmed that there is a God-given law and that humanity has freedom to obey or disobey it. This moral challenge can be interpreted as very static, as though each generation is faced with the same laws and the same temptations and there is no process of development. Perhaps we should read the theme of divine blessing in Genesis 1 and 2 as making it more dynamic; Irenaeus, anyway, is quite explicit about it. In his argument against the doctrine of the fall, he denies that the creation was at first perfect but then went wrong. Instead, he argues that Adam was morally, spiritually and intellectually a child.[19] God equipped humanity with free will in order that we would come to resemble God more and more:

God had power at the beginning to grant perfection to man; but as the latter was only recently created, he could not possibly have received it, or even if he had received it could he have contained it, or containing it, could he have retained it.[20]

Instead, we are encouraged to use our freedom to grow into perfection:

This, then, was the [object of the] long-suffering of God, that man, passing through all things, and acquiring the knowledge of moral discipline, then attaining to the resurrection from the dead, and learning by experience what is the source of his deliverance, may always live in a state of gratitude to the Lord, having obtained from him the gift of incorruptibility.[21]

Those who accept the New Testament as authoritative scripture should pay attention to the reasons why these books were included and others left out. Many of the reasons were to do with defending the omnipotent, omniscient and good God of Hebrew tradition, and the goodness of the created order, against the alternative theories which were popular at the time.

For these reasons I think it is fair to say that optimistic theology, as I have defined it in this chapter, has strong roots in the bible and the early Christian Church, in addition to a wide range of representatives throughout the history of Christianity. Many people, today as in the past, would agree with much or all of it. Nevertheless I suspect that a great many, even of those who would initially say they agree with it, also accept other doctrines which contradict it. Nobody is entirely consistent in their beliefs; we all live with contradictions, most of them unintended. In order to appreciate fully the implications of optimistic theology, we must be clear about what it denies. This will be the subject of the next chapter.

---

1   So many scholars have commentated on this text that all I can hope to do is to follow the general consensus. I have depended most heavily on C Westermann, *Genesis 1-11*.

2   C Westermann, *Genesis 1-11*, pp. 25f. According to the text, chaos was there from the beginning. Later Jews and Christians taught that God created the world from nothing. But even here in Genesis, it plays no active part. There is no equivalent of Tiamat.

3   1 Chron 21:1.

4   A major bone of contention has been the 'dominion' text, where God blesses humanity and gives us dominion over other forms of life (Genesis 1:26-28). Modern technology-lovers often invoke it to justify suppressing nature.

Nature-lovers often accept the interpretation and condemn the bible for being against nature. This flies in the face of the text, which tells us — six times — that everything God creates is good. Part of the world's goodness lies in the opportunity we have been given to use what nature provides, and develop our creativity. But why use it to set ourselves *against* what God has created? 2500 years ago, when the texts were written, they were aware of their newest technologies, chief among them agriculture and the domestication of cattle. Did they make God angry? The question was probably a common one, and the text seems to say that they do not; but it hardly makes sense to transfer this judgement to the completely different technologies of today, of which the writers knew nothing.

5   E.g. S T Davis, Ed., *Encountering Evil: Live Options in Theodicy.*
6   C Westermann, *Genesis 1-11*, pp. 2ff.
7   An example is D Griffin in S T Davis, Ed, *Encountering Evil*, pp. 101-136.
8   *Metaphysics* 4.8, 9.8.
9   T C Vriezen has analysed the wide variety of theories about what the serpent is supposed to represent. Westermann summarizes them in *Genesis 1-11* pp. 237-40. Today scholars generally agree that the text is far too monotheistic to allow for a devil-in-disguise. As Westermann puts it, the serpent does argue against God's command, but 'we are not justified by the text in seeing behind these words a complete orientation of the serpent against God or a being at enmity with God'.
10 C Westermann, *Genesis 1-11*, pp. 248f.
11 C Westermann, *Genesis 1-11*, pp. 48-55.
12 The only exception I know of is the occasional refrain in Deuteronomy which hints that laws have a deterrent value, e.g. 17:13, 'All the people will hear and be afraid, and will not act presumptuously again'.
13 For some explorations of this theme, see H B Acton, *The Philosophy of Punishment*, T Honderich, *Punishment: The Supposed Justifications*, W Moberly, *The Ethics of Punishment* and N Walker, *The Aims of a Penal System.*
14 Num. 35:33-4 is the clearest example.
15 B Chilton and J I H McDonald, *Jesus and the Ethics of the Kingdom*, pp. 12f, 25f, 68.
16 Mk. 10:6 = Mt. 19:4; Mk. 13:19 = Mt. 24:21; Mt. 25:34; Lk 11:50; Jn. 17:24; Acts 14:15-17; Rom. 1:20, 4:17; 2 Cor 4:6; Eph. 1:4; Heb. 4:3; 9:26; 11:3; 1 Pet. 1:20; 2 Pet. 3:4; Rev. 4:11; 10:6; 13:8; 17:8. The verb used for God's act of creating is *ktizo*; *demiourgeo*, the word normally used by Platonists to describe the creative act of the demiurge, is avoided in order to stress the absolute sovereignty and creativity of God.
17 2.2.1.
18 2.5.4.
19 5.6.1; 5.16.2; 3.23.5; 4.28.1-3.
20 4.38.2
21 3.20.2. This passage is discussed by J Hick, *Evil and the God of Love*, p. 219, in the context of Irenaeus' theodicy. Irenaeus is not altogether consistent with his theology, and sometimes accepts positions which are being denied by the passages cited here. However, his main concerns are clear enough. See J N D Kelly, *Early Christian Doctrines* pp 171f.

Chapter 3

Heavenly conflict and an evil world

IN THE LAST chapter I described a particular way of evaluating the world. It was created by a good God with complete power and knowledge, and it follows that we should evaluate it as good. If we do not, we are wrong. This is what I mean by 'optimistic theology'. In this chapter I shall describe what I mean by 'pessimistic theology'. Pessimism agrees with optimism that there is an objective standard of goodness, provided by some kind of supreme and good god who lays down the way things ought to be. The difference is that pessimists believe the world does not live up to this standard. There is an element of evil which is not simply the result of human sin; it is built into the way things are, and produces conflict and tragedy which are not part of the good god's intentions and therefore have no redeeming features.

On the level of cosmology, the difference between optimism and pessimism can be very fine. Any limitation of God's power, knowledge or goodness will turn an optimistic theory into a pessimistic one. If the Creator acted either in ignorance, or against competition, or with limited powers, or with evil intent, built-in evil becomes a real threat and demands a completely different account of reality and our place in it.

The history of religion has produced a huge range of pessimistic theologies. I have chosen examples which will also show how pessimism was established within Christianity.

The world was created by good and evil gods

One possibility is that there always has been conflict between good and evil gods and both make their mark on the world. This was the teaching of Zoroaster. Zoroastrianism was the religion of the ancient Persian empire, which governed Jerusalem from 538 to 332 BC.

Zoroaster lived, at the very latest, in the sixth century BC, possibly much earlier. Most of our information comes from documents written in the ninth century AD, and we cannot be sure that all the beliefs described there are as old as they claim, but at the time the Persians governed Jerusalem they probably held the doctrines I shall describe here.

There is one God, Ahura Mazda, all-wise, completely just and good, the creator of all that is good. Since wisdom, justice and goodness are utterly different from wickedness and cruelty, there exists another uncreated god, Angra Mainu, wholly ignorant and malign, who created all that is evil. Both these original gods made a free choice between good and evil, though in each case the choice was in accordance with their nature. Each god commands a vast array of heavenly beings, angels and demons respectively, in an ordered hierarchy.[1]

Ahura Mazda created the world knowing that Angra Mainu would attack it; but he also knew that in the end he would win, destroy evil and establish a universe which was good for ever. The creation was in two stages. First, Ahura Mazda brought all beings into existence in a spiritual, immaterial state, in which they could not be attacked by Angra Mainu. However, he then went on to give them material existence, despite the threat from Angra Mainu, because it is better to have material existence than not to have it.[2] Since both good and evil spirits shared in the initial work of creation, the world is full of conflict between good and evil.

History is divided into stages. One characteristic account describes four ages of 3,000 years each. In the first, Ahura Mazda produced the creatures which will enable him to be victorious over evil, though they remained invisible. In the second, he created the material world, despite opposition from Angra Mainu, and combined the bodies of humans with their spirits. In the third — the present one — Angra Mainu has gained control. At the end of this age there will be massive conflict between the two powers, including earthquakes, wars and social and cosmic upheavals. A descendant of Zoroaster, born of a virgin, will appear as a deliverer, defeat Angra Mainu and bring in the fourth age. Creation will be purified, with the evil elements removed, and humanity will live for eternity in a state of perfection.

Both gods created animals. Angra Mainu created beasts of prey, scorpions, wasps, ugly toads and anything judged harmful or repulsive to humanity, so people were encouraged to kill them.[4]

Humanity's task is to choose between the two powers and live accord-

ingly. We have a real part to play in overcoming evil and restoring the
world to its original perfection, by proper worship and righteous behaviour. When we die our lives are judged and we are sent to heaven or hell
accordingly, for a limited time. Afterwards everything will be restored to
its original perfection.

We must allow for the uncertainties with regard to dating, but Mary
Boyce may well be correct in claiming that

> Zoroaster was thus the first to teach the doctrines of an individual
> judgement, Heaven and Hell, the future resurrection of the body, the
> general Last Judgement, and life everlasting for the reunited soul and
> body. These doctrines were to become familiar articles of faith to
> much of mankind, through borrowings by Judaism, Christianity and
> Islam; yet it is in Zoroastrianism itself that they have their fullest
> logical coherence, since Zoroaster insisted both on the goodness of
> the material creation, and hence of the physical body, and on the
> unwavering impartiality of divine justice.[5]

Here, then, is a radical dualism of good and evil. Everything, whether
material or spiritual, is the work of either the good god or the evil one, and
the two are set *against* each other. Let us now note the differences
between this type of theological system and the optimism I described in
the last chapter.

Firstly, Ahura Mazda is not the same as P's God. For P, there is no
question of any other being existing without God's permission. Ahura
Mazda is faced with an opponent and is powerless to destroy him. His
power is limited.

Secondly, the origin of evil lies in an eternally existent evil god. This
creates a problem. We find it easy enough to believe that an eternally existent god should be motivated by goodness, or even by selfishness: but why
should a god systematically engage in doing evil? It does not satisfy us to
state that choosing evil was in Angra Mainu's nature: *why* was it in his
nature? How did an evil-prone deity come into existence?[6] In the last
chapter I noted that the origin of evil is the most difficult problem for optimistic theology. But if it is difficult to account for *human* wrongdoing in
an otherwise perfect world, is not *divine* wrongdoing in the same circumstances even harder to explain?

Thirdly, we are trapped in evil. We do have the choice between doing good and evil, but even if the entire human race always did good, the world would still be riddled with the powers of evil. There is a *tragic* dimension to life: the existence of evil forces is outside the good god's plan and has no redeeming features. From the human point of view, the existence of evil is inescapable.

Fourthly, the black-and-white view of heavenly powers tends to produce a black-and-white view of humanity. Even today, when we are horrified by other people's crimes, it is easy enough to decide that they are wicked by nature and need a stiff punishment. This attitude is bound to be reinforced if one believes that other people's actions are influenced by spirits who spend their time provoking evil. At its worst, this type of theological system is a bit like the cheap television thrillers of today, in which the goodies never do anything wrong, the baddies never do anything right and the conflict between the two never completely ends.

Finally, the ethical task — to do good and resist evil — is an unfortunate result of Angra Mainu's activities. The good god did not intend us to be faced with it. For the writers of Genesis, by contrast, it is part of God's good creation, the means through which we can become holy.

An originally perfect creation has been spoilt

The Persian Empire ended with the conquests of Alexander of Macedon. A more unified, cosmopolitan culture followed, in which ideas from Greece, Egypt, Palestine, Babylon, Persia and even India spread widely and influenced each other. It is called the 'Hellenistic Age'.

Among the Jews, the very idea of being open to foreign influence was a matter of debate. On the whole, those who upheld P's tradition, as described in the last chapter, were faithful to the one supreme God and the Old Testament law. This meant they emphasized the difference between the Jews and everybody else. Other Jews were more open to new ideas.

Hellenistic culture generally thought of the world in very gloomy terms: it was full of evil beings, ranging from supreme gods like Angra Mainu to the local spirits we find in the gospels of Matthew, Mark and Luke. Human life was constantly up against them. Characteristically they were held responsible for death, sin, illness, possession and natural disasters. Had they not entered the world, these things would never happen.

Within this context, Jews developed the literature known as 'Apocalyptic'. The best known examples are the biblical books of Daniel

and Revelation, but most of it was excluded from the bible. It is marked
out by its bizarre style — full of angels, beasts, numbers and calculations.
Some of the documents are difficult to date, but the range of Jewish
Apocalyptic is roughly from the middle of the second century BC to the
end of the first century AD. After the destruction of Jerusalem in 70 AD,
it was suppressed by Rabbinic Judaism; but in Christianity the ideas
survived, flourished and provided the new religion with some of its central
doctrines.

Characteristically the Jewish Apocalyptists depict heaven and the
world as full of good and evil forces. There are many detailed descriptions
of the angels and demons. Wars between nations reflect parallel wars in
heaven, fought by their respective guardian angels. The leader of the evil
forces is often called Satan.

There are many accounts of world history. Usually it is divided into
fixed stages. Because the world is controlled not by God but by the forces
of evil, there is much speculation about when God will intervene to
triumph over evil and impose a new age of justice.[7] Often the central
message is that the end of the age is coming very soon. God's action will
overcome Satan and the demons, bring about the end of history and begin
a completely new order.[8]

There are many similarities with Zoroastrianism: the heavens full of
spirits, the stages of history, the good god who will intervene in the future.
One difference is the heightened expectation that the new age is coming
soon. Another is that, as Jews, they believed that there is only one supreme
God. They refused to believe in an eternally existent evil god. But if a
good God created a perfect world, where does evil come from? Something
must have gone wrong *after* the world was created. Thus arose the
doctrine of the fall: at first the world was perfect, but later on evil entered
it.

Many of the early Christians accepted this theological structure and
adapted it to account for the work of Jesus. Jesus either was bringing in
the new age, or had already done so. Unfortunately there is no consensus
about what Jesus himself believed. In the last chapter I mentioned one
possibility. Alternatively, many scholars today believe he taught that the
end was nigh and would be an unmistakeable, public event.[9] Others
believe that Jesus saw himself as the one who was bringing in the new age,
within his own ministry.[10]

Whatever Jesus himself believed, some New Testament authors certainly thought he was bringing in the new age. Mark's Gospel captures the mood of excitement. There is one sequence of four miracles which he seems to have grouped together to express the comprehensive range of the victory. By stilling the storm (4:31-41) Jesus proves his power over the forces of nature. By healing the Gerasene demoniac (5:1-20) he proves his power to exorcise evil spirits. By healing the woman with the haemorrhage (5:25-34) he proves his power to heal. By raising Jairus' daughter (5:21-4, 35-43) he proves his power over death. In each case Mark uses Greek words which imply that Jesus is counteracting an active power of evil. It is not that Jesus was good at exorcising, but that the powers of evil have been once and for all *defeated*. The age of rule by evil spirits is over, the new age is coming in, and things will be different.[11]

The writings of Christians in the first and second centuries often claim that Christ achieved a great victory for the whole human race. What sort of victory, and what difference did it make? There are not many references to the fall. In the New Testament we only hear of it in Paul's Epistle to the Romans (5:12-14 and 8:18-23), and even here it is only mentioned in passing; Paul's concern was with justification and salvation. Nor do the Christians of this era give much support to Mark's idea of a battle against evil spirits: instead they emphasize that Christ gave them immortality, new life, fellowship with God and the new law.[12] Irenaeus, for example, taught that Christ 'became what we are in order to enable us to become what he is'.[13] In other words, at this stage in its history the Church emphasized the themes of optimistic theology rather than spiritual conflict.

It was not until the fourth century that doctrines arose to explain how Christ brought about a real change by overcoming forces of evil. By then, of course, the new age was old hat. Death, sin and illness had not gone away. If Christ had brought about a real change, it was no use looking for its effects in ordinary human life. Where else could they look for it, but in the heavenly world? Fourth century theologians developed two theories of the work of Christ. They have been read into the New Testament ever since and remain popular among Christians today.

One is that Christ offered himself as a ransom to the devil. According to Gregory of Nyssa, Adam's sin caused the fall and put us into the devil's power. The devil would not give us back to God without compensation, so God offered Jesus as a ransom. The devil knew that Jesus was born of a virgin and renowned as a miracle-worker, and so accepted the exchange. He was tricked: what he did not know was that Jesus was also divine. As a result the devil could not hold onto him. As Gregory puts it, he was outwitted and caught 'like a fish by the bait'. Was God acting unjustly? Gregory argued that even the devil would be saved in the end, so it was in his interests too.[14]

The other is the 'realist' theory. God's anger was provoked by human sin and justice demanded punishment. Christ offered himself as a substitute. According to Cyril of Jerusalem, the reason why Christ's sacrifice was adequate is that he was divine.[15]

Since then Christianity has incorporated these two theories of atonement, juggling between them from time to time, and has thereby turned itself into a *polytheistic* religion. What has been established is *a myth about conflict between the gods*. I realize that this is a major criticism to make of the Christian tradition and I do not make it lightly. Defenders of the ransom theory may argue that the devil is not an evil god but a fallen angel. However there is no significant difference between the two: the devil functions as a heavenly being who can ruin the created order and render the good God helpless as he does his evil deeds. Defenders of the realist theory may argue that Jesus and God only cooperate on a saving plan, and do not really enter into conflict with each other; but then they have to explain why a saving plan is needed at all. Characteristically, they argue that God's justice demands punishment but God's mercy desires to let us off. In order to close the gap between God and Jesus, then, they increase the population of heaven: a saving plan is needed because God and Jesus are *constrained* by higher authorities, 'God's justice' and 'God's mercy'.

Whichever version we choose, there is more than one heavenly being and they do not act in harmony. No one god is in complete control. What has happened, in redemption, results from the interaction between these heavenly beings, not from a single master plan.

In these theories the redeeming work of Christ is a counterpart to the fall. The same fourth century movement, which worked out how Christ saved us, also worked out how we fell. God must have created a perfect world. Athanasius, for example, taught that Adam and Eve had supernatural knowledge and rationality before they sinned, and would not suffer illness or die.[16] So why did they ever sin? Augustine concludes that, at the time of temptation, they must have already possessed an evil will. Within themselves, they had already fallen away from original perfection before they committed a sinful act.[17] Augustine's move illustrates what happens when we try to explain how an original perfection developed a flaw. Whenever a particular point in the story is selected as the moment when things began to go wrong, the question arises 'Why did they go wrong *then*, since all was perfect before?' The only satisfactory answer is that some other flaw must have already existed. As we analyse the theology, we keep pushing back the moment when the first flaw developed, to a time nearer the original creation.

The same happens if we put the blame on the serpent, as Satan in disguise. Because Jews and Christians refused to accept the Zoroastrian idea of an eternally existent evil god, they developed myths about how God originally made the angels perfect, but some of them rebelled and fell.[18] Why did they rebel, if all was perfect before? Again it was Augustine who explored the problem most fully. Since the original creation was perfect, all evil deities must be fallen angels. Some angels fell but others did not. Angels who are saved must surely know they are saved — after all, saved humans know as much. They must, then, have had full wisdom and reason from the start, and known with certainty of their eternal bliss. On the other hand the angels who were destined to fall must have either not known whether they would fall, or known that they would fall, or been in error. None of these possibilities is compatible with perfect bliss. Therefore there must have been a distinction between the two types of angel right from the time of their initial creation. God must have *predestined* them to fall.[19]

It is difficult to fault Augustine's argument. In effect, he has inherited the concept of an original perfection which later developed a flaw, and pursued its logic to the point at which the original perfection disappears and God is directly responsible for creating evil. Since his day, Christians have tried to rescue the doctrine from this flaw, but its logical structure must defeat every attempt: any successful solution must, like Augustine's, move away from the idea of an original perfection which later fell, towards a completely different theological system. If the origin of evil is not explained by an eternally existent evil god, the idea of a fault arising in a perfect world does no better.

Elsewhere in this book I shall refer to this type of theology as 'fall-redemption theology'. The entire human race has fallen into an evil state and the work of Christ was to redeem us from it. The focus of attention is on three critical moments: when the world was first created, when it fell and when it was redeemed.

It is popular among Christians today and many believe it can be harmonized with a God who is omnipotent, omniscient and good. I hope to have shown that it cannot. Genesis describes how God permitted human evil as *part of* the world's goodness. Fall-redemption theology, on the other hand, has to affirm either that God's plans went wrong — which denies divine power — or that God deliberately created evil — which denies divine goodness. In either case, God's character is radically changed.

One line of defence is that God remains totally in control but permitted the rule of evil spirits for a limited time only. Against this argument it would be difficult to improve on Irenaeus' reply, noted in the last chapter. Why did God not stop the evil right from the start? Not to stop it is to deliberately permit evil; God, then, would be to blame for it.

Another argument may run: if God gives humans free will to do good or evil to each other, why not also permit angels the same freedom? The answer lies in the practical implications. According to optimistic theology, God permits us to harm each other because this is how we can grow spiritually and morally. By being hurt, we learn what it is like to be hurt, and reflect on what it might be like for other people to be hurt by us. We might speculate that this argument may equally apply *within* the spiritual realm: but it does not apply between evil spirits and humans. We simply do not know enough about them. Our senses invite us to assume that if being punched on the nose hurts us, it will hurt other humans just the same. We cannot apply the analogy to evil spirits. We do not know whether they have noses, or even whether they exist at all. In practice, those who believe in evil spirits rarely discuss how our responses to them may help them to repent or develop spiritually, let alone how our spiritual development can grow through being nice to them. Usually they are written off as eternally hostile, like the baddies of television cartoons, to be exorcised rather than forgiven.

Fall-redemption theology, then, is quite different from optimistic theology. When it comes to explaining the origin of evil, it fares no better than the other systems we have considered so far.

A good creator had limited power

I now turn to a different theory: that there is one supreme creator god, whose power is limited by the nature of reality. This is the main explanation of evil in Plato's *Timaeus*, his most theological work, written in the fourth century BC. The material world has been created by a 'demiurge' — a maker, or craftsman who, unlike the God of Genesis, worked within limitations. In order to create, he used pre-existent materials and followed a pattern already available in the world of *forms*.

Plato's theory of forms is central to his philosophy. The ancient Greeks were fascinated with the relationships between permanence and change, between oneness and diversity and between the intellectual and the material. According to Plato, when we observe the world we perceive many different objects which are not permanent and therefore cannot represent eternal truth. Our minds put them together into groups and provide us with concepts of them. These concepts are the 'forms', or 'ideas'. Everything in the physical world — human artefacts, animals, plants, virtues and even abstract concepts — are reflections of their form. The form of each thing is not only a concept but something which really exists, unchanging, in the eternal world. What is good about the material world is that it reflects the pattern of the forms.

Why did the demiurge create the world at all? Because he was good, and therefore wished all things to be as like himself as possible. It was an act of goodness to change the world from a disorderly and unharmonious state into a state of order. This is the best world he could possibly make.[20]

Why, then, is there so much wrong with human life? Plato's main answer is that body and soul are made of radically different materials and do not fuse together easily. The world may be the best possible world, but it is still made out of *matter*, and anything material is inferior to the spiritual. The human *soul,* on the other hand, is not material. It properly belongs to the world of forms, but is incarnated in the body. The task of the soul is to control the bodily passions. Every person's life, then, has the character of a moral test.[21]

Plato's demiurge, then, is just as well-intentioned as the God of Genesis and Ahura Mazda. Like Ahura Mazda, his power is limited, but it is limited by the nature of reality, rather than another god. There are three original principles of reality: the demiurge, the forms and matter. The demiurge and the forms are entirely good, but matter is inferior.

Plato's account of reality is just as dualistic as Zoroaster's, but it draws a different line: the material is inferior, the spiritual and intellectual are superior. Bodily desires and passions do not have a positive function: they result from the unfortunate conflict caused by the fusion of body and soul. Human life is therefore an arena of conflict, between the intelligent and eternal soul on the one hand and the material and mortal body on the other. While we live, there is no escape from the conflict.

Does Plato offer a better explanation of the origin of evil? At first sight he does: compared with the other theories we have considered so far, God remains entirely good but evil results from the nature of reality. The way things are is nobody's fault: it just happens to be this way. On closer inspection, however, Plato's system is really a compromise which solves nothing. Of the three original principles, one is a god and two are impersonal. If they had all been impersonal, the cosmology would be a neutralist one, of the kind I shall discuss in Part 2. If they had all been personal, it would have been of the Zoroastrian type. The compromise, in which the good things are caused by a god and the evil things by impersonal matter, simply makes us ask why such a good god should have used such poor materials. Could he not have used something else? Or found some way to improve the quality of matter before embarking on the universe-creating project? Whatever the answers, it is the intelligent, purposeful agent who must take responsibility. If I make an omelette knowing that the eggs are rotten, it will be my responsibility; nobody will blame the eggs.

The world was created by evil gods

Another possibility is that there is a good supreme god who is the source of all true value, but that the world was made by other gods, acting either ignorantly or with evil intent. This theology has traditionally been attributed to the Gnostics, who flourished in and around the Roman Empire from the first to the third centuries AD. Their last great exponent, Mani, founded a religion which remained popular for hundreds of years, spread across Asia and survived in China until the twentieth century. Another Gnostic sect, the Mandeans, survives in Iraq today.

Until the middle of the twentieth century, most of our information about the Gnostics came from the writings of hostile Christians, including Irenaeus, who disliked their elaborate cosmologies and negative attitudes to the world. More recently a number of their manuscripts have been discovered, of which the most important were found at Nag Hammadi in 1946. This means we now have documents written by Gnostics themselves, not their enemies. As a result scholars today are much more sympathetic towards the Gnostics than they used to be. Comparing the new evidence with the old, most scholars consider that what the early Christians said about them was on the whole accurate, but of course Nag Hammadi is far more sympathetic, and there was much more to Gnosticism which did not interest their Christian opponents.[22] The more extreme Gnostic beliefs may have been exaggerated by their opponents, or only held by a few, or even developed within Christianity. However, my concern here is not with Gnostics in general but with a particular type of theology which is found within their writings. It is the type against which the early Christian Church reacted, and although Nag Hammadi has shed much light on it the main doctrines were already known to scholars.

Many Gnostic texts consist of elaborate cosmologies. Each document has its own theory, but what characterizes them is the dualism between the one good God, who is distant and powerless, and the creator or creators of the world, who are evil or ignorant.[23] Some theories begin with two gods, one good and one evil. Others begin with one good god, and describe how evil develops as other gods are created. In either case the world has been created by one or more evil gods, and the documents often make fun of their stupidity.[24] Some texts identify the creator with the God of the Jewish scriptures, and proceed to point out Old Testament texts which depict him as cruel and oppressive.

After the world was created the heavenly Spirit, or Soul, fell into it. Being evil, the creators of the world set about keeping it, to prevent it going back to heaven where it belonged. To do this they broke it into small pieces and put each piece into a separate human body.[25] This explains how human spirits are sparks of the divine but our bodies are evil.

Once they have achieved this, the rulers of the world deceive humans into forgetting our real nature and believing that our true home is in this world. We can see the logic of the system: if evil powers are responsible not only for the material world but also for the laws of nature, the norms of society and human powers of reason, they can stop us understanding our true condition. The onus is on the supreme god to devise a rescue plan. Many texts describe a messenger, or redeemer, sent from the realms above into the world, to alert humanity to its real condition. The plot is often like a modern spy thriller: as the messenger enters the world governed by evil beings, he disguises himself with a human body in order to outwit them and pass on the message. He is often described as lost and homesick.[26]

Characteristically, the message consists of information about the heavenly realm, the true nature of human life, and how our spirits may escape from this bodily and earthly prison, outwit the evil powers and reach our true home where the supreme god is.[27] A famous Valentinian formula summarizes the agenda:

> What liberates is the knowledge of who we were, what we became; where we were, whereinto we have been thrown; whereto we speed, wherefrom we are redeemed; what birth is, and what rebirth.[28]

This is why they claimed a superior understanding of reality. The word 'Gnostic' comes from the Greek word *gnosis*, 'knowledge'. Only the knowledge which comes from outside the world is reliable; all else comes from 'this world' and therefore misleads us.

There were two types of ethical system. What they had in common was the determination to reject the *natural* because it was the work of the evil creator. 'Ascetics' avoided natural activities. 'Libertinists' deliberately broke worldly norms and laws. Both groups singled out sexual activity as particularly evil, because it caused new humans to be born and thereby perpetuated the scheme to entrap the divine Spirit on earth.[29]

The recently discovered documents show us that Gnosticism covers a wide range of ideas. Despite the fascination with cosmology, many texts are interested in other matters and offer no cosmology at all. What is more representative of Gnosticism in general is the tendency to turn away from the outer, material world and concentrate on the inner self.

However, this in itself is revealing. The inward turn fits the negative cosmology like a glove. If the material world is evil, and if the only good element is the inner human spirit, what else is there to do but to turn one's back on the public world and concentrate on the inner self, the rituals of the sect and the hope of life after death?

Of course, the inward turn does not necessarily mean rejecting the outward. It is legitimate to explore the inner for its own sake. No doubt many did: but my present concern is with those who did evaluate the world negatively. There is a sharp contrast between the good supreme God and the evil creators of the world. Everything is evil except the distant, supreme deity and the human spirit. The agenda for human life is, therefore, to reject the worldly and material. What is left is the inner self, the knowledge derived from the supreme god, and life after death. Then as now, people who accepted this type of theology would band together in small groups where they would express their beliefs in rituals, pass on spiritual knowledge and reinforce each other's hostility to the big bad world, that constant source of temptation which needs to be resisted.

Elsewhere in this book I shall refer to this system as 'anticosmic theology'. Scholars debate how much New Testament authors, particularly Paul and John, were influenced by it.[30] Most of the later epistles seem to be opposing Gnostic theories of one sort or another, and the goodness of the created order was a point at issue.[31] As I noted in Chapter 2, it was opponents of anticosmic theology who determined which texts were to be included in the New Testament. Nevertheless, it continued to develop within western Christianity. Over time it took over the myths of creation, fall and redemption, and reinterpreted them to fit its own account of reality. It is in this form that western Christianity is most familiar with them today. The main reinterpretations are these:

(a) The material world cannot be redeemed. For many of the first Christians, Christ was bringing in a new age and life on earth would be radically different. Experience proved otherwise, but instead of abandoning their hope, they kept reinterpreting it until there was nothing left of its this-worldly content. The process is almost complete in the writings of Augustine. From time to time he echoes hopes of real this-worldly change; for example, he expresses surprise that people get excited when engaging in sexual intercourse, even after they have been baptized.[32] But apart from occasional remarks like this, he does not expect Christ's redeeming work to produce any visible changes. It was his opponents, the Donatists and Pelagians, who kept demanding moral perfection of Christians. Augustine had no such expectations. The benefits of redemption will be enjoyed in the next life, and even then only by those who have been baptized. Thus a fall-redemption message — of a this-worldly new age — was transformed into an anticosmic message of how the individual soul may gain salvation after death.

(b) The original perfection loses its relevance. Once Christians gave up expecting to return to it, its only function was to be a backdrop against

which the wickedness of sin would stand out. What is of practical significance is not that God created a perfect world, but that after it had been
created it fell, permanently and irretrievably.

(c) The saving work of Christ is not to change the world order, but to
provide believers with information. True, Christ overcame Satan, or nego-
tiated with him, or with God: but that achievement was completed at the
time of his death and resurrection. Thereafter, what counts for the
Christian is to *know* that he did it. Thus Christ becomes much more of a
Gnostic messenger than a Jewish Messiah. Christian faith becomes *gnosis*
about what the heavenly beings did and how Christ can save our souls.

(d) Christian *gnosis* has its own, uniquely reliable, source of heavenly
information. God's message of salvation, which did not come through an
unmistakeable cosmic Messiah riding to earth on the clouds of heaven,
came instead through an emissary from heaven who looked just like any
other human being but was really divine. The message, once given, is
passed on by the teaching of the bible and the Church.

Thus an anticosmic version of the fall-redemption myth came to be
established in western Christianity and is as popular as ever today. It is
something of a mismatch, and tension still arises. Institutional churches
often encourage their members to affirm anticosmic slogans such as
'Christ is my personal saviour'. Scholars point out that the New Testament
tells a different story: Christ is the saviour of *the whole world*. But they are
rarely heeded. After all, how would the world be different if he were not?
The scholars of today, like those of Augustine's day, cannot cash out those
New Testament doctrines as meaningful statements about reality. But the
anticosmic interpretation, unbiblical though it is, works: individuals can
at least *feel* that Jesus makes a difference to their inner selves.

Conclusion

I have now considered a range of theories which fit my definition of
pessimistic theology. According to Zoroaster, the world was created by
two gods, one good and one evil. According to the fall-redemption tradition, an originally perfect creation fell. According to Plato, the world was
made with imperfect materials. According to anticosmic theory, it was
made by evil gods. All four agree with optimistic theology, against
neutralism, that there is a supreme deity who is the source and standard
of true goodness. Thus there is an absolute, objective truth about what is

good and the way the world ought to be. They differ from optimistic theology by denying that it meets this standard.

I have given a tight definition to optimistic theology: God has complete power and knowledge and is perfectly good. Pessimistic theology covers a wide range of possibilities, both in theory — because of the way I have defined it — and in practice, in the history of religious ideas. Instead of categorizing all the possibilities into two types, I could have described them in terms of a spectrum. At one extreme would be the optimistic theory that the world is altogether good. At the other would be the theory that it is altogether evil. Dotted about at various points in between would come the huge range of theologies, like the ones in this chapter, which describe the world as partly good and partly evil.

When we examine the issues, however, the wide range of cosmologies, evaluations and agendas do fall into two distinct types. P attempted a thoroughgoing description of a good world created by a good God. I argued that the intention was not entirely fulfilled, but the attempt has at least been made, not only by P but by many others. When it comes to the other extreme, I doubt whether the attempt has ever been made. There is no complete antithesis to Genesis, in which reality is totally evil without remainder. Even the anticosmic theologians made room for the divine spark. This is hardly surprising: humanity needs hope. The greater the emphasis on evil, the more we need to believe that *somewhere* there is something better to hope for.

The vast majority of theologies, then, are between the extremes. Part of reality is good and part is evil. Although there is an infinite variety of possible mixtures, they all have certain features in common which make them quite different from optimistic theology.

(a) If the creator is omnipotent, omniscient and good, the created order has *security*. God will never be attacked by other gods, or make mistakes, or do things to spite us. If we limit God's omnipotence, omniscience or goodness in any way, the absence of security provides a completely different agenda for human life. It is a bit like giving a child a computer game. As long as he is confident that the game works properly, he can happily start playing. His goal is to win. Often he will lose, but that is not a tragedy: it is an intended part of the game. On the other hand, if he finds a fault in the program, which prevents it being played properly, a completely different agenda arises. The difference between winning and losing the game pales into insignificance. Now is not the time to practice the art of shooting down the aliens. Before anybody plays, the manufacturer must be asked to correct the bug.

So also with the nature of reality. Suppose the world was made perfectly good by a good god, with the intention that we should practice the art of holiness. Then God's plans went wrong, a flaw developed and evil messed up the system. This creates insecurity. The appropriate response is to concentrate on coping with the fault: practising the art of godly holiness will have to wait. Thus, once we allow any limitations at all to God's power or knowledge or goodness, the questions characteristic of pessimistic theology are bound to arise and *cannot be given optimistic answers*. The pessimistic agenda *overrides* the optimistic agenda.

(b) If the creator is omnipotent, omniscient and good, the way things are is the way a good God *intended*. When we recoil in horror at other people's crimes, we accept that they are within the range of events which have been permitted by a good God for the greater good. We may wonder why God permits them — this is the problem of evil — but whatever happens has been permitted by God for good reasons, even if we do not understand them. In pessimistic theology, on the other hand, evil is not permitted for the greater good. It has no redeeming features. It is pure *tragedy*. God stands helpless in the face of it, and so do we.

(c) In optimistic theology, part of the world's goodness lies in the opportunity we have to choose between good and evil. Disciplining ourselves to overcome our bad habits, forgiving others when they hurt us and patiently enduring undeserved suffering, are *part of* what it means to be good. In pessimistic theology, they are an additional burden which was never intended by the good God. Ahura Mazda, for example, did not originally intend humanity to be faced with it. Plato's god would have fitted body and soul together more easily if he had been able to. Therefore even moral goodness is not what it ought to be, because in real life it is up against evils it was never designed to cope with.

(d) In optimistic theology, evil exists only to the extent that humanity causes it. To overcome it is precisely the task we have been given by God, and it is a real option. In pessimistic theology, the cause of evil lies beyond us: from our point of view, we are trapped in it. It is *inescapable*.

For these reasons, it seems best to categorize the range of theologies into two types. In optimistic theology, the fundamental nature of reality is goodness, and evil takes place within the context of an overall goodness. In pessimistic theology, the fundamental nature of reality is not complete evil — humanity cannot cope with that possibility — but rather, *conflict* between good and evil. Whatever is good, and whatever is evil, occurs within the context of an overall state of conflict. For human life, this conflict is inescapable and tragic. It leads to an agenda for human life which is concerned, not with making the most of it, but with finding ways to resist evil and protect whatever remains good.

The history of Christianity has produced a wide range of theological traditions and I have only mentioned a few. Were we to examine others, I would expect a similar pattern to emerge. Living traditions generally incorporate some ideas from optimism and some from pessimism. At the points of intersection between the two, there are bound to be unanswered questions. Optimistic theology will have no way of dealing with them, but pessimistic theology will always be able to invent another story about the gods or appeal to the inferior quality of human understanding. The questions will eventually be resolved by being given pessimistic answers. As the tradition develops over time, its pessimistic elements will, so to speak, invade the territory of its optimistic elements.

Nevertheless, pessimism is quite different from optimism. However fine the differences may be on a cosmological level, in practice they tell humanity to do completely different things. I shall consider the practical implications in the next chapter.

1   D S Russell, *The Method and Message of Jewish Apocalyptic*, pp. 258-61.
2   M Boyce, *Zoroastrians*, pp. 20-25.
3   D S Russell, *The Method and Message of Jewish Apocalyptic*, pp. 228f.
4   M Boyce, *Zoroastrians*, p. 44.
5   M Boyce, *Zoroastrians*, p. 29.
6   An influential heresy, Zurvanism, reflected on the origins of Ahura Mazda and Angra Mainu. But its answers produced no new ideas: they are of the type which refer back to other gods (M Boyce, *Zoroastrians*, pp. 67-70).
7   D S Russell, *The Method and Message of Jewish Apocalyptic*, pp. 224f, 230f, 241-5.
8   J J Collins, *The Apocalyptic Imagination*, pp. 5-17; D S Russell, *The Method and Message of Jewish Apocalyptic*, pp. 379-385. Earlier in the twentieth century scholars believed that the imminent end was the central doctrine of the whole Apocalyptic movement. About half the documents now available expect it.
9   It was popularized by Schweitzer at the beginning of the twentieth century,

and has remained popular since. E P Sanders, *Jesus and Judaism*, is a recent defence.

10 C H Dodd, *The Parables of the Kingdom*.

11 Fisher, Kathleen, 'The miracles of Mark 4:35-5:43: their meaning and function in the Gospel framework', *Biblical Theology Bulletin*, January 1981, pp. 13-16.

12 J N D Kelly, *Early Christian Doctrines*, pp. 163-188.

13 *Against the Heresies* 5. pref.

14 *Or. Cat.* 22-4.

15 *Cat.* 13,1.

16 J N D Kelly, *Early Christian Doctrines*, pp. 346-8.

17 Augustine, *City of God*, 14.13.

18 D S Russell, *The Method and Message of Jewish Apocalyptic*, pp. 254-5.

19 Augustine, *City of God*, 11.11.

20 Plato, *Timaeus*, 28-30, pp. 41-2.

21 Plato, *Timaeus*, 42-44, pp. 58-60.

22 P Perkins, *Gnosticism and the New Testament*, pp. 9-19; H Jonas, *The Gnostic Religion*, p. 33.

23 H Jonas, *The Gnostic Religion*, pp. 49-51.

24 Sometimes, for example, the creator boasts 'I am the Father and God, and there is none above me'. This is followed by a voice from the sky declaring that he is wrong because such-and-such a god is above him. One instance is *On the Origin of the World*, II, 103, J M Robinson, Ed., *The Nag Hammadi Library*, p. 175.

25 For example, *On the Origin of the World* II, 112-3, J M Robinson, Ed, *The Nag Hammadi Library*, p. 180.

26 H Jonas, *The Gnostic Religion*, pp. 81, 114.

27 For example, *The First Apocalypse of James* 33-5, J M Robinson, Ed, *The Nag Hammadi Library*, pp. 265-6.

28 *Exc. Theod.* 78. 2, quoted in H Jonas, *The Gnostic Religion*, p. 45.

29 H Jonas, *The Gnostic Religion*, pp. 55-6.

30 J Dunn, *Unity and Diversity in the New Testament*, pp. 275-308. P Perkins, *Gnosticism and the New Testament. Theology Digest* 41, Spring 94, pp. 47f discusses the theme of Christians as strangers in the world.

31 E.g. 1 Tim 1:4, 7; 4:7; 6:20; Titus 1:14f; 3:9; Jude 4,7.

32 J N D Kelly, *Early Christian Doctrines*, p. 363.

Chapter 4

Good and evil worlds: contrasting implications

IN THE LAST two chapters I have described what I mean by optimistic and pessimistic theology and why they produce very different evaluations of the world. In this chapter I aim to draw out some of the practical implications and show that they lead to quite distinct programmes of action.

It might have been most helpful to use illustrations from modern political and economic debate, since these so often dominate public discussions about what humanity ought to spend its time doing. However, these debates pay little attention to either optimism or pessimism: they are dominated by neutralism, which I shall consider in Part 2. Optimism and pessimism survive best in the world of 'religion', which has become a distinct area of discourse. In this other world, religious belief explains the nature of reality. Optimists and pessimists produce different theories; there are times when they agree about what we ought to be doing, but even then they usually have different reasons for doing it.

Most of my examples, then, will come from religion. I will refer briefly to a wide range of beliefs. Some come from traditions I have already described in this book. Most come from personal experience. I realize that some of the beliefs I mention may seem very strange and I may be suspected of exaggerating, or setting up 'Aunt Sallies'. For this reason — at least, to satisfy myself — I have restricted the more extreme examples to ones which I have had a personal opportunity to discuss with people who sincerely believe them.

Living in the world

For pessimists, reality contains serious evil. It is tragic: it is only there because things are not the way they should be. It is also inescapable: whatever we do, our lives are up against it. We cannot make the world a better place. We ought not to become too comfortable in it. Instead, we need to clarify what counts as evil and protect ourselves against it. If the means of protection are to be trustworthy they must not be tainted by the natural order; they must bypass it and come directly from God. For this reason pessimists tend to be very concerned with *uniqueness* and *distinctiveness.* The wider the separation between the holy and the ordinary, the better.

The uniqueness of Christ is central to most pessimistic versions of Christianity. It can be explained in a number of ways, but what makes him so important is precisely that he was *not* just one more human being. Other religions produce similar variants, which look for a divinely appointed person with unique powers.

Usually, Christ is not the only unique feature. Pessimistic theology trades in many uniquenesses: the bible, holy actions performed by the true church and properly ordained priests, the prayers and miracles of true Christians. In each case the emphasis on the special nature of the holy downgrades everything natural.

It follows that believers must also be distinct from nonbelievers. Pessimists often draw sharp dividing lines between the two. This leads to a persistent problem: the need for observable differences. For a long time Calvinists were wont to treat wealth as a sign of divine blessing. Today pessimists often seek the signs of a true Christian in personal morality. Unfortunately, observable differences in moral standards rarely correlate with membership of a church. A common solution is to focus on one or two sins which are well known in the host society, and conduct fierce campaigns against them. Abortion and homosexuality head the list at the moment; a generation ago alcohol did. In this way they can generate an appearance of moral superiority, provided that sect members do not succumb to the sin of the day.

Optimists believe that the whole of life, and the world around us, are good gifts from a good God. The world is good as it is, in its normal, everyday manifestations. Within it there is much evil, caused by the human misuse of freedom, but even the need to oppose evil takes place within the context of an overall goodness. The emphasis, then, is on *affirming* and *celebrating* God's goodness and the goodness of the world.

Optimists have no need to draw sharp boundary lines. The whole world is of God and is capable of reflecting God's glory. Different people are more or less sinful: it is a matter of degree, not of making simple distinctions. It is still possible to believe that Jesus was sinless, or that he had some divine characteristic which nobody else has ever had, but this is no reason for setting him apart from the rest of humanity. On the contrary, we should positively *welcome* the possibility that other people may have lived similar lives and achieved just as much, or may do so in the future.

The same applies to other aspects of religious life. We should *welcome* the fact that the elements of Holy Communion come from ordinary bread and wine, and that the bible was written by ordinary people, because they show us that God affirms the value of normal, natural life.

Sources of knowledge

Optimists and pessimists have different attitudes to authority, roughly following the lines of the traditional Christian debate between *natural* and *revealed* theology. In general, pessimists have reason to doubt the reliability of our natural faculties. Some anticosmic myths, for example, tell us that they were created by evil gods specifically to deceive us. Reliable information comes from sources which are untainted by the natural order. The Pope's encyclicals, or the the bible, or the 'word of prophecy', are reliable precisely because they do *not* come from ordinary humans, but tap into an unnatural source of authority. The theories of evolutionists are mere human opinion, but the bible gives us the facts.

In its extreme form this pessimism undermines all science. In religious circles it sets up a sharp distinction between those who accept the other-worldly authority and those who do not. This is why pessimists so often split into competing sects: each one has its own theory about the truth, and since each theory has to be accepted as it is without being subjected to mere human reason, there is no means to resolve disagreements.

Optimists value the range of human faculties: reason, the senses and instinct all provide information about reality. They are given to us by a good God and are therefore capable of doing whatever God expects us to do with them. In general we should expect to seek truth about God and religion in much the same way as we seek truth about anything else. For example, students of economic theory or medical technology character-istically believe *both* that they are standing in a tradition, learning from the past and adding to it, *and* that any feature of the current consensus may be overturned in the future as new discoveries come to light. Similarly, the writers of Genesis and the Gospels could not have produced creative and meaningful theology unless they were prepared *both* to make use of their traditions *and* to challenge tradition with their own insights. The value of the bible, then, does not depend on a unique method of production. If it was written by ordinary people, using their natural capacity to reflect on life and respond to God, it is none the worse for that. We should not be afraid to ask of it the questions we might ask of any other book.

Responding to evil

To optimists, evil exists, but within a universe which is fundamentally good. It is allowed for the sake of a greater good. There is no completely unredeemable evil. Ultimately, — at the level of how-God-created-the-world-to-be — to desire the triumph of good over evil is to flow *with* the grain of the natural order, not against it. There is a real sense in which virtue is its own reward. Evil is caused by humans, each of whom has good qualities and is capable of overcoming his or her weaknesses. We do not overcome evil by using force to make it impossible, or to restrain the people who are likely to commit it. God could have done that, but chose the better way of giving us free will. Rather, we overcome it by doing what God does: encouraging and developing the good qualities of evildoers, working towards the day when they freely choose good.

For these reasons, forgiving wrongdoers and patiently enduring evil are creative acts of goodness in their own right. When we respond to evil with good, or simply refuse to return evil for evil, we are helping to make the world a better place. By contrast, when we suppress or punish evil by force, we may well be simply indulging a desire which is itself evil. Two wrongs do not make a right.

To pessimists this is far too weak a response. Evil, far from being permitted by God, undermines God's control. From this perspective, forgiveness and endurance are not constructive responses at all. We need to actively oppose the forces of evil, to stop them doing harm. We cannot stand on niceties: what we need is *victory* by the forces of good, to impose a new world order. Triumph over the powers of evil is a matter of spiritual warfare and has its own importance, over and above the moral duty to live a good life.

Ethics

To optimists, God has given us freedom to do good or evil because it is an opportunity to become holy, if we so choose. Since the choices are made available within God's good world, living an ethically good life is to live with the grain of nature, not against it. We should aim to live in harmony with our bodies, other people and our environment. The ethical life is not a battle against human nature as such, but against our wrongdoing. In the long run and from a universal perspective, it is in our interests to live the way God has designed us to live.

Pessimists, because they tend to draw sharp distinctions between true believers and outsiders, often have a two-tier ethical system. One set of rules is for how to relate to the outside world with its evils. Our lives are inescapably up against them — whether the evil of the natural world, or demons, or unsaved neighbours, or our inner natures. The question is how to endure valiantly without falling by the wayside. The other set of rules governs relations with other believers and carves out a sphere of holiness which contrasts with the life of the world outside.

Because pessimists understand ethics in these terms, they may see little point in dialogue with outsiders about moral standards. Outsiders do not recognize the true nature of good and evil and therefore cannot be expected to accept the rules. They have no business discussing the internal affairs of the sect. Thus pessimistic ethical systems characteristically teach that outsiders must be converted first, before any sharing of views about right and wrong becomes possible.

Life after death

Life after death is important to pessimists for three main reasons. Firstly, the turn away from what is evil in the world generally requires a turn towards something else. If our present existence is 'a vale of tears', somewhere there must be something better.

Secondly, pessimism often inherits the Zoroastrian doctrine of rewards and punishments. The conflict between good and evil in this world means that the good often suffer more than the evil. These injustices are tragedies caused by the forces of evil. They have no redeeming features, let alone any ultimate purpose. The next life is the obvious place to settle old scores. This doctrine adds another element of divisiveness to pessimistic theology: the good news for some will be bad news for others.

Thirdly, life after death will vindicate true believers. This idea stems from the anticosmic agenda. Members of pessimistic sects often teach that they alone understand the true nature of reality; but they die with their wisdom unrecognized by the vast majority of people. After death, perhaps, they will receive their reward. Again, the good news for some will be bad news for others.

The idea that some will go to eternal bliss and others to eternal damnation is the clearest example of how the pessimistic agenda, once accepted, overrides the optimistic agenda. Here we are, in a temporary life, for a mere seventy years or so, and what happens within it will determine our destiny for the whole of eternity! Even if post-death conditions were not so extreme — if, say, the issue was between being a milkman or a postman for eternity — the very fact that it would last for eternity would make its importance override all this-worldly considerations. *Every* aspect of earthly life would pale into insignificance beside it. So much the more if the differences are much greater, as we are so often warned. In the shadow of eternity, this life ceases to have any significance in itself: the *only* thing which matters about it is passing That Great Exam.

In the history of Christianity pessimists have often backed up their theories with action. At the time of the medieval Inquisitions, it seemed clear to the torturers that a brief period of intense pain in an earthly torture chamber was far better for the sufferers than an eternity of divine punishment. The torture was for their own good. The logic is impeccable, if only we accept the theology. In the affluent west today, politeness and decency forbid such extremes. There is no excuse: those who really believe that their next door neighbours are going to suffer agony for the whole of eternity for not accepting the Christian faith, are guilty of the most extreme negligence if they do not treat the matter with the greatest urgency, as the Inquisitors did. Nobody goes this far, of course. Despite the rhetoric, the pessimists of today do not take the doctrine as seriously as its content demands.

Optimistic theology has no reason to accept any of the pessimist's reasons for believing in life after death. We should not look forward to the next life as a way of turning away from this one, since this one is to be valued as it is. Unresolved injustices can be forgiven, and there is no need for a cosmic 'Prize Day' with public announcements of those who believed the right things. No doubt we are all partly right and partly wrong.

However, as I noted in Chapter 2, there is another, quite different, reason for optimists to believe in life after death. It is the simple fact that we die. If our lives are of real value, it seems odd that God should discard us at death as though we were worthless. God's purposes for us must continue.

Heavenly rewards and punishments are less likely to figure in the speculations of optimists. If they are there at all, they will not threaten us. This life is to be lived and valued for its own sake, not as a test in preparation for the next one. Perhaps this is why God keeps so quiet about what the next life will be like.

Evangelism

Optimists believe in promoting their views for practical reasons. Human society is part of God's good world, but people's misdeeds cause many things to go wrong and at any one time many people are suffering because of the wrongdoing of others. Life is better lived when we understand the truth about reality and make our decisions accordingly. This general concern for the world is reflected in socially concerned activity — voluntary care, pressure groups, politics. They engage in these things just like concerned non-Christians, and with them. The difference their Christianity makes is that they think their beliefs about God provide a truer understanding of life and therefore a truer understanding of what needs to be done. Within the course of their socially concerned activities they will welcome opportunities to explain why they believe what they do. Still, their faith does not entitle them to claim a special divine authority. Truth may emerge through the meeting of minds, but believers have no trump card to play.

Pessimists are more likely to believe they *do* have a trump card to play: divine revelation. Because it is the only reliable source of truth, there is a sharp distinction between the people who accept it and the misguided ones who put their trust in their own rationality. Evangelism, therefore, is a distinct, one-sided form of communication. There is no equality between believer and unbeliever. If the believer listens carefully to the unbeliever and tries to enter the unbeliever's world sympathetically, there is a danger of being led astray by the devil's influence. The aim is not to show how one's own position is reasonable, but to play the trump card: the appeal to a divine authority which overrides every conversation and every rational conclusion.

Worship

When optimists attend church services they expect to celebrate and enjoy God's goodness and develop their commitment to living a godly life. There is an analogy with voluntary societies: in the same way, an environmentalist attends a Friends of the Earth meeting to find out information about the environment, receive inspiration and encouragement and go home again with new ideas about how to put the vision into practice.

When pessimists worship, there is a greater sense that they are coming together to engage in their distinctive religious activities *away from the wicked world*. At its most extreme, the element of mutual reinforcement will become a kind of debriefing. The outside world is constantly tempting believers to stray from the narrow way: within the safe, supportive group the important thing is to reaffirm the truths which are unknown to outsiders and warn waverers against doubt. The group often tells itself that it is rejected by the outside world. This helps accentuate the distinction between members and outsiders, and encourages members to reject the outside world in return.

In addition pessimistic worship is often the means to acquire special spiritual gifts, or grace, which is not available at all to non-worshippers. Among Catholics one thinks of the grace acquired through the sacraments; among Charismatics, specialist forms of prayer in the context of healing or exorcism. To this extent, worship has an objective focus. What matters is not whether you feel uplifted, but whether you really did receive God's grace through the sacrament, or whether God's healing power really did work through you. For this reason the experience must be *valid*. Like magic, whether the act achieved its objective intention often depends on whether the ingredients, words and actions were exactly correct. The printed order of service must be followed precisely, prayers must be offered in the name of Jesus, the priest must be validly ordained, the candidate for healing must have the right kind of faith.

Prayer

The function of prayer varies along the same lines. For pessimists, it characteristically focuses on persuading God to do something which God would otherwise not have done — forgiving one's sin, perhaps, or healing an illness. With their clear distinction between the ordinary workings of nature and the interventionist acts of God, they appeal to one to override the other. This presupposes that the praying Christians know what to pray for and that God will perform the required intervention only after suitable prayers have been offered. Pessimists construct theories to explain why God will not do what needs to be done if it is not prayed for, or not prayed for 'in the name of Jesus', or with enough faith.

To optimists, all this inverts the proper relationship between us and God. It is God who knows what needs to be done, and humanity which has been given the power to do it. When we pray we do not need to tell God what needs doing, but we should give God the opportunity to tell *us* what to do. Prayer, then, is a way of relating to, or coming into harmony with, the divine. The overall intention is to become more like God. There will be more emphasis on celebration, thanksgiving, praise and reflection on our lives.

Church structures

Pessimists are likely to treat the church, or their own sect, as a boat in a storm: it is the place where one is safe from the influence of the outside world. What matters about it is that it possesses that divine revelation which sets it apart. It would be quite wrong to combine with a church or sect which does not share one's own version of the truth. The whole point of having a church at all would be undermined if the ways of the unsaved were to prevail — if the Eucharistic Prayer was said by an invalidly ordained priest, or if the sermon was preached by someone who was not a true biblical believer.

There is no question of 'keeping up with the times'. Changes will be designed to keep the world's influence out, not to let it in. The general stance towards the outside world will be a matter of gaining converts from it, not caring for it for its own sake: after all, what is most important about other people is not how rich or healthy they are, but whether they are saved or damned. Money and effort will be concentrated not on social service but on whatever is perceived as the specific task of the church — evangelism, perhaps, or the administration of the sacraments.

Optimists are more inclined to think of the church as part of the world, not separate from it. What matters is not that it should have a particular structure, but that it should fulfil its purpose as well as possible. There is less need for clear boundaries between what is acceptable and what is unacceptable, or between insiders and outsiders. The church's money and energy is best spent when it expresses concern for the world. Optimists may get irritated by expenditure on the local church building or its furnishings, and accuse the church of being inward-looking instead of doing something for the poor, the Third World or the environment.

Caring for the world

Perhaps most obviously of all, different evaluations of the world lead to different views about whether and how to care for it. To optimists the natural order, as created by God, has value in itself and is just what we need to live fulfilled lives. We should use it, but not suppress it or transform it into something else.

For pessimists, this does not apply. There is real evil in the world. Depending on what it is, it needs to be killed, or suppressed, or transcended. I have noted how Zoroastrians believed in killing certain animals because they were created by an evil god. Plato taught that the bodily passions need to be controlled by the soul. Later I shall refer to Francis Bacon's view that the whole of nature was corrupted at the fall and needs to be suppressed by science and technology. Somehow or other, pessimistic theories set up an opposition between humanity and at least part of our environment, because of the evil in it.

Not all pessimistic theories seek to destroy part of the natural order. Instead, some recommend having as little as possible to do with it. To this extent, they are allies of modern ecological concern. The alliance, however, is accidental: they are not interested in protecting or developing nature's goodness. What is fundamental to pessimism is the presence of evil in the world, which in some way or other sets us against it. What we do about being against it varies from one theory to another, but the stance of being against it denies that we should value it positively.

Conclusion

These are some of the ways optimistic and pessimistic theology, with their different evaluations of the world, produce different doctrines and recommend different actions. We could add endlessly to the list, but I think they should provide a strong enough basis for the following observations.

Firstly, there is no tradition within Christianity which represents either extreme perfectly. All living versions of Christianity are to some extent compromises. We cannot, for example, pick out post-Vatican 2 Catholicism, or the House Church movement, as a perfect example of one or the other. Supporters of a particular tradition may respond to some of my examples along the lines of 'I agree with it to some extent, but I wouldn't go to that extreme'.

Secondly, although each tradition within Christianity compromises between the extremes, the compromises vary immensely. Some approximate to one extreme, some to the other.

Thirdly, when we look at any actual expression of Christianity, its value judgements about the world are reflected in a huge range of beliefs, rituals and practices which did not at first seem to be anything to do with value judgements about the world. Contrary to appearances, the doctrine that God is completely unknowable, or transubstantiation, or particular styles of evangelism, do in fact presuppose particular value judgements about the world. Many people, for all sorts of reasons, accept the doctrines without sharing the matching value judgement; but it is those who do share the matching value judgement who will most strongly feel that the doctrines make sense.

Fourthly, the western Christianity of today is dominated by the elements I have described as pessimistic. Some of the views I have described as optimistic will strike many people as barely Christian at all.

I suspect that there has been a long-term drift towards pessimistic theology within Christian history. I mentioned some possible reasons in Chapter 3. Whenever there is conflict between two doctrines, one pessimistic and one optimistic, pessimistic theology can accommodate it more easily because it already includes a theory of conflict. Whenever we are faced with two different agendas, a pessimistic one and an optimistic one, the pessimistic one generally presents itself as more urgent. I think there is another reason too. When optimism is in the ascendant, it justifies itself largely by appealing to reason. When pessimism is in the ascendant, reason plays less part and the church appeals more to its own authority. It therefore needs to lay down authoritative statements which declare where it stands, so that it can then say to waverers, 'If you do not accept this, you are not one of us'. For example, early Anglicanism produced a revival of optimistic theology in the writings of Hooker, Andrewes, Herbert and others. In their day, they expressed the soul of the Church of England. Yet none of their writings were formally established as authoritative teachings in it. On the other hand, the Thirty-Nine Articles, with their overwhelmingly pessimistic theology, have been. Even today, priests are required to assent to them. Over time, authoritative pessimistic doctrines have accumulated.

The history of Christianity contains a huge range of different doctrines, which have been combined in countless different ways to produce a wide variety of theologies. My analysis should indicate why some groups of doctrines combine together more easily than others. I would anticipate that the same type of analysis could be applied to other religious traditions too, with comparable results.

This completes my analysis of optimistic and pessimistic theology. Both appeal to a true standard of goodness, sanctioned by a supreme good god. Optimists believe that, according to this standard, the world is good. People who evaluate it as good are right and people who evaluate it differently are wrong. This evaluation is justified by the belief that the good God also has complete power and knowledge and has deliberately created the world to be a good one. Pessimists believe that the world is not this good. They draw attention to the widespread existence of evil, and conclude that there must be a tragic and inescapable source of evil, over and above human wrongdoing. The world cannot have been made by a God of complete power, knowledge and goodness.

The third option is that there is no absolute standard by which to judge the goodness of the world. This is what I shall consider in Part 2.

PART 2

Chapter 5

God, matter and the laws of nature

I~T IS A SUNNY~ summer evening. The workmen have gone home and the building site, surrounded by its high wire fence, has been locked up. This does not deter the local youngsters. It is a poor area, with many young people and little for them to do. In no time at all, half a dozen are over the fence. A pile of bricks is rearranged to serve as goal-posts. A plank of wood, broken in half, serves as two cricket bats. A bath is inverted and the youngest member of the group is pushed inside it.

After a while a quarrel breaks out between two of the boys. Joe has a roll of electric wire. He claims that as he got to it first, it is his. Nick insists that he saw it first, and had called out, 'See that wire up there? That's mine!' If he had not, Joe would not even have noticed it. He appeals to the gang leader. The leader calls the others and asks which of them heard Nick call out his claim for the wire. Two of them say they heard it, so the leader pronounces judgement: Joe must give it to Nick. Then somebody spots the arrival of a policeman, and suddenly the site is deserted.

Later, back home, the question is raised again by their older sisters. But the sisters bring a completely new dimension into it. According to them, the wire does not belong to either of the boys. It belongs to the workmen and should be given back. The boys point out that before the workmen arrived, there was a row of derelict houses on the site and they had played there undisturbed. It was the only interesting place in the neighbourhood where they could go. They had had many good times there, and were never consulted when the workmen arrived to put the fence up.

'But it's the law!' scream the sisters.

'Since when have you been so concerned about the law?' reply the boys. 'What about all those things you take from the shops?'

'That was a long time ago. We've stopped doing that. It's wrong.'

'You only stopped because you got a job and you could afford to pay for things. If you lose your job, what will you do then? Will you stop using lipstick and hair spray?'

'That's not the point. The wire doesn't belong to you.'

This story can be told over and over again in every inner city area. These are the conflicts which arise in deprived communities, and the value systems which people develop in order to cope with them. The boys have a point which needs to be taken seriously. They have no money, and the political establishment which decided to erect buildings on the site did not take their needs into account, let alone consult them. From their point of view the law is hostile to their interests and the question 'Why should I obey the law?' needs an answer. Given their deprived circumstances, the only way they can make something of their lives is by trying to carve out for themselves a realm of meaning and excitement, even though it conflicts with the law. Within this realm of their own, they develop their own value judgements and methods for settling disputes. Others read the headline 'Callous Vandals Wreck Building Site'. Most have no idea what life in deprived inner city areas is like; they express anger and think it self-evident that everybody should always obey the law. But this only expresses *their* interests, and their lack of concern for the deprived.

The elder sisters, too, have a point. They naturally want to share the social life of their peers, and if that means shoplifting, and all their friends shoplift, they will do the same. Once they are offered a job and can afford to buy the things they want, they have a stake in society. Emotionally, they are only too glad to resolve the conflict caused by stealing. Their hypocrisy, so evident to their younger brothers, reveals that they are learning to adopt the values of adults.

In ways like these, we all allow our lives to influence the kinds of value judgements we make. In a sense we are all like the boys in the building site: if we find ourselves in a situation where there seem to be no moral norms, values or purposes, we invent them quickly enough.

In Part 1 I considered the types of theory which lead to the conclusion that value judgements are *objective*. If they are, there is a truth about what is of value, over and above the evaluations people actually make. On this basis it is possible to make a distinction between right and wrong values. We can say that the boys were wrong to take the wire and the sisters were right that they should give it back. People who campaign against abortion would have precious little influence if their only reason for opposing it was 'My hormones make me feel like this'. What they tell us is that abortion *really is* wrong, whether or not the majority, or the government, think so.

As we saw in Part 1, the idea of objective values is justified by appealing to a higher authority. It makes sense to accept the authority of a superior being who has our best interests at heart and understands them better than we do. But what if there no such being?

In Part 2 I shall consider weaker, *subjective* evaluations. I propose to define 'neutralism' as the belief that there are no objective values. It therefore covers all types of evaluation which are not covered by optimism and pessimism. It is justified by any cosmology which does not contain a divine being whose evaluations are authoritative. If there are no gods at all, only humans can create values. Alternatively there may be gods who do not evaluate. Even if they do evaluate, according to some theologies there is no need for us to accept their judgements. An example would be the Babylonian gods described in Chapter 1. In all these cases there is no objectively given truth about value; if we judge life to be valuable, we do so only on our own authority.

Neutralists, then, have the option of refusing to make any evaluations at all, either positive or negative. In the 1960s it became fashionable for a while to treat all value judgements as unjustified. One was forever being *accused* of making them, as though a rational person never did such a thing. In practice human beings find it quite impossible to live without them. Philosophers today discuss a wide range of neutralist theories of value, as I shall indicate in Chapter 7.

Throughout history there have been neutralists. As far as we know they have usually been in a minority; but over the last three centuries a neutralist tradition has dominated western Europe and now influences the whole world. Because it offers a world-view, or 'paradigm', which affects every aspect of our lives today, we often fail to realize that we share it; it just seems to us to be 'common sense', and it often surprises us that anybody could think otherwise. At a popular level it is most influential in the way we understand the world around us and the way we think science operates. Critics often describe this as 'the mechanistic paradigm'.[1]

In Part 2 I will concentrate on this neutralist tradition. It characterizes the 'modern' age, and some critics describe themselves as 'postmodern' to contrast their own ideas with it. My analysis will agree with some of the critics but not all; in my view, some theories which are described as postmodern are really the logical consequences of modern neutralism and should be seen as part of modernism even if they help unravel it.

Chapter 5 will explore the mechanistic paradigm as it has been propounded between the seventeenth century and the present day. I do not wish to blame the seventeenth century mechanists for the problems of today; if we carry on taking for granted the ideas of three hundred years ago, even though they now cause us to destroy the world, that is our folly, not theirs. Nevertheless if we are to stop doing the damage, and do something more sensible instead, we will need to understand where we have gone wrong.

The mechanistic paradigm

The seventeenth century mechanists were largely reacting against the *occult*. They produced a new set of theories which borrowed and adapted the ideas of the fourteenth century sceptics. The sceptics, in turn, had been trying to settle the dispute between 'faith' and 'reason'. As medieval scientists studied the world they produced theories which contradicted the Church's teachings, and sometimes the bible. A debate developed between 'faith' — the inherited teachings of the Church — and 'reason' — the theories of scientists. Many philosophers tried to reconcile the two, but not even Thomas Aquinas, the greatest of the thirteenth century theologians, could satisfy both sides.

The sceptics gave up trying to reconcile them and instead separated them into distinct worlds, each with its own methods. The truths of religion are revealed by authority — the Church and the bible — and are to be accepted by faith. No amount of human reasoning, they taught, can increase our understanding of religious matters, because God is beyond all reason. William of Ockham believed that God is completely free and can do anything at all, even to the extent of overturning the categories of good and evil or cause and effect, or awarding salvation at random. Among his followers, Robert Holcot and Adam of Woodham defended God's freedom to lie and sin.[2] The natural order, on the other hand, is to be studied by human reason. Just as no amount of reason can tell us anything about religious truth, so also the Church and the bible cannot tell us anything about the world around us.

In effect this meant emptying the world. Throughout the Middle Ages, the ordinary folk of Europe had taken for granted that the natural order was full of processes and forces which they did not understand. Many a village had its 'wise woman' or 'sorcerer' whose herbs, spells and prayers were recommended for healing the sick, recovering lost property or pronouncing a verdict on suspected criminals. Generally they did not distinguish as we would between natural, magical and spiritual remedies; in either case, nobody could explain how they worked, and in that sense they were occult. Often enough the same was said of the Church's prayers.[3] The sceptics rejected this rich and uncertain world. Reason was supreme in the natural order. Nothing was occult. Everything was completely accessible to human observation and understanding.

If the fourteenth century sceptics, led by Franciscan friars, emptied the world, the pagans of the fifteenth century Renaissance filled it up again. Astrology, fatalism and magic became popular and taught people that their lives and the world around them were controlled by hidden powers beyond the scope of human understanding. As a reaction against fourteenth century scepticism, no doubt, it was a great relief: but the price was a world full of hidden forces and a powerless humanity. Pessimistic theology dominated the Christianity of the time and reinforced the general picture: the devil and evil spirits were all around us. The doctrine of the fall was all too real.[4] Many people felt a strong *fear* of the natural environment. Luther was one:

> Our body bears the traces of God's wrath, which our sin has deserved. God's wrath also appears on the earth in all creatures... And what of thorns, thistles, water, fire, caterpillars, flies, fleas, and bedbugs? Collectively and individually, are not all of them messengers who preach to us concerning sin and God's wrath?[5]

At the same time European society was becoming more aware of the advances it was making in the arts, mathematics, science and technology. There was a sense of excitement: humanity was making *progress*. Every society looks for ways of overcoming its problems, and this generally means revealing and manipulating natural processes which were previously hidden. There was less and less need to cringe in fear at the natural order.

Seventeenth century society, then, not only inherited a divided reality, split into 'faith' and 'reason', but was faced with a conflict between the two. Theology, largely pessimistic, took a gloomy view: humanity was in the grip of hostile forces. Secular philosophy offered hope: science was learning how to control nature. The dominant answer was to treat one doctrine as the solution to the other.

It was most clearly expressed by Francis Bacon. According to Bacon, God gave humanity dominion over the world (Genesis 1:26) but this dominion was lost at the fall. We can overcome the effects of the fall in two ways: by the grace of Christ, as taught by the Church, and by learning, through scientific research, how to control nature.[6] In his day there was much speculation about a new age, which many believed was just beginning. Bacon adopted the idea and proposed a 'great instauration' — a restoration to humanity of the power over nature which had been lost at the fall. There were to be no occult powers: everything was to be open to human investigation.

> That the state of knowledge is not prosperous nor greatly advancing, and that a way must be opened for the human understanding entirely different from any hitherto known, and other helps provided, in order that the mind may exercise over the nature of things the authority which properly belongs to it.[7]

Bacon's language has an aggressiveness going far beyond the search for understanding. In the witch hunts of the time, torture was common, and Bacon used images from it to express how science should dominate nature. Nature was to be 'hounded in her wanderings', 'bound into service' and 'put into constraint' so that the scientist may 'torture nature's secrets from her'.[8] Given that Luther's fear of nature was common, we can understand how Bacon's aggressiveness rang like a message of hope.

Thus arose the mechanistic paradigm. Reacting against an oppressive nature, full of occult and fearsome forces, they went to the other extreme and set out to oppress it in turn. They were inspired by the prospect of *controlling* nature. Through scientific research, they declared, humanity has the power to discover nature's every secret. In this way they pitted humanity, with its scientific knowledge, *against* a hostile natural order, confident that they would win.

In order to make the project credible they needed to believe a number of things. Although many people believed the universe was full of self-willed spiritual beings, everything would need to function according to regular and predictable patterns. Although it seemed very complex, it would need to be simple enough for the human mind to understand it. Although it seemed to have countless hidden properties, it would need to be entirely accessible to human observation. They therefore described the universe as *determined, simple* and *observable*. They learned to think of it as a sort of gigantic machine, with every movement caused by a prior movement and causing something else in turn. They often described it as a clock, since clock technology was developing at the time.

Given the historical context, we can sympathize. Yet these ideas are still with us, over three hundred years later. Are they still credible and do they still proclaim a liberating message? Newton proposed that there were four elements of reality: God, absolute space and time, matter and eternal laws of nature. Later physicists dispensed with absolute space and time. What has happened to God, matter and the laws of nature as the implications of determinism, simplicity and observability have been worked out in scientific theory?

Determinism

It is virtually impossible for science to make any headway within a pessimistic theory of reality. Science depends on the assumption that the future will be like the past in some ways. If the universe was made by erratic gods with no consistent purposes, or if its fate depends on wars between gods, it may be that not even the gods know what will happen next. Or perhaps some of them do, in which case we may be able to get some information by communicating with them. Knowledge, in this case, will depend on prayer, or perhaps magical rituals. There will be no point in keeping records of observations and looking for patterns of regularities.

Some of the ancient Greek philosophers proposed an alternative view of reality. Even though they generally believed in gods, they denied that the gods affect the way the world works. Instead, nature functions according to *impersonal and eternal laws*. Therefore it makes sense to puzzle out what these laws are, and scientific research becomes meaningful.

If impersonal laws of nature are to function as the basis for science, they must be reliable. We need to be confident that the gods do not intervene to override them. The ancient Greek philosopher Aristotle believed that God is the 'unmoved mover', without parts or passions, who set the universe in existence but does not concern himself with it. Instead, he contemplates the only object worthy of his contemplation — himself.[9] In this way the foundations of neutralism were laid down: humanity relates not to concerned and evaluating gods but to impersonal nature, 'the way things are'.

Basil, the fourth century bishop of Caesarea, adapted Aristotle's theory to fit the Christian doctrine of creation. According to Basil the laws of nature do exist, but only because God created them. The regularity of nature is *caused by* God's deliberate, and good, provision. In this way he justified scientific research by appealing to a good God. His theory remained popular until the eighteenth century.[10] It reflects optimistic theology in two key ways.

(a) If science is to be possible, we need to believe two things: that the created order functions according to regular patterns and that the human mind is capable of perceiving them. Aristotle had affirmed the first. Basil combined the second with it: God, being good, has not only laid down laws of nature, but has also made us capable of discovering them. The same God does both, so they fit.

(b) To the Greek philosophers, nature's laws imposed regularity by their own power. To Basil, on the other hand, they were created by God to carry out God's commands. What God imposes is goodness, and regularity is one expression of it. In this way Basil reconciled the Greek emphasis on regularity with the Christian emphasis on goodness. By doing so, we might say that *from an optimistic perspective* he changed the concept of 'laws of nature' more than he changed the Christian doctrine of God's activity. What, after all, is the difference between saying that a good God acts regularly, and saying that a good God sets up a system of regular laws? The idea of placing a set of laws between God and nature only seems to explain regularity if we assume that impersonal laws act more regularly than a personal agent. In our own case this is usually true: hand-made products tend to vary more than machine-made products. We may also presuppose that time-consuming regular activities become boring and are best done by labour-saving devices. These analogies do not apply to God. We do not know whether God uses some kind of device to produce regularity, and from the point of view of optimistic theology it makes no difference. The phrase 'laws of nature' is basically a way of saying that God acts in a regular way.

A thousand years later, the sceptics of the later Middle Ages disagreed. In their view God was always free to act either regularly or irregularly. The laws of nature *contrasted with* God because they were reliable and comprehensible. It was the laws of nature, not God, which brought that all-important assurance that the world was an ordered and comprehensible place.

By the seventeenth century, the laws of nature had become part of Europe's mental furniture as principles which were quite distinct from God. Isaac Newton could assume that the way to defend the existence of God was to show that the laws of nature could *not* explain everything, so God must intervene from time to time.[11] This idea is often called 'the God of the Gaps'. Although it flourished for a long time, it did not fit the mechanistic paradigm: if we are to control the natural order, all its operations must be *determined* by the laws of nature.

Determinism involves two concepts. One is *regularity*. Only if things function according to regularities can we hope to predict what they will do in the future. The other is *causation*. There have been various theories about causation: do things function the way they do because their actions are caused by a divine being, or by impersonal laws of nature, or are they freely chosen by the thing itself, or completely random?

Processes may, of course, be caused without being predictable, if whatever causes them does not operate regularly. They may also be predictable without being caused. It may be, for example, that every time the ice cream van drives past my house I buy an ice cream; it does not follow that the van's arrival *causes* me to buy one. The mechanistic paradigm, however, with its desire to control the natural order, needs to believe that natural processes are both regular and caused. It characteristically claims that all regular processes must be caused by laws of nature, and processes which do not seem regular must be regular really — it must be just our lack of knowledge which stops us mapping them as regularities.

Are these beliefs justified? We need to examine what we mean by the laws of nature. If they are not God's regularities, what are they? If they are nothing to do with God, what we seem to be left with are self-existent entities which somehow cause things to happen in regular and predictable ways. As soon as we present the matter in this way, it is clear that we have created as many problems as we have solved. What do they consist of, and how do they make things behave the way they do?

In popular language we often speak of the laws of nature as if they *force* their effects to happen. A law 'brings about' its effect, or 'makes it happen'. Scientists often enough think along these lines too, and philosophers of science sometimes discuss the possibility of 'powers' or 'necessitations' of some sort.[12] If so, the laws of nature have some kind of *power* over physical events; we might picture them as 'machines in the sky', automatically producing particular effects in particular situations.

Most philosophers of science have not been convinced. As David Hume pointed out in the eighteenth century, when we say that one event causes another what we actually observe is only that one event is habitually followed by another. However often we observe the second event following the first, we never perceive the first *causing* the second.[13]

Characteristically, scientists describe laws in terms of observed regularities. Every morning the sun rises in the east. Whenever a solid is dissolved in a liquid, the boiling point of the liquid is raised. When a magnetic iron rod is broken in two, the pieces are magnets again. Thus the characteristic form of a law of nature is 'When the conditions are x, y happens'. When Newton 'discovered' the law of gravity, his discovery consisted of accounting for two sets of observations — things falling to the earth and planets circling the sun — according to the same mathematical principles. It was a great achievement indeed, but he did not observe an entity called 'gravity' forcing anything to do anything.

Most philosophers of science have followed Hume's lead. They avoid speculating about unobservable causal powers and concentrate instead on definitions which fit the observable phenomena: that is to say, the laws of nature are simply *formulae for describing observed regularities*.[14]

In that case, do they really *explain* why things happen the way they do? If you ask me 'Why do you eat so much ice cream?' you will probably not be satisfied with the answer 'Because when the ice cream van comes, I buy an ice cream'. The arrival of the van does not cause me to buy one. Tomorrow, you will point out, I could stay indoors. In the same way, if the statement 'Whenever a solid is dissolved in a liquid, the boiling point of the liquid is raised' *only* tells us what has been observed in the past, does it really explain anything?

This raises the question of what counts as an *explanation*. Explanations need to respond to the motivations behind our questions. Ancient religion was mainly concerned to *evaluate* the processes in the world around us. From this perspective, to posit an impersonal law of gravity as the cause of water flowing downhill does not explain anything. The question is simply shifted: we then need to ask who created the law of gravity, and why. The mechanist, on the other hand, wants to *control*. To this end, an observed regularity of the type 'When the conditions are *x*, then *y* always results' usually provides all the information required. To say 'water cannot flow uphill' helps us work out where to fix our gutters. If that is all that concerns us, so much the better if the laws of nature are impersonal and make no moral judgements on our actions.

In the mechanistic paradigm, then, a useful law of nature simply describes regularities in a way which helps us make predictions. Do past regularities, though, justify the assumption that they will continue in the future? Realist accounts of the laws of nature may offer reasons for predictability. If the reason why the sun has risen every morning so far is that God has made it rise, whether it will rise again tomorrow depends on God's intentions. Alternatively, if there is an impersonal 'machine in the sky' forcing the earth to spin, predictability depends on whether any screws are getting loose or any parts need oiling. Once we reject all realist notions, and the law 'the sun rises every morning' means no more than 'the sun has so far been observed to rise every morning', we have no way of knowing whether it will rise again tomorrow.

Although determinism is now widely taken for granted, the attempt to establish it has not succeeded. The part of the project which has made progress is the attempt to show that processes which at first seemed irregular can usually be mapped as regularities. On the other hand, in the process of establishing these regularities scientists have discovered ever more processes which have *not* been reduced to regularities. The faster they run, the further there is to go. Most now think it is not even theoretically possible to map every process as a regularity, and even if it is, the prospect of doing so is as remote as ever.

As for causation, Hume stands unrefuted: all we observe is sequences of events. We continue to *assume* that causation is a real process, and the assumption works, but we cannot prove it.

In practice we *trust* that there are regularities, that we can understand them well enough for most purposes and that they will continue in the future. Life would be impossible otherwise, but they remain acts of trust: we have not proved them.

Simplicity

In the seventeenth century it was far from obvious that the universe was simple enough for the human mind to comprehend. If scientists were to learn all about it, it would need to be far simpler than it seemed. Theory developed accordingly. Gassendi and Galileo revived the ancient Greek 'atomic' theory, according to which the world consists of atoms in motion in an infinite void. Atoms are hard and indestructible particles of different shapes and sizes. Fundamentally all reality reduces to shape, size, weight and motion. These are the 'primary qualities' of things. The only way one thing can act on another is by mechanical impact: one thing *pushes* another.[15] 'Secondary qualities' are the other characteristics which things seem to have, such as colour, taste and temperature. These do not exist objectively: they are simply the way our minds interpret the sensations we get when bodies of matter impact on our senses. According to Galileo,

> I think, therefore, that these tastes, odours, colours, etc., so far as their objective existence is concerned, are nothing but mere names for something that resides exclusively in our sensitive body, so that if the perceiving creatures were removed, all of these qualities would be annihilated and abolished from existence.[16]

Similarly, Descartes described matter as entirely passive. It is made up of corpuscles with definite sizes, shapes and speeds, and has no innate qualities. There is no weight, gravity or causation: what we observe is bodies of matter in relative motion, continually re-created by a consistent God.[17]

It was an extreme reaction, but we can see why it was popular. It meant that science was basically *mechanics*. They could already measure shape, size, weight and motion, and according to the theory nothing else was needed for a complete account of the natural world.

Since then the world has turned out to be more and more complex. In order to retain the theory of simplicity, mechanists have developed the idea of 'reductionism'. Descartes, using mathematics as a model, argued that we should break down every problem into its constituent parts until each part is so simple that the questions can be answered by direct intuition.[18] Similarly, in order to understand a complex organism — say an animal — scientists should see their task as a matter of dividing it into its parts and examining each part until they reach the most basic and simple constituents. Behind the theory lies the assumption that once they have got down to the constituent parts, and mapped them at the lowest possible level, they have achieved a complete understanding of the animal: in other words, that it is nothing but the sum of its parts. To suggest that there is anything else in addition would be to invoke something occult. This scientific reductionism easily leads to a reductionist *value judgement*, that every material thing is of no more value than the parts of which it is composed.

Does reductionism work? The debate continues. Granted that there are far *more* things and processes than the seventeenth century philosophers ever imagined, can they all be described according to a simple model of reality which can be understood by the human mind? As the world has turned out to be ever more complex, a *hierarchy* of sciences has developed. This hierarchy is usually described with physics at the 'lowest' level and above it chemistry, botany, biology and so on. Towards the top we might locate human sciences such as sociology and economics. Each science relates to a particular level of reality, and has its own set of theories, concepts, descriptions and techniques, but also depends on the laws of the sciences 'below' it. For example, what makes botany a separate science from chemistry is that it is a distinct level of activity, with methods and theories of its own which do not exist at the level of chemistry.[19] The question is, can the laws of each science be *reduced to* (described in terms of) the laws of the sciences below it, or not? If we knew enough about physics, chemistry and botany, would we be able to describe the laws of botany as special cases of the laws of physics and chemistry? The same question is asked all the way up the hierarchy. Total reduction would account for everything in terms of physics.

Scientists have had much success in splitting complex wholes into more easily understood component parts. To this extent Descartes was right. But they have not been successful at reducing processes.[20] This general failure, despite persistent attempts, is now a significant feature of science. The more they try and fail, the more likely it seems that that reductions of processes are impossible.

Opponents of reductionism have developed an alternative theory, known as 'emergence'. Emergentists accept that higher level processes cannot be reduced to lower level processes. Instead, when the processes involved in the lower level reach a particular intensity, a new pattern of behaviour 'emerges' which *could not be foreseen* by the laws of the lower level. For example, when chemical activity reaches a certain level, a process which we describe as 'life' emerges. When we say that life is an 'emergent' quality what we mean is (a) that the processes at work in living things cannot be described by the laws of chemistry — they need a separate science to describe them — and (b) that the emergence of life could not be foreseen by the laws of chemistry.[21]

We should not exaggerate the significance of emergence theory. When the processes in the lower level develop the appropriate intensity and the new processes emerge, the higher processes emerge *out of what was going on at the lower level*. To claim that the laws of one science cannot be reduced to the laws of another is to say that human scientific research cannot describe the link. In other words, what emergence theory achieves is that it retains the underlying unity of reality and the ability of scientists to explore it, while abandoning the idea that it is simple enough to understand.

In the twentieth century, quantum theory has done more than anything else to make the world appear more complicated. Perhaps the best example is the EPR effect. Einstein, Podolsky and Rosen established that once two quantum particles have interacted with each other they retain a power to influence each other even after they have been separated. Measuring one of these infinitesimally small particles produces an instantaneous effect in the other, even if the other has been moved to the far side of the world. The result was so astonishing that it has been subjected to a great deal of examination and is now well corroborated.[22]

The early mechanists could not have been more wrong about the world's simplicity. Since their time, scientists have discovered an ever more complex world, with a greater variety of processes than any Renaissance magician ever imagined. The complexity of reality is so far beyond our present understanding that even if a complete account of it is theoretically possible, we have no ground for expecting that we shall ever achieve it.

Observability

To say that nothing is occult is to say that everything must be observable. The early mechanists were so strongly committed to observability that, when Newton first published his findings about gravity, he refused to accept that there was a force acting on matter at a distance. Such a force would have to be occult and was therefore unacceptable.[23]

Although denying unobservables helped the cause of science then, it is more of a hindrance today. Scientists hypothesize the existence of many things which cannot be observed, such as electrons and black holes. To complicate the matter, many scientific experiments are conducted within complex machines and the results, instead of being directly seen by the human eye, are printed out by the machine. There is such a wide variety of these processes that it is impossible to draw a clear dividing line between observables and unobservables.[24]

The question of unobservables has generated a debate among philosophers of science. There are four main positions.

(i) 'Realism' is often described as the 'common sense' view: when scientists postulate the existence of electrons or black holes, they mean that these things really do exist, whether or not scientists know about them. In philosophical language, there is a *correspondence* between the scientist's concepts and the real world. Realists generally argue that this is the only way to defend science: scientists have to work on the basis that they are trying to find out about a reality which is already there.[25]

(ii) 'Empiricists' refuse to accept unobservables. There is one central argument. The reason why scientists postulate unobservables is that it helps them account for what they do observe. At one stage, for example, the puzzling orbit of Uranus provided the observed data and the existence of an unobserved planet — later called Neptune — was postulated to account for it. Often a theory which postulates unobservables can be tested by experiments. If the results fit the theory, this is taken as evidence that the theory is correct. However it presumes too much. In fact, whenever an unobservable is postulated to explain observed data, it is always possible to produce alternative theories which account for the same observables, *and would be confirmed by the same results of experiments.* In the case of Uranus and Neptune, one could imagine all sorts of undiscovered entities in the solar system. In practice scientists generally opt for the simplest solution, but there is a long list of simplest solutions which have later been refuted.

This part of the empiricist argument is generally accepted. Empiricists go on to conclude that, because observed data can always be explained by more than one set of unobservables, we cannot know anything at all about unobservables.[26]

(iii) 'Constructivists', or 'idealists', emphasize the role of theory. When scientists make observations about the world, they already presuppose theories about the nature of reality. If they did not, they would not be able to interpret their observations. Because different theories lead to different interpretations of the same observations, the reality which scientists discover largely depends on the theories with which they began. It is possible for contrasting theories to differ so much that they cannot even agree on a rational method to resolve disagreement.[27]

Does this mean that there is no objective reality apart from what our minds 'construct'? Some believe so: Henry Margenau, an American physicist, claimed that the neutron did not exist until it was 'discovered' in 1932,[28] but it is more common to believe that reality is an unstructured chaos and our theories provide ways of structuring it. Constructivism has been less popular among scientists than philosophers and I shall return to it in Chapter 6.

(iv) 'Pragmatists' argue that successful hypotheses about unobservables should be accepted simply as pragmatically useful features of scientific practice, not as true descriptions of reality.[29]

The disagreement between these schools of thought arises from a weakness within the mechanistic paradigm. The early mechanists rejected the occult and set out to show how everything is observable. What scientists have now found is quite different: when we study the things we can observe, we are led to the conclusion that other things exist, which we cannot observe. Each of these four theories in its own way abandons the idea that there is an objective physical reality which is entirely observable. Whichever theory we accept, the fully observable material world proclaimed by the seventeenth century mechanists is no longer an option.

Conclusion

Without doubt, modern science has explored reality far more impressively than anybody could have predicted in the seventeenth century. It has blossomed under the auspices of the mechanistic paradigm, and many people assume that the mechanistic paradigm must therefore be right. In fact, every major element in it has been rejected. The determined, simple, observable world we were promised, with its finite list of calculable laws of nature, has been refuted as conclusively as anything could be.

It is time to abandon determinism, simplicity and observability. We will always be surrounded by forces we do not understand, and will never establish complete control over nature. Does this mean we must return to that pre-modern age, when they lived in fear of nature and its occult forces?

There is a difference between now and then. It is evaluative. Then, mechanism reacted against oppressive pessimistic theology. It was a way of saying that we do not need to live in cringing fear of the forces of nature. Against the view that humanity cannot understand them, it insisted that we can. Against the view that they are hostile to us, it insisted that they are available to us and we can use them.

Today, the pessimistic theology which was then so oppressive is a minority interest. On the other hand scientists have observed, measured and explained so much that they themselves have come up against the limitations of determinism, simplicity and observability. It turns out that the world is more complicated than the human mind is ever likely to describe, let alone understand. There really are more forces at work than we can count, let alone understand. We probably never will reach a complete understanding of a single living thing, however minutely we split it into its parts. However, all this hidden complexity of nature has turned out to be *just what we need* if we are to live and flourish.

Today, those who stick rigidly with the mechanistic paradigm are no longer liberating us from a gloomy sense of oppression by the occult. Instead they are doing the opposite: with their perverse insistence that, against all appearances, the natural order contains nothing of intrinsic value, they are stopping us delighting in its goodness.

The motivation behind the mechanistic paradigm — the desire to control nature — is still with us. Western society has stopped worrying about demons and the occult, but the programme of establishing ever-greater control over nature is now treated as a self-justifying activity. As long as this urge persists, people will believe that nature has no value or purpose except to be available for use by humans.

Yet this is only part of the story. The relentless destructiveness of modern neutralism has even undermined its own programme of controlling nature. In the next chapter I shall show how.

1   This term has been popularized by F Capra, *The Turning Point.*
2   G Leff, *Medieval Thought: from St Augustine to Ockham*, pp. 286-294.
3   K Thomas, *Religion and the Decline of Magic*, Chapter 2.
4   K Thomas, *Religion and the Decline of Magic*, Chapter 1.
5   Werke Kritische Gesamtausgabe (Schriften) (Weimar), 39.1.205, quoted in P Santmire, *The Travail of Nature*, p. 125.
6   *Novum Organum*, Bk 2, Aph 52.
7   Preface to *The Great Instauration*
8   C Merchant, *The Death of Nature*, p. 169.
9   *Metaphysics*, 4.8, 9.8.
10   C Kaiser, *Creation and the History of Science*, pp. 4-34.
11   C Kaiser, *Creation and the History of Science*, p. 180.
12   D M Armstrong, *What Is a Law of Nature?*, pp. 121-3; P. Gasper, 'Causation and explanation', R Boyd, P Gasper & J D Trout, Eds, *The Philosophy of Science*, p. 290. Boyd defends the idea on p. 368.
13   D Hume, *Enquiries Concerning Human Understanding and Concerning the Principles of Morals*, 7.2.60.
14   R Boyd, P Gasper & J D Trout, Eds, *The Philosophy of Science*, pp. 355-68.
15   John Dunn, J O Urmson, and A J Ayer, *The British Empiricists*, pp. 95-105.
16   *The Assayer*, M R Matthews Ed., *The Scientific Background to Modern Philosophy*, pp. 56-7. Galileo also argued that it is as absurd to locate the colour in the body as to locate the tickle in the hand that caused it (John Dunn, J O Urmson, and A J Ayer, *The British Empiricists* p. 99).
17   J Cottingham, *The Rationalists*, pp. 116-22.
18   R Descartes, *Discourse on Method and the Meditations*, pp. 41f.
19   A R Peacocke, *Creation and the World of Science*, pp. 112-119.
20   A O'Hear, *An Introduction to the Philosophy of Science*, p. 189.
21   A O'Hear, *An Introduction to the Philosophy of Science*, pp. 177-201.
22   J Polkinghorne, *Reason and Reality*, p. 94.
23   John Dunn, J O Urmson, and A J Ayer, *The British Empiricists* p. 98.
24   A O'Hear, *An Introduction to the Philosophy of Science*, pp. 97-105.
25   R Boyd, P Gasper & J D Trout, Eds, *The Philosophy of Science*, pp. 195-221.
26   R Boyd, P Gasper & J D Trout, Eds, *The Philosophy of Science*, pp. 196-202.
27   R Boyd, P Gasper & J D Trout, Eds, *The Philosophy of Science*, pp. 12-13. The most influential constructivist account has been T Kuhn's *The Structure of Scientific Revolutions* (1970). As examples of incommensurable traditions Kuhn cites the transition from Ptolemaic to Copernican astronomy and from Newtonian mechanics to special relativity.
28   J Polkinghorne, *One World: The Encounter of Science and Theology*, p. 21.
29   An example is B von Fraasen, 'To save the phenomena', R Boyd, P Gasper & J D Trout, Eds, *The Philosophy of Science*, pp. 187-194.

Chapter 6

Humanity and nature: who controls whom?

IN THE LAST chapter I described the 'mechanistic paradigm' of the early Enlightenment philosophers. The natural order, they believed, is determined, simple and observable. At the time they were reacting against the idea that humanity is trapped in a hostile world full of occult powers. Instead of nature having power over us, they declared, we should have power over nature. They often described their age as the beginning of a new stage in history. They now had the will to establish control, and they understood how to go about it. By scientific study of the natural order they would accumulate more and more information.

How could they be sure their programme of transforming nature would work? Bacon, as we saw, believed we would be putting right what had gone wrong at the fall: God has designed the world to be dominated by us, so it must be possible. Later generations dispensed with the fall and God's intentions, and this left them without his reason for confidence. What if our efforts do more harm than good? Could the project be pure arrogance by a bigoted society, over-confident in its own powers? The dominant answer was to promote humanity every bit as much as they demoted nature: we are capable of acquiring *complete* and *certain* knowledge. Once we have it, they believed, the possibility of error will not arise. Since knowledge resides in the mind, they needed to show that the human mind is capable of receiving accurate information, understanding it and judging wisely how to use it. In this chapter I shall summarize modern theories of knowledge and the mind in turn.

The search for certainty

If certainty was to be possible, there must be a *method* for acquiring it. The seventeenth century mechanists, in philosophy as in science, tried to establish simple and universal procedures. Two types were proposed: *rationalism* and *empiricism*. Previous philosophers had of course recognized that we use both reason and the evidence of the senses in order to understand the world around us. These faculties were now refashioned into the tools of certainty.

Rationalism

Descartes provided the most influential seventeenth century account of rationalism. Reason, he believed, should be based on strict logical deduction from first principles. Each of us has an innate power to discover the first principles. We all have certain basic 'clear and distinct perceptions', which he called 'intuition'. Provided we proceed step by step from correct first principles, making no errors on the way, we can reach ever more complex conclusions.

To establish the first principles Descartes used his method of radical doubt. Doubting everything he could, he found himself left with the proposition 'I think, therefore I am'. This became his first principle. His next step was to deduce the existence of God. To do this he borrowed medieval arguments but turned them into strict logical deductions. Since his aim was to provide the means to certainty, the existence of God had to follow from his first proposition as surely as any geometrical proof. Once that had been proved, he appealed to the reliability of God — who would not engage in wholesale deception — to guarantee the truth of his intuitions and the reality of the 'external' world outside his mental images.[1]

Descartes' theory has had immense influence. It captured the mood of the age and gave people confidence in their own ability to discover new knowledge. On the other hand it has not stood up well to critical analysis.

One weakness is the role of God. In the last chapter I noted Basil's belief that the same God created both the material world and the human mind, so our minds are designed to understand the world. Some of the medieval scholastics elaborated the idea.[2] For them, however, faith in God always came first; there was nothing 'behind' faith to justify it.

When Descartes argued that God would not deceive, he was of course drawing on this medieval tradition. Earlier in his argument, however, he parted company with medieval theory by dispensing with faith and establishing God's existence by strict logical deduction. In this way he inverted the relationship between God and human reason. Human reason became supreme: the existence of *everything*, even the supreme divine being, was to be derived from it. Critics asked how he could prove the existence of God from his intuitions, if his intuitions could only be guaranteed *after* God's existence has been proved. On the other hand, if he could rely on intuition before he had proved the existence of God, then why not afterwards as well? In this case, does not God become irrelevant?

Later philosophers have tried to restate the argument, leaving God out, but this does not solve the problem. Whatever the first principles, we need assurance that we correctly understand them; and whatever we deduce from them, we need assurance that our deductive logic is valid. These assurances must be provided before the process begins, not after. Since this cannot be done, it seems that we cannot deduce knowledge with certainty from self-evident first principles.[3]

Empiricism

Whereas the rationalists began with the capacity to reason, the empiricists began with the information provided by the senses. Early Enlightenment empiricists often described the mind as being in its own 'box', containing the faculty of reason, but separated from the material world. The senses penetrate into it with information. The mind then uses reason to make sense of the information and build up a picture of the world. To John Locke, for example, what is contained in the mind is *ideas*. At birth, the minds of children are blank like white paper. The first marks on the paper are caused by the natural impact of particular ideas through the senses. These ideas are simple and in general cannot be wrong. The mind joins simple ideas together to create complex ideas, and at this point we can make mistakes.[4]

Although their starting point was the evidence of the senses, they did not mean to accept every claim to have seen an angel or demon: on the contrary, they wanted to show that stories like these were unscientific. What is real, they taught, is not what one, possibly misguided, person claims to have seen, but publicly available observations which can be checked — observed and measured — by others. All true knowledge, then, was to be restricted to what is known 'intersubjectively': that is, public information which, in principle, can be verified by anybody with the means to do so. The idea is still popular today: many believe that the only types of information which are really true are publicly observable and measurable 'facts'. If the doctor's measuring instruments indicate that there is nothing wrong with you, there really is nothing wrong with you.

How do we know that the senses provide true information? Locke answers that they reinforce each other by providing mutually compatible information, but this does not add up to proof. To strengthen his case Locke, like Descartes, appealed to a good Creator who would not deceive.[5] In his day such appeals were common. However we should note the theological implications. If God expects us to love our neighbours it is reasonable to assume that God will not deceive us about whether our neighbours exist and how we might show our love for them. If, on the other hand, we do things which God does not expect of us — such as acquiring complete and certain knowledge about the universe — we cannot take for granted that our minds are up to the task. The assumption that God would not deceive us only works when we are doing godly things.

Scepticism

Neither rationalism nor empiricism could produce a complete account of reality. At the very least they needed to be accepted together: the senses provide information about reality and the mind can reason about it. Combining the two, it was still possible to believe that everything which exists can be discovered in one of these two ways. Hume's conclusion to the *Enquiry Concerning Human Understanding* is a good example:

> If we take in our hand any volume; of divinity or school [scholastic] metaphysics, for instance; let us ask, *Does it contain any abstract reasoning concerning quantity or number?* No. *Does it contain any experimental reasoning concerning matter of fact and existence?* No. Commit it then to the flames: for it can contain nothing but sophistry and illusion.

Hume was pleased to dispense with God but persisted with his logic. As I noted in the last chapter, it led him to doubt causation as well. He went further still: we believe there is a world around us, and think we see and hear things, but all we really know is that we have perceptions in our minds. We have no way of checking whether these perceptions match the reality outside us.[6]

Modern scepticism is generally dated from Hume. There are many versions of it. We might describe the starting-point as the belief that reason and the senses can provide complete and certain knowledge. On this basis, what turns out to be non-existent? The mechanistic philosophers had intended to deny the existence of occult and spiritual forces. By the end of the eighteenth century, many said the same of God too. The same argument leads just as surely to denying 'metaphysical' concepts like causation. To cap it all, there is no absolute certainty even about the knowledge which reason and the senses do provide. If we must deny the existence of everything which cannot be proved to exist, then nothing exists at all.

Three kinds of response are possible. One is to accept the general framework of Enlightenment rationalism and empiricism, but find some way to fill the gaps. This was Kant's approach. Another is to keep the principle and deny whatever cannot be proved. This has led to logical positivism and non-realism. The third is to abandon the framework and give up the hope of certainty. I shall consider them in turn.

Idealism

Kant's 'idealist' theory classified judgements into three types. Two were inherited from the rationalists and empiricists respectively: reason provides secure statements about logic and mathematics and the senses produce new information. Kant argued that there is a third class, which add information but are not dependent on the senses. These he called 'synthetic *a priori*' judgements.[7] He believed that there are many instances of them, including most of mathematics and the basic presuppositions of the natural sciences and moral thought.[8]

According to Kant, then, the human mind — *all* human minds — naturally provide us with certain types of information. His theory has had an immense following and has spawned alternative versions of idealism. Today, however, few philosophers agree with him. One key problem is: since the synthetic *a priori* concepts are derived from a mental world quite separate from the material world, how do we know they are true? As Kant has maintained the gulf between mind and matter, his system does not provide a satisfactory answer. To those committed to the search for certainty, of course, there is no evidence that Kant's realm of mental constructs exists at all.

Logical positivism

The logical positivists flourished in the 1920s and early 1930s. They reaffirmed Hume's scepticism but concentrated more on linguistic analysis. Their central theory was the Verification Principle, which states that the meaning of a statement is the method of its verification. Meaningful statements can be verified, by either reason or the senses. Any statement which cannot be verified in either of these ways cannot be verified at all and is therefore meaningless.[9] Not only were they keen to dispense with God: they were willing to kill off causation too.[10]

In philosophical circles logical positivism has now been widely discredited. The Verification Principle stands accused of being self-refuting,[11] and in practice it empties reality far more drastically than even its authors intended: not only God and causation become meaningless, but also scientific axioms, mathematical formulae, the rules of logic, statements about the past,[12] other people's minds and statements about feelings. The writings of logical positivists express much concern that we can verify the existence of our own minds and feelings, but not those of others. They examine questions like 'Is another person's toothache "toothache" in the same sense as mine?' The answer must be no.[13]

Non-realism

The logical positivists accepted that the evidence of our senses produces knowledge. Even this, however, has never been *proved*. For those who demand certainty, we do not know that anything exists outside our minds.

In the current debate on realism, the main classification is between realists on the one hand and various versions of non-realism on the other. Realists believe that the big wide world outside their minds really does exist independently of whether our minds think about it. Yet how do we know our mental concepts represent the way it is? Non-realists point out that we have no way of independently checking. We cannot have any idea of *reality* at all, without it being an *idea* of reality. Since our own mental concepts are as near as we shall ever get to accessing it, we can never know whether they tell us the truth about it.

'Idealism' describes the view that the external world *depends on* human minds. Kant's idealism did not argue that the whole of reality is created by the mind; George Berkeley's version and more recent ones do. Berkeley, writing in the first half of the eighteenth century, was reacting against the atomic theory of his day. According to Gassendi, Galileo and Locke, all matter consisted of atoms and there was a sharp distinction between their primary and secondary qualities. Only their primary qualities — shape, size, weight and motion — really belonged to them. Their secondary qualities — colour, feel, smell, sound and taste — only existed in our minds. Berkeley pointed out that secondary qualities are all we ever experience of the outside world. We cannot see or feel matter directly. So why assume it exists? According to Locke, God created matter for the purpose of making it impinge on our senses — in an inexplicable way — so that our senses would then — again in an inexplicable way — produce images in our minds. Why, Berkeley asked, should God use such a round-about method for producing these images in our minds, instead of simply creating our mental images directly, without using matter?[14]

This theory produces the question of continuous existence. If things only exist as mental images, do they cease to exist when we stop looking at them and come back into existence when we look in their direction again? Similarly, a stick poked into water appears bent. If there is no objective reality behind our mental images, does it really become bent? Did nothing exist before humans evolved? Berkeley had a simple reply: when humans are not looking, everything stays as it is because God is still looking.

Berkeley's theory was a minority view in his day. In the twentieth century it has become more popular, but stripped of God's involvement. As a result the question of continuous existence needs to be asked again. Of the various versions of idealism, perhaps the most common is the view that reality is there, even when nobody is looking at it, but it is an unstructured chaos. Our minds, using the concepts available to us, provide the distinction between the water and the stick, and between a straight stick and a bent one.[15]

For this reason idealism tends to lead to *relativism*. If there is no objective truth behind our constructions of reality, what happens when my construction of it differs from yours? We must conclude that what is real *for me* is not real *for you*. Relativists face the problem that they have to apply their theory to their own relativism: if I am a relativist and you are a realist, I accept that realism is true for you.[16]

Some philosophers have tried to solve these difficulties by analysing the way language is used. However, whatever theory of linguistic analysis they apply, they still need to explain how language relates to the objective reality outside it. One possible answer is that it does not. In this case, the meaning of words is to be understood entirely within the language, and we must give up trying to relate them to a world outside it. Some non-realists have concluded that language is the only thing which really exists.[17]

In general, non-realist theories make it harder for us to make sense of our lives. They offer explanations of what is going on when, say, we clean our teeth, but these explanations leave us wondering whether our mental concepts, the movements of our hands, the shape of the toothbrush and the sense impressions in our mouth all combine to form an intelligible and useful activity. Nevertheless failure to make sense of our lives does not refute them: it may be that there is no external world and our mental images do not make any sense.

As the debate continues, without any sign of resolution, both sides can see quite clearly that the other side must be wrong. Non- realists are right to say that we cannot look behind our concepts to reality-as-it-is. Realists are equally right when they look down the abyss of non-realism and conclude that human society depends absolutely on presuppositions which non-realists cannot provide.

Knowledge without certainty

The search for certainty has seemed credible for a long time, largely because of the countless successes of science. Every day brings new knowledge and it can easily seem as though complete and certain knowledge is on its way. It is not. Scientists provide knowledge without certainty. They use *induction*, a humbler and more tentative process altogether. In induction, we generalize from what we have observed, to make hypotheses about what we have not observed. What makes science successful is that these hypotheses often turn out to be right. Nothing, though, is certain: even Newton's laws of physics turned out to be mistaken, despite centuries of accumulated evidence in their favour.

Many twentieth century philosophers have therefore abandoned the search for certainty. Instead they describe knowledge in more modest terms. Today theories of knowledge are generally classified as 'foundationalist' or 'coherentist'. Classical rationalism, empiricism and Kantian idealism are foundationalist because they aim to derive knowledge from self-justifying foundations. Foundationalists face the twofold task, firstly of showing how their foundations are self-justifying and secondly of deriving all else from them.

Coherentism does not depend on foundations. All we have is a number of different theories, any or all of which may be wrong. We build up our understanding of reality by observing the world around us and reflecting on our observations. As we do so, we often have to make small changes to our theories, and occasionally big ones. The larger our set of observations and reflections, the less likely we are to have a consistent understanding of reality which is wrong.

To illustrate the difference we might compare foundationalism with a new team of managing directors. We arrive at Head Office, unfamiliar with our surroundings. Our first task is to understand the operations of the firm as a whole. We are able, in principle, to talk to any number of people, ask any number of questions and look in whichever cupboards we will. When we are ready we will proceed to the second task — to make decisions.

Coherence theory is more like being kidnap victims. We regain consciousness we know not where. We look around us and try to puzzle out what might have happened. We collect as much information as we can and ignore whatever we guess will not be useful. New events and observations help build up our picture and test our theories. We are not certain of anything at all; but once we have a theory which is repeatedly confirmed by new observations, we gain confidence. At each moment, we know that our theory may be disproved by the next observation. Even so, we cannot afford the luxury of doing nothing until all has been revealed. Any moment may be the best chance to run for it. All we can do is weigh up the evidence and make a decision.

Many philosophers locate the end of modernism and the beginning of postmodernism at the point where foundationalism is abandoned.[18] Foundationalism encourages the view that there is one set of true beliefs and that this set of beliefs is basically public. Coherence theory, on the other hand, is better able to explain why different societies hold different beliefs with equal conviction. Coherentists may or may not be realists, but in either case their claims to knowledge are humbler.

Coherentism is not a new idea. The reflections of ancient near eastern culture, as it asked questions about God or the gods, may be described as coherentist. Gradually, as their traditions developed into the colossal medieval systems of Judaism, Christianity and Islam, confidence increased and they described reality in hierarchical systems with God at the top. God had complete 'foundational' knowledge and could see everything. Humanity did not: but the faithful could come closer to a 'God's eye

view' through submission and prayer. The seventeenth century philosophers, reacting against oppressive, pessimistic interpretations of this
hierarchy, demanded direct access to the God's eye view. In order to get
it, they promoted human reason to the top of the hierarchy. God became
superfluous and was later removed from the scene, leaving reason as a self-
justifying foundation. However, since reason is not self-justifying, the
system collapses and leaves us trapped in ignorance.

The mind

So far this chapter has taken for granted that the human mind really exists
and thinks. The mechanistic paradigm undermines this too.

Early Enlightenment philosophers made a sharp contrast between the
rational, active, subjective human mind — or soul — and the non-rational,
passive, objective material world. It was a dualistic picture: value was
located in the mind, not in matter. We can see why they liked it. The mechanistic, determined universe was not the whole of reality. It depended on
another, non-mechanistic, world of reason and value, the home of God
and the soul, where the writ of science did not run. Into it mechanists could
slot secondary qualities, values, morality and whichever parts of reality
they deemed beyond the scope of science. From this dualistic point of view,
the only conceivable relationship between rational minds and the natural
world was one of complete *domination*. Humanity did not owe anything to
it. To respect or even venerate it was mere superstition.

If soul and body are so radically different, how do they relate to each
other? Descartes suggested that they connect in the pineal gland.
Scientifically this was no worse than many theories of his time, but it did
not overcome the problem: if the two elements are so different, what kind
of process could there possibly be within the pineal gland? This, he
admitted, was 'very difficult to explain'.[19]

Over time philosophers solved it by abandoning dualism. They
emptied, and then abolished, the spiritual world. I have already noted how
the role of God declined. In addition the mechanistic paradigm became
so popular that it was set to work on the mind as well. New sciences like
sociology were developed, and old ones like economics were adapted, to
study human minds on the understanding that they are part of the determined, mechanistic world. The new mood was proclaimed by La
Mettrie's thesis that the mind is a machine.[20]

The immaterial world, home of God and the soul, which the seventeenth century had accepted as the source of all value, meaning and purpose, could now be discarded altogether. The mechanistic attitudes which they had applied to the natural world could now be directed to humanity as well. Humans, like animals, became parts of the world-machine, nothing but the sum of their bodily parts, every action determined, simple and observable. It followed that the way to find out about the mind is by scientific analysis of the body. Whatever is not found there must be taken to be non-existent.

Society had grown used to the mechanistic idea that the world of matter has no intrinsic value and we can therefore use it in whatever way we choose. Now the logic was taken one stage further: human beings are also part of that world of matter. Over time others would work out the implications.

Our minds and other minds

Dualistic theory invited people to think about the world from the perspective of a 'detached observer'; whatever theories we held about the world, they did not affect our theories about our own minds. Once the observing mind is relocated as *part of* the world being observed, theories of the mind ought to became self-referring. For example, if I believe that mental thoughts are meaningless and determined, I should conclude that this belief of mine is meaningless and determined. In practice human beings refuse to believe that we ourselves are automata, even when we have been persuaded to believe it of other people. By making an exception of ourselves, we create contradictions.

There is no shortage of them, even in the most respectable literature. One example is Charles Darwin's *The Descent of Man*. On the one hand he described the 'higher' human faculties, including social behaviour and moral and religious convictions, as developments from simple animal instincts. For example, religious feelings are derived from the kind of feeling dogs have for their masters. The implications were clear enough at the time: religion and morality were being reduced to nothing but successfully evolved patterns of behaviour, useful for particular groups in particular situations but devoid of objective truth.[21] On the other hand, when he used his theory to support the programme of eugenics which was being proposed by his cousin Galton, he used the language of moral imperatives just as though his own moral commitments were *not* devoid of objective truth:

> Man scans with scrupulous care the character and pedigree of his horses, cattle, and dogs before he matches them; but when he comes to his own marriage he rarely, or never, takes any such care... Yet he might by selection do something not only for the bodily constitution and frame of his offspring, but for their intellectual and moral qualities. Both sexes ought to refrain from marriage if in any marked degree inferior in body or mind...[22]

A more recent example is B F Skinner's *Beyond Freedom and Dignity*, published in 1971. Skinner was the leading behaviourist of his day. According to his theory all human behaviour results from 'conditioning'. When a particular piece of behaviour is followed by pleasant or unpleasant experiences, these experiences function as positive or negative 'reinforcers', respectively encouraging or discouraging the behaviour in question. All human behaviour is caused by conditioning; we have no real freedom and the mind is nothing but an explanatory fiction.[23]

Skinner's motivation shines through his writing clearly enough. There is a consistently expressed, keen concern to improve the lot of human life. This should be done by abandoning the false ideas of freedom and dignity and instituting a regime of positive and negative reinforcers to condition behaviour.

> In what we may call the pre-scientific view... a person's behaviour is at least to some extent his own achievement. He is free to deliberate, decide, and act, possibly in original ways, and he is to be given credit for his successes and blamed for his failures. In the scientific view... a person's behaviour is determined by a genetic endowment traceable to the evolutionary history of the species and by the environmental circumstances to which as an individual he has been exposed... As we learn more about the effects of the environment, we have less reason to attribute any part of human behaviour to an autonomous controlling agent. And the second view shows a marked advantage when we begin to do something about behaviour... The environment can be changed, and we are learning how to change it.[24]

Behaviourists explicitly sought control of other people's behaviour — for example in penal policy — by rigid systems of rewards and punishments, convinced that their subjects' mental thoughts were meaningless accompaniments of determined actions, while their own mental thoughts were full of wisdom and insight, working out what needed to be done. Skinner noted the problem,[25] but without offering a solution.

In this way Descartes' dualism of mind and matter was transformed into a dualism between 'our' minds on the one hand and 'their' minds, together with matter, on the other. This development has encouraged that paternalistic attitude which has been so common in modern politics and social theory: *we* understand the position and *we* know best, while other people's opinions and desires are merely the result of their upbringing and education.

Mind and brain

Even if we accept that other people's minds are as real as our own, it remains the case that scientists have not observed a separate entity, called a 'mind', over and above the brain. What does the mind consist of? Is it simply a stream of brain events, or is it something in addition to the brain, or is it some kind of 'private place' where mental events happen?

It is generally accepted that the mind depends on the state of the brain, since drugs and brain damage affect the mind. A thoroughgoing reductionist will describe the mind entirely in terms of brain activity. What else could it consist of, except parts of the brain? What kinds of processes could there be, except brain processes? Mechanists may argue that, in theory, if scientists could learn enough about how the brain works, they would be able to read the entire contents of a person's brain and thereby know what that person is thinking. Whether it is possible in practice is another matter: the point is that the contents of the mind consist entirely of the contents of the brain, with nothing left over.[26]

An alternative view, still mechanistic, is that we should count mental events as real even though they are nothing but the products of brain events. The reason is that our language about the mind is meaningful, and makes sense in ways which language about the brain cannot replace. If we were able to measure all of a person's brain states, we might find that each brain state correlates with a particular mental state; but we do not know, and whether they do or not, we can still make sense of our mental thoughts and relate them to other mental thoughts. This kind of defence is now commonly accepted by philosophers of mind. It means that, even if the mind is nothing but a convenient way of describing brain events, mental language is still meaningful.[27] On this basis, some linguistic analysts have argued that the mind can be reduced to language.[28]

A more generous theory treats the mind as an *emergent* property, similar to the types of emergence I discussed in the last chapter. When brain processes reach a certain degree of complexity, new patterns of activity emerge at a 'higher' level, with their own characteristics which cannot be explained at the lower level. As the plant can do things which molecules cannot do, the mind can do things which the brain cannot do.[29]

This theory solves many of the problems which dog other theories and I prefer it. It explains how the mind behaves in ways which cannot be fully explained in terms of brain events, without needing to claim that some other substance exists. However, it leaves open the question of determinism. Are all mental events determined brain events, parts of the universal sequence of mechanistic causes and effects? Or does the emergent property of the mind create the potential for free will?

Free will

The word 'freedom' is used in different ways. In debates on free will, the key distinction is between *voluntariness* and *open futures*. Voluntariness describes the situation where we do something because we want to. When offered a choice between tea and coffee, I choose tea *because I want to*. This is quite compatible with determinism. What determinists deny is that the choice was genuinely open. Contrary to my inner feelings, they believe, a truly uncaused event is impossible. My choice of tea is part of a determined sequence in which every event is caused by a previous event and causes others in turn.

Determinists generally accept that if our society abandoned its belief in free will, we would have to change our way of thinking in a number of important ways.

(i) Most theories of determinism emphasize the importance of human *wants*. What we *want* is an essential ingredient of what our minds cause us to do. Our wants come to be treated as a basic given: it becomes difficult to explain how we might change our minds about what to want.[30]

(ii) Many common thoughts and attitudes, such as appreciation, gratitude, resentment and anger, presuppose that the other person was free to do otherwise than they did.[31]

(iii) Many mental activities, like choosing and trying, function on the assumption that we ourselves have free will. Determinists can explain why non-determinists, when choosing or trying, *think* they are making a difference to what would otherwise have happened; but these explanations do not serve so well when we ask why determinists themselves choose and try. If we were all committed determinists, we would gradually learn not to think so much about our choices or try so hard to achieve objectives.

(iv) All moral judgements, of ourselves and others, presuppose free will. Some people welcome determinism for this reason: it is an argument against heavy sentences for particular kinds of crime, as nobody ever deserves to be punished. Yet few of us would welcome a society in which there were no judgements of right or wrong.

Because of these problems, some philosophers argue that belief in free will is necessary even though it is misguided.[32]

The ancient Greek Epicurus argued that determinism is self-refuting. Determinists must believe that their own beliefs are determined, so their objection to free will is merely the result of determined causes. Determinists may reply that determined opinions are not on that account false: most of us would like to think that one of the causes of our opinions is the fact that they are true.[33] This reply seems acceptable as long as we think about one opinion at a time. However, determinists characteristically believe that all opinions which have ever been held and ever will be held are determined. In that case we can never get outside our network of caused opinions to an open, undetermined vantage point from which to check which of our opinions, if any, are caused by the truth. The opinion 'My opinions are caused by the truth' is a caused opinion and we do not know what causes it. Such a conclusion can be accepted — it does not refute determinism — but it does mean that determinism leads to complete ignorance, as we can never know which of our opinions is caused by the truth.

Determinism has been taught in Departments of Psychology and the Social Sciences for so long that it has now become thoroughly respectable. Yet it continues to baffle, because it does seem to deny a very basic awareness of how we do the things we do; indeed, in Departments of Law, free will is equally strongly taken for granted. Within ourselves we feel confident that our futures are open. Our evidence that we have free will is direct. Yet we cannot prove it in the rational, deductive way demanded by mechanistic philosophers.

Conclusion

The philosophers of the mechanistic paradigm have now spent hundreds of years pursuing their search for complete and certain knowledge. Have they produced any results? By now we can confidently say that they have. They have shown us that we now have all the knowledge we can possibly get, and we know it with certainty: namely, that we cannot know anything at all. The purpose of seeking it was to gain a complete understanding of reality. We now know all there is to know about reality: it consists of nothing but the images in our minds. The motivation behind the search for certainty was the desire to control the natural order. Complete control has indeed been established, down to the tiniest detail. But it is not we who control nature: it is nature which controls us.

The exaltation of humanity, with which the modern period began, has resulted in a more systematic self-abasement than pessimistic theologians have ever devised. In the process of reaching these conclusions, we have been led through many bizarre and conflicting opinions. Western philosophy has gradually lost credibility, largely because it has spent so much time doubting the existence of things which we have no option but to take for granted in our daily lives. We cannot live as though we were sitting on a distant star, mentally emptying the world like a doll's house and examining each item for proof of existence before putting it back in. When we get up in the morning we have to believe that the real world exists, we have minds, rationality and freedom, and other people have them too. If philosophers raise doubts about these things, they do not make us go back to bed and start the day again: we simply ignore philosophers.

In our daily lives, when we are trying to do more humble things than dominate the world, we accept that we do not know everything, we know nothing at all with absolute certainty and we have no absolute control over our environment. Instead we have enough knowledge, with enough confidence, to do the things which really need doing. We *trust* the reality of what cannot be proved. This act of trust breaks the rules of the mechanistic paradigm, but it works much better than waiting for the proof.

This chapter has explored some of the more extreme implications of the mechanistic paradigm, with its theory that the world is determined, simple and observable. Most people, of course, have never taken them seriously. Yet this is where the mechanistic paradigm leads. In addition it leads to another set of problems, which we must also consider. It seems that all the much-vaunted achievements of modern technology are nothing but the determined effects of physical causes, operating according to impersonal laws of nature. If all our thoughts and actions are determined, does that mean there is no right or wrong, no purpose to our lives and no real value? These are the questions to which I shall turn in the next chapter.

1   The arguments are contained in *Discourse on Method* and *Meditations*. J Cottingham, *The Rationalists*, pp. 31-46 contains a summary.
2   Especially Anselm. G Leff, *Medieval Thought*, pp. 98-100.
3   J Cottingham, *The Rationalists* p. 49.
4   J Locke, *An Essay Concerning Human Understanding*, 1.2.15; John Dunn, J O Urmson, and A J Ayer, *The British Empiricists* p. 72.
5   John Dunn, J O Urmson, and A J Ayer, *The British Empiricists* p. 73.
6   John Dunn, J O Urmson, and A J Ayer, *The British Empiricists* pp. 219ff.
7   'Synthetic', as opposed to 'analytic', means that they provide information; 'a priori', as opposed to 'a posteriori', that they are independent of the senses. He dismissed the fourth possibility, of analytic *a posteriori* judgements, as he believed there were no examples of them.
8   S Körner, *Kant*, pp. 17-26.
9   O Hanfling, *Essential Readings in Logical Positivism* pp. 1- 8.
10 A O'Hear, *An Introduction to the Philosophy of Science* pp. 108-9.
11 It must either be a truth contained within the meaning of its words, or empirically verifiable; and, clearly, it is neither (O Hanfling, *Essential Readings in Logical Positivism*, pp. 8,34).
12 O Hanfling, *Essential Readings in Logical Positivism*, p. 10.
13 O Hanfling, *Essential Readings in Logical Positivism*, p. 111. See also Carnap's analysis of the statement 'I am thirsty' on p. 158.
14 John Dunn, J O Urmson, and A J Ayer, *The British Empiricists* pp. 114-124.
15 N Rescher has explored this idea. R Trigg, *Reality at Risk*, p. 5.
16 R Trigg, *Reality at Risk,* pp. ix- xi and 124-152.
17 R Trigg, *Reality at Risk*, p. xvii; O Hanfling, *Essential Readings in Logical Positivism*, p. 16.
18 Michael Polanyi's *Personal Knowledge* has been influential in the change; knowledge is seen no longer as a public accumulation of certainties but as more subjective, varied and relative.
19 J Cottingham, *The Rationalists*, pp. 124-7.
20 Dale Jacquette, *Philosophy of Mind*, pp. 62-4.
21 T Cosslett, Ed, *Science and Religion in the Nineteenth Century*, pp 8f, 157-65.
22 T Cosslett, Ed, *Science and Religion in the Nineteenth Century*, pp. 169f.
23 B F Skinner, *Beyond Freedom and Dignity*, p. 29.
24 B F Skinner, *Beyond Freedom and Dignity*, p. 101.

25 B F Skinner, *Beyond Freedom and Dignity*, pp. 101f.
26 R Rorty, *Philosophy and the Mirror of Nature,* defends this view.
27 T Honderich, *How Free Are You?*, pp. 24-6.
28 R Trigg, *Reality at Risk*, p. 49; A Kenny, *The Metaphysics of Mind*, p. 4.
29 Dale Jacquette, *Philosophy of Mind*, pp. 19-21.
30 T Honderich, *How Free Are You?*, pp. 87ff.
31 So Honderich admits: 'Gratitude, what I may think of as real gratitude, has to go' (*How Free Are You?*, p. 90).
32 G Graham, *Philosophy of Mind*, p. 159.
33 T Honderich, *How Free Are You?*, p. 76.

Chapter 7

Who creates values?

HILARY AND JANE were thrilled. They had been working on their science project for three years and at last it had worked! None of the students of the previous year, 2695, had succeeded, but Hilary and Jane had finally done it.

The project was to create a universe, complete with beings who could feel pain and pleasure and act freely, and had a moral sense. They had designed it in such a way that it was best for everybody if they all looked after each other, but individuals could benefit themselves by hurting other people. Each individual could choose for themselves which to do.

Hilary was getting excited. 'Aren't they cute and cuddly? Look at this one over here. He's really nice. He's doing everything he can to help the others. Keep it up — you're doing brilliantly! Those two over there aren't so nice, they are hammer and tongs against each other. Somebody's going to get hurt soon. Do you think we ought to do something to break them up?

Jane laughed. 'You're getting carried away, aren't you? They're not *real* people! They are only beings we've made. They haven't got real feelings. They don't have real problems of right and wrong to worry about, like we have.'

'Yes they do. That was the whole point of the project — to make beings with freedom and a moral sense like us. Do you think we've left something out?'

'No, but what I mean is — they only exist because we made them. They don't have a purpose, except for us to pass our exams. At the end of term all this is going to be poured down the plug-hole and we'll have to start on next term's project. This little chap you're so pleased about, who's anxious to be nice to everybody so that they all live together happily — I know we made them so that it could work, but it doesn't really *matter* — not like it would in *our* world. We don't really care whether they get on well together or not!'

'I do,' said Hilary.

Do we think our universe is a bit like that one? If we do, does it make a difference whether it was created by Jane or by Hilary? All through history, people have believed that their lives have value. To feel that it does not is to be miserable. But what does it mean?

The word 'value' is used in different ways. We often use it to refer to *morality*. In these cases, to say we have values is to say that we distinguish between right and wrong and we think the distinction matters. To have moral values is to be on the side of good against evil. At other times we may refer to *purpose*. This invokes the idea that our lives have an overall direction and it is important that we should proceed according to it.

The word 'value' also has an additional meaning, over and above these. We speak of things *having value* or *being valuable*. I referred earlier to the distinction between things which are 'intrinsically' valuable — for their own sakes — and things which are merely 'instrumentally' valuable, because they contribute to the value of something else. If music has intrinsic value, a piano has instrumental value. In order for some things to have instrumental value, there must also be some things which have intrinsic value.

In the last two chapters I have described how the mechanistic paradigm sees the universe as nothing but impersonal matter operating according to deterministic laws of nature. The way it operates, which seems so complex, is nothing but automatic responses to causal laws. We ourselves, even as we examine it and wonder at it, are nothing but some of the atoms, and our behaviour is nothing but some of the determined effects of causes. Even if we leave aside the more extreme conclusions of Chapter 6, and continue to believe that we have bodies, minds, freedom and knowledge, it seems that there is nothing in the whole of reality which can be a source of value, purpose or moral significance. What can these concepts possibly mean, in a world where everything is just matter moved by impersonal processes? Are they just the residue left over from earlier theories of reality? In this chapter I shall argue that they are, and trace how they lost their power and meaning as the implications of neutralism were worked out. For convenience I shall refer to purpose, morality and intrinsic value collectively as 'values'.

They could still make sense within the earlier, dualistic version of the mechanistic paradigm, as part of the non-material realm where the soul related to God. Once that other realm had been abolished, the whole of reality was reduced to matter. No scientist had ever observed any entity called 'value' or 'purpose' or 'morality', so it seemed that they did not exist.

Such are the logical implications of neutralism. It has taken a long time for them to be recognized. If there is one slogan which stood out as the flagship of the Enlightenment, it was 'progress'. In the nineteenth century there were only a few dissidents, like Nietzsche, who could see the direction in which neutralism was heading. Today philosophers defend a wide range of positions about value, purpose and morality, some more neutralistic than others. They had their roots in theology. Neutralism cut off their roots. Without them, they have gone their separate ways. They flourished for a while and then began to wither.

To illustrate how this has happened, I shall concentrate on two key questions which need to be asked of all theories of value. The first is: who determines what it is? Who decides what counts as valuable, or what the purpose of life is, or which actions are morally good or bad? The second is: why should anybody pay any attention to it? Even if I know that it is wrong to steal, or that other people's lives have value, why should I respond accordingly? I shall describe five characteristic positions on a realist-nonrealist spectrum and note the strengths and weaknesses of each one. Philosophers' theories are much more varied, but they all fit somewhere on this spectrum. Most of the illustrations come from moral theory, as it provides a wealth of material, but the points I will make usually apply to values in general.

Theological theories

In Part 1 I discussed how theologies evaluate the world. Optimism and pessimism agree that there is a superior being who understands the nature of reality and sets a standard of true value. In general, theologies justify their account of value by their cosmologies: when we know how and why the world was made and how we relate to God, it becomes clear what is valuable and what is not. Different cosmologies produce different values.

It we accept intrinsic value as a real part of the way things are, we may believe that it provides a purpose for us. It makes sense to believe that we fulfil the purpose of our lives when we aspire towards true values. This purpose in turn provides a framework for moral principles. For example, by 'stealing is wrong', religions do not normally mean 'I personally would prefer it if people didn't steal', or 'I contract with society that I shall not steal from others on condition that they do not steal from me'. They mean 'Within our understanding of the purpose of life, stealing is destructive. To become more honest is more in keeping with the purpose of life, and therefore realizes higher value'.

Values, then, are derived from our beliefs about how and why the world was made. As such they are founded in a reality which transcends human life. They stand apart from us and provide standards by which we may direct our lives. Whether we do or not is up to us, but they are there anyway. However they do not fit within the mechanistic paradigm. We cannot control them: on the contrary, *they* claim authority over *us*. In addition, they cannot be deduced by reason or observed by the senses.

Within the modern period values have often been used as an argument for the existence of God. From the seventeenth to the nineteenth centuries there was a flowering of natural theology, particularly in England. It was led by people — often clergy — with a strong interest in scientific exploration, who found in every new discovery yet another reason to praise the Creator. The order of nature on earth was the result of benevolent *design*.[1] As scientists observe the natural order, they reveal a world which shows every sign of being full of *purpose*.

The last great work of this tradition was William Paley's *Natural Theology* (1802). His key argument was the famous watch analogy: a person who had never seen a watch before but happened to find one and examine it, would conclude that it had been designed for a purpose by an intelligent being. Similarly, when we examine the world around us, we see evidence of intentional design.[2] Later generations, influenced by Thomas Huxley's anti-religious campaigning, have lumped the design argument together with the very different arguments of those who opposed evolution, and treated them as though they were all equally refuted by Darwin.[3] Darwin did disagree with Paley, but his arguments undermined Paley's over-static science rather than his theology.[4] Defenders of design replied that their theory fitted Darwinism just as well. If anything, Darwinism implied the continually active God of the Jewish and Christian traditions, rather than the distant First Cause of the Deists.[5]

What really mattered to the design argument was whether the appearances of design were misleading. Darwin believed they were, but he was not a good philosopher and did not produce good arguments. His main point was to emphasize the struggle for existence and the large amount of waste and suffering, rather than the harmony which the natural theologians observed.

> I cannot persuade myself that a beneficent and omnipotent God would have designedly created the Ichneumonidae with the express intention of their feeding within the live bodies of Caterpillars, or that a cat should play with mice.[6]

The issue is not, however, settled by observable facts. Nature can provide more than enough examples of both harmony and suffering. The disagreement is really one of evaluation: whether ichneumonidae or watch, Paley infers benevolent design and Darwin does not.

In most societies, throughout the history of humanity, people have responded to the world around them by believing it is full of value and purpose. In this sense, Paley was speaking for the majority. However, as neutralist evaluations of the world bit deeper into Europe's consciousness, people trained themselves to dismiss everything they saw, however exciting or valuable it seemed, as nothing but a collection of atoms obeying impersonal laws of nature. Paley and Darwin agreed that they were faced with a choice: either mechanistic science could not account for everything, or there is no design. Paley plumped for one, Darwin for the other.

Today, secular ethicists have a characteristic reply to theological accounts of value. Let us take, for example, God's command that we should not steal. Is stealing wrong because God forbids it, or does God forbid it because it is wrong? If the only reason why it is wrong is that God forbids it, God's law seems arbitrary. If we decide to obey God's arbitrary law, it is *our* decision to do so. On the other hand, if God forbids it because it really is wrong, then God's forbidding adds nothing: God or no God, we should not steal. Similarly with purpose and intrinsic value: it is up to us to decide whether to accept God's judgement on these matters, and why.

Even the most religious people in western society today are so imbued with neutralist presuppositions that it is difficult to escape from them, and within the neutralist view of reality the point is unanswerable. In my discussion of theological values in Part 1, however, it did not arise because the neutralist presuppositions were not there. What is being assumed in this argument is (i) that the nature of reality can be completely described without mention of God, and (ii) that humanity is capable of gaining complete and certain knowledge about it. From this perspective, God has nothing to offer. Here we are in *our* world, getting on with things, and if God comes along and imposes extra rules, we do not see why we should pay any attention. Who is this stranger, after all?

For this reason it has become standard procedure for theories of value to avoid referring to God. Like theories of rationality or the laws of nature, they must stand on their own and be justified in their own terms, even if God put them there. This leads to the idea that values are independent of God and humanity, but their existence is still real.

Realist theories

Realist values, then, stand apart from us and provide standards for us whether we recognize them or not, and our task is to discover them.

This is a common view in moral theory. We have seen how the regularities of nature were attributed at one stage to God, later to God's laws, and eventually to independent laws without reference to God. In the same way, 'human rights' and 'moral rules' could slide from being God's decrees to being independent laws passing judgement on human action.

Contractual rights have long been recognized. A contractual right is a permission granted by a specific law or agreement: when you buy a bus ticket, you have a right to ride on the bus. The idea of *natural* rights has developed by analogy with it, though natural rights describe a status which may *not* have been agreed. Today many people believe that rights have an existence of their own even when they are not legally recognized: in moral debate, for example, people appeal to 'the unborn child's right to life' or 'the woman's right to choose'. These appeals depend on the assumption that rights really exist, whether we recognize them or not, and pass judgement on the things we do. We might think of them as 'shields in the sky', protecting people from unjustified harm.

If we take seriously the idea that there are shields in the sky, and they are our moral authorities, it follows that the way to settle moral disagreements is to find out what the shields actually protect. Either the baby's right to life really exists, or the woman's right to choose really exists; what we need to know is, which one is there? We need some way to find the shields and 'read' them.

Rights theory is still popular today, but not even the most realist moral philosopher seriously considers looking for rights in this way. Usually they concentrate on linguistic and logical analysis, in the hope of establishing a rights-based moral system which would be internally consistent and produce credible moral commands.[7] In other words, they do not believe there are any shields in the sky, but they do believe that the *idea* of rights produces a useful model for constructing a moral theory. When they proceed in this way, they are only using the language of rights as a useful framework for creating a non-realist moral system.

Moral philosophers have generated many different theories of rights. The reason for the variety is that none of them is convincing. Even if they do succeed, will it help? Suppose moral philosophers reach a consensus that a particular rights-based theory satisfies all the criteria: even if it produces a decisive verdict that the unborn child has a right to life, pro-abortionists can simply point out that they have only given us a conceptual scheme which works within its own terms. There will still be no shields in the sky, no moral authority telling us what to do.

Let us admit, then, that there are no independent entities, called 'rights', setting standards for human behaviour. There are no shields in the sky. Even if there were, we would still be faced with that other question: why should we pay any attention to them? We are so used to hearing people emphatically claiming a right to one thing or another that we tend to over-look this all-pervasive gap in the logic. Suppose I declare that there is a *blik* against electric cookers. Because of this *blik*, I myself never use the cooker on Wednesday afternoons and I am horrified with my neighbour who does. What might the neighbour think? A rational neighbour will want to know firstly what a *blik* is, secondly what evidence I have that it exists, and thirdly how it relates to Wednesday afternoons. These are the questions which need to be asked of natural rights. Even if I accept that you have a right to life, I need to understand what a right to life is, and how it relates to killing, before I understand why I should not kill you. What is the logical connection between 'You have a right to life' and 'I ought not to kill you'?

The same weaknesses apply to all realist theories of value. We might think of moral laws, for example, as 'notice boards in the sky'. If we believe God put them there, we can ask why, and consider why we should obey them. If, on the other hand, they just stand there, demanding our allegiance by their own say-so, blind to circumstances or consequences, we need some additional reason why we should pay attention to them.

Other realist theories avoid appealing to an additional 'thing-in-the-sky'. Perhaps 'good' and 'bad' are descriptions of real *qualities* which actions and things possess. Systems of this type need to explain how we can recognize goodness or badness when they are there, and theories of 'moral sense' or 'intuition' have developed accordingly. The most influential has been G E Moore's *Principia Ethica* (1903). Moore argued that the word 'good' stands for something which is basic and simple, and therefore undefinable. When we explain or define things we usually refer to their constituent parts. Those constituent parts can themselves be defined in the same way. The process of defining or explaining things must depend on a bedrock of concepts which are so simple that they cannot be defined further. 'Good' is one of these. Moore suggests 'yellow' as another: 'Just as you cannot, by any manner of means, explain to any one who does not already know it, what yellow is, so you cannot explain what good is'.[8]

Unlike rights and moral rules, intuition does not have to postulate the existence of an unproven thing-in-the-sky. On the other hand, it replaces it with equally unproven moral qualities which things are supposed to have. It addition it shares that other weakness, of not being able to explain why its judgements should carry any weight. Even if I intuit that stealing is wrong, what is it about my intuitions which means I should pay any attention to them?

Realist theories of intrinsic value have recently been developed by environmental ethicists, particularly Holmes Rolston III. It is not surprising that they should be revived in the context of environmental issues; realism, unlike non-realism, can at least attribute value to nature even when humans do not value it. Outside environmental theory, however, they largely remain unpopular for the reasons I have already given.

Realist theories, then, appeal to objective standards which exist whether or not humans recognize them. Their strengths are that they present themselves to us as authorities which we ought to obey, whether or not it suits us, and they can explain why we should all hold the same values.

On the other hand they share two weaknesses. One is that the really existent standards to which they appeal have never been shown to exist. The second is that, even though they invite our obedience, we are not told why we should give it. Secular philosophers are usually quick enough to point out that if value, purpose and morality have been put there by God, it does not automatically follow that we ought to respect them. But if they just happen to exist, invisible things-in-the-sky, handing out instructions for no known reason, these hesitations apply all the more. It is as though the clouds in the sky were to form the words 'There is buried treasure under the oak tree'. Anybody who saw it and started to dig for it would reveal at least a suspicion that there is some controlling power which has deliberately caused the writing. Those who were absolutely convinced that the movements of the clouds created the writing by pure coincidence, would not dig.

If true values have been created by God, we can ask why God created them, and this gives us a basis upon which to consider how to respond. If, on the other hand, they just happen to be there, and we can say nothing about how they came to be there, the decision to obey them will have to depend on other reasons, which we must decide for ourselves. Thus non-realists argue that all our values are human constructs.

Social construct theories

If we abandon the attempt to derive values from outside ourselves, they must be created by us, either socially or individually. Perhaps the most influential social construct theory is the one developed by the seventeenth century philosopher Thomas Hobbes. According to Hobbes there is no objectively given morality. What is 'good' is whatever anybody desires. People have desires for many different things and real conflicts of interest are only to be expected. If everyone tries to gratify their own desires without considering others, the result is conflict and few will have their desires gratified. On the whole we are better off in a peaceful and law-abiding society, and we therefore accept legal and moral limitations. The rules are not good in themselves, but are necessary conditions for gratifying our desires.[9]

The strength of this approach is that it does not appeal to invisible entities which may not exist. The reason why some things are moral and others immoral is that this is the way to gratify desires. Its weakness lies in what replaces those doubted moral authorities: the state.

Compared with realist 'things-in-the-sky', the state is more local. This creates the possibility of irresolvable conflict. For example, one country values maximizing industrial production and produces acid rain which falls on another country. The other country values clean air. If values are created by the state, there cannot be any solution to the conflict: the government of each country is the supreme creator of value within that country and cannot be wrong.[10]

Within the state, the question arises: who decides what is to be counted as moral? Hobbes did not have any starry-eyed hope of everybody agreeing to the same moral judgements. Coercion would be required. In practice, as Marx could see, the decisions are made by those with power, in their own interests, and imposed on the powerless. If we attribute to the ruling powers the right to create not only the legal rules but the moral rules as well, the powerless find not only that the laws are against them but that morality is against them too.

This is not merely a practical difficulty. It undermines all social construct theories. According to Hobbes the reason for constraint, whether moral or legal, is that it is the way to gratify our desires. Desires are fundamentally the property of *individuals*. The success of any moral or legal system should therefore be judged by the individuals within it. The way to answer the question 'Is the present moral consensus — or government — successful at gratifying desires?' is to do a social survey, asking each inhabitant for their personal experiences.

Let us suppose that a survey of this type was conducted and everybody in the state except Fred Jones supported the moral consensus. Fred believes that it hinders the gratification of his desires more than it helps. Since morality is a social construct designed to gratify the desires of people like Fred, there is no higher court of appeal than Fred's judgement. Hobbes may think that Fred's interests are best served by obeying the moral laws, but if Fred thinks otherwise he cannot be wrong. His views are perfectly legitimate, *whatever his reasons*.

Paternalistic accounts of knowledge make social construct theories seem more credible. If the experts — the scientists who study human behaviour — really know what will gratify Fred's desires better than Fred himself knows, the problem can be solved. Without doubt this type of paternalism has had immense influence on the policies of western governments in the twentieth century. It is quite unjustifiable. Each individual knows best how to gratify his or her own desires. No government psychologist will ever do as well.

Social construct theories, then, suffer from two weaknesses. On an international level there are many creators of value, none of which has universal authority, and there is no method for resolving conflict between them. Within the state the creator of value justifies its pronouncements by appeal to the individual, but is not itself the individual. When morality is based on self-interest, individuals who judge their self-interest differently can only be expected to make different moral judgements. Social construct theories therefore tend to reduce to individualistic theories.

Individualistic theories

Individualism accepts that the highest court of appeal is the individual person. This solves the problem of why we should obey moral authority. We feel we ought to do what is right because we have decided for ourselves what counts as the right thing to do.

The idea that 'we create our own values' is popular today. It benefits from two common errors. One is that 'we create our own values' is taken to mean 'we create our own values on the basis of our most deeply held convictions'. This confuses the issue, because when we speak about our values in this sense, they *are* our most deeply held convictions. The statement would be better rendered 'We *derive* our values from other, already-held, values'. The question then becomes clear: where do the already-held values come from? The whole point of 'we create our own values' is that we create the starting point, the initial set of criteria from which all other judgements are derived.

Secondly, 'we create our own values' easily slides into 'we *ought* to create our own values'. Don Cupitt writes:

> Our task is to make our own faith come true by building the Kingdom of God on earth. We do it all... Ethics is not a matter of fitting into a ready-made moral order, but of designing and building a better one... We are objectively valueless, but we give each other value when we love one another. And the most rational faith to adopt and to act upon is that which leads us to value each person, each aspect of the world and our life, as highly as is self-consistently possible.[11]

'Our task is to...' clearly means 'we ought to'; Cupitt writes with a moral urgency *as he insists* that there is no ready-made morality and we need to create our own. Any argument of the type 'There are no obligations and therefore we must...' clearly contradicts itself. Cupitt looks forward to a 'better' moral order. The idea of comparing two moral orders, and pronouncing one better than the other, presupposes that there already is a moral standard by which they can be judged. Yet the whole point of the argument is that no such standard exists.

On what basis do I decide which moral rules to accept? Suppose I am deciding whether to count stealing as wrong. What reasons might there be? I am free to choose my own reasons, of course, but if I tell myself not to steal because it would be against a moral rule, or my intuitions, or the well-being of other people, I would be appealing to a different moral theory and my objection to stealing would no longer be individualistic. Consistent non-realism about value must insist that there are no values before we create them. This means that, before we create them, there is no good reason for creating them. The only possible reasons for creating them are reasons which can exist without values. Reasons of this type would be that our hormones make us feel like creating them, or that we think creating them will satisfy our desires, or that we decided at random to create them. Most of us would think that values created like this are so weak that they are not values at all: rather than dignifying them with the description of 'values', we might call them 'habits' or 'whims'.

In the absence of an alternative, individualistic theories tend to emphasize the role of what people *want*. Some moral philosophers argue that, as individuals, we can be left to decide for ourselves how to weigh immediate desires against long-term happiness, or our own well-being against the well-being of others; whatever we want becomes the basis of our morality.[12]

Wants, though, have their own problems as a moral system. Usually, when we catch other people changing their moral principles in the light of their wants, we condemn them for it. But we do sometimes change our wants in the light of moral principles, and when we do we give ourselves a moral pat on the back. According to wants theory it should be the other way round: because morality is based on wants, we should adapt our moral principles to suit what we want. Individualistic theories therefore tend towards inviting us to live self-centred lives.[13] Do value, purpose and morality boil down to spurious justifications of what we were going to do anyway?

Many moral philosophers now argue that they do. The basis for all values is the individual's experience of life. I value pie and chips: you value giving money to the poor. I value the local park: you would value an amusement arcade far more, if it was built on the site. This, of course, is the kind of account which dissolves values into nothing, since they really only echo what we want to do, and leave us with no way of justifying our preferences to others. Different people inevitably have conflicting values, and there is no way of resolving the conflicts. However strongly I feel about racial justice or protecting the rainforests, the reason for my value system is simply that *that is how I feel*. If others feel differently, all I can do is engage in emotive attempts to manipulate their feelings, or just shout in frustration.

Emotivism accepts this conclusion. Emotivist theory arose out of the ideas of the logical positivists, for whom all moral talk was meaningless because it cannot be verified.[14] C L Stevenson developed the first systematic account in *Ethics and Language* (1944). To Stevenson, each moral statement is a combination of a factual statement with a statement of attitude. 'This is wrong' means 'I disapprove of this; do so as well'. The factual statement is a statement about one's own feelings and can be taken to be true. The other part is an imperative.

So what are we really talking about when we say that something is good? On an analytical level, Stevenson notes,

> We seem forced to a distressingly meagre conclusion: if a man says 'X is good', and if he can prove that he really approves of X, then he has all the proof that can be demanded of him.

How, then, can we *justify* our moral beliefs? Stevenson discusses what happens when we try to persuade others to change their moral views. It is a matter of using facts to show how our preferred situation will satisfy the other person's desires. When we are told to do something, and ask 'Why?', a reason is something which makes the imperative attractive. The speaker does not *give reasons* for a change in the hearer's attitude, but *causes* them. In this way emotivism reduces moral debate to psychological manipulation.[15]

Value-denying theories

Just as the weaknesses in social theories make them dissolve into individualistic theories, individualistic theories dissolve into expressions of self-interest, so that the only reason for upholding any values at all is to manipulate the behaviour of other people for one's own benefit. By this stage we cannot help wondering whether all value, purpose and morality is a big mistake. Friedrich Nietzsche foresaw this conclusion in the nineteenth century:

> No one is accountable for existing at all, or for being constituted as he is, or for living in the circumstances and surroundings in which he lives... He is *not* the result of a special design, a will, a purpose; he is *not* the subject of an attempt to attain to an 'ideal of man' or an 'ideal of happiness' or 'an ideal of morality' — it is absurd to want to hand over his nature to some purpose or other. *We* invented the concept 'purpose': in reality purpose is *lacking*.[16]

His view became popular in the twentieth century. J L Mackie, in *Ethics: Inventing Right and Wrong* (1977) reviews the different kinds of moral theory and rejects them all. Moral discussions, he argues, presuppose that there is a right and wrong, but there is no right and wrong. He describes his proposal as an 'error theory'.[17] The implication is that we have to live without values altogether: any attempt to hang onto them is a refusal to face reality.

It is tempting to conclude that values have developed because it suits human interests to develop them, and that we should therefore create new values designed for our mutual benefit; but this would only take us back to social construct theory. Mackie does in fact take this line, but has been much criticized for it: what his error theory indicates is that social construct theories are just as erroneous as the others.[18]

Conclusion

I have described five types of response to the questions 'What values exist?' and 'Why should we respect them?' We might summarize by saying that non-human sources are best for setting up objective standards, but we cannot show either that they exist or that we ought to respect them. Social construct theories produce standards, though not objective ones, and can offer reasons why individuals should obey them by appealing to self-interest; but they cannot give dissidents convincing reasons to conform. Individualistic theories can state more simply that we should obey our principles because we have chosen them ourselves; but we cannot expect people to agree with each other, or even to be consistent over time. Finally, it can be argued that all appeals to values are simply errors and the only honest thing to do is to live without them.

To simplify even further, we could reduce the five alternatives to two.

Values are established by an authority, either non-human or human. In either case, what claim has it got on our allegiance? What reasons can anybody give us to convince us that we ought to do as it says even when we do not want to? At the very least, we will need to be persuaded that the authority understands the nature of reality better than we do, foresees the future better than we do and is committed to our well-being. If the authority is non-human, only the God of optimistic theology will do. If it is human, we *may* choose to trust other people but we know only too well that they will let us down. As soon as the judgements of other humans do not suit us, we will have every reason to withdraw our allegiance and make our own judgements.

Alasdair MacIntyre compares the decline of moral values with the development of taboo in eighteenth century Polynesia. Captain Cook and the English visitors were amazed by the moral behaviour of the Polynesians. On the one hand their sexual habits seemed very liberal; on the other, they strictly forbade men and women to eat together. When the visitors asked why, the answer was that it was *taboo*. They asked what 'taboo' meant, but they received no answer which they could understand. It did not mean simply 'prohibited'; the Polynesians explained that eating together was prohibited *because* it was taboo. Yet forty years later, the taboos were abolished without causing any significant social consequences. So — what did 'taboo' mean, and why was it so important to one generation and so unimportant to another?

Anthropologists have proposed an answer which is well illustrated by Valeri's study of Hawaii, where the word for taboo was 'kapu'. Originally, the moral rules followed rationally from the people's understanding of the world and their place in it. Like traditional societies all over the world, their rituals expressed and reaffirmed their understanding of the gods and the hierarchical order of society with its kingship, family relationships and relationship to the land. Anything which was considered divine, or closely related to the divine, was kapu. People with higher positions in the hierarchy were closer to the divine, and therefore kapu. There were many laws regulating the relationships between what was kapu and what was not. We could think of parallels in religious life today: for example, many churches protect what is holy by forbidding women to join the choir, enter the sanctuary or become priests. In both cases, only within the original theological setting do the rules make sense.

In the second stage, the kapu rules were gradually separated from their original function and came to be understood as commands and prohibitions in their own right, like European rights and duties. Once this began to happen, it became possible for kapu rules to change, so that they ceased to share the original underlying harmony. Instead they became a set of separate commands and prohibitions with no common purpose. The Hawaiians came to understand kapu as a simple, basic, unanalysable concept which could not be explained in terms of anything else but was essential for the life of society — just like Moore's definition of 'good', but a hundred years before him.

There are other parallels. As the original theological setting was lost, the rulers manipulated kapu rules to govern trade with the Europeans. Kapu came to represent the interests of the ruling classes. On the other hand, individuals began using it to claim property rights, *as individuals*, independently of their position in the traditional hierarchy. Kapu rights were claimed *against* other people. Finally, in 1819, the kapu rules were abolished. There was no social upheaval: by this stage, Hawaiians were happy to live without them.[19]

When modern Europe, like Hawaii, separated its moral rules from their theological setting, morality lost its rational basis. It has taken a long time to admit the fact, because precious few welcome it, but within the terms of modern neutralism all talk of purpose, morality or value is bound to be a mistake. The suspicion has been lurking for a long time. A great deal of the academic moral philosophy being written today could be described as a struggle to find some meaning for value within the terms of modern secular thought. There cannot be any. Values perform a function which cannot be performed by anything which we create ourselves. They stand beyond us, setting standards which reveal to us the best within ourselves, and inviting us to direct our lives towards them. They speak to us with an authority which transcends our self-interest, and they tell us to do what we do not want to do. The early Enlightenment dualists relegated them to a separate world where the soul and God could interact beyond the reach of science. The radical Enlightenment abolished that other world. As long as we accept their view of reality, there cannot be any room, anywhere in the universe, for value, purpose or morality. Step by step and quite rationally, modern secular theory has abolished value.

Where does this leave us? In practice our society is full of values. We do the things we do because they seem to be valuable, or to have a purpose, or to be morally good or bad. If there are no true values, is anything at all worth doing? In the next chapter I shall consider some practical implications.

1   C J. Glacken, *Traces on the Rhodian Shore,* 375-428.
2   Ch. 1; T Cosslett, Ed, *Science and Religion in the Nineteenth Century*, p. 27.
3   Huxley was to represent the public storm over the *Origin of Species* as a debate between science and religion, a representation which is still common today. However, there were far too many clergyman-scientists on both sides of the debate. See T Cosslett, Ed, *Science and Religion in the Nineteenth Century*, pp. 1-24; C C Gillispie, *Genesis and Geology.*
4   C J. Glacken, *Traces on the Rhodian Shore,* 415-21.
5   E.g. Charles Kingsley, another clergyman-naturalist (T Cosslett, Ed, *Science and Religion in the Nineteenth Century*, pp. 2-7).
6   T Cosslett, Ed, *Science and Religion in the Nineteenth Century* pp. 7f.
7   J Waldron, Ed, *Theories of Rights*, pp. 1-20.
8   W D Hudson, *Modern Moral Philosophy*, pp. 67-8.
9   D H Monro, Ed, *A Guide to the British Moralists*, p. 14.
10 It is possible to escape this conclusion by including international organizations — just as rule by the state can help gratify our desires, so can international treaties — but this only draws attention to the state's failure to gratify desires. Because we have conflicting desires, we create conflicting organizations with conflicting value systems, not just a single harmony-generating authority.
11 'The greening of faith in a damaged world', *The Guardian*, 3 October 1988. See also my reply in the issue of 17 October.
12 For example, P. Foot, *Virtues and Vices*, 1978, discussed in W D Hudson, *Modern Moral Philosophy*, pp. 314-9.
13 Foot tries to escape this conclusion by recognizing the desire to help others as part of our wants; she hopes people will see themselves as 'volunteers banded together to fight for liberty, etc.' and come into 'the moral cause' (W D Hudson, *Modern Moral Philosophy*, pp. 324-333), but this kind of theory can never provide a moral reason for doing so.
14 W D Hudson, *Modern Moral Philosophy*, pp. 107-111; A J Ayer, *Language, Truth and Logic*, pp. 110-6.
15 C L Stevenson, *Ethics and Language*, pp. 21-28.
16 *Twilight of the Idols*, 1889, quoted in J Kent, *The End of the Line?*, p. vii.
17 J L Mackie, *Ethics: Inventing Right and Wrong*, e.g. pp. 48-9.
18 For example, S. Blackburn makes the point in T Honderich, Ed, *Morality and Objectivity*, pp. 1-3.
19 A MacIntyre, *After Virtue: A Study in Moral Theory* pp. 111-2; A MacIntyre, *Three Rival Versions of Moral Enquiry*, pp. 178-86.

Chapter 8

Living in a value-free world

OVER THE LAST three chapters I have described what I mean by 'neutralism'. Unlike optimism and pessimism, it believes that only humans can create values. It is justified by any type of cosmology which does not believe there is a higher, objective source of true value.

In this chapter I shall offer examples of the practical implications, as I did for optimism and pessimism in Chapter 4. If we believe in the neutralist evaluation of the world, what does it lead us to do?

The modern western culture which began in Europe has now spread round the world. Compared with other cultures it is quite distinct, and knows it. There is a strong sense of superiority. We have been taught to think we have a far better grasp of of reality than other cultures have had. We have made *progress*. What we mean by progress is what the early Enlightenment philosophers taught us to mean: that the natural order is not the way we would like it to be, so we should exercise dominion over it. We should find out how the world works, in order to control it. Because our science and technology have been so successful at doing it, we think of ourselves as more civilized than past ages.

What has made modern western culture so different from others, then, is its massive programmes to improve the way things are. Many commentators now believe that the modern era is coming to an end because these programmes are collapsing.

In this chapter I shall describe how the rise and fall of modernism relate to a neutralist evaluation of the world. It rose when neutralism was applied to the whole of the physical world, but there still existed another, spiritual world where God gave the human soul the task of dominating nature. It declined when neutralism took over the whole of reality and there was no valuing, purposeful authority to tell us what needed to be done.

I shall first describe some of the grand programmes of improvement, and then note how the justifications for them have declined, following the pattern of Chapter 7. Thirdly, I shall describe the role of religion in a neutralist theory of reality.

The rise of the grand programmes

In Chapter 5 I described how the seventeenth century mechanists set out to exercise dominion over nature. Their theories made the physical world seem determined, simple and observable. They set out to observe and measure everything, so that in time they would know everything about it and be able to control it completely. At the time, many Protestant sects expected God to bring about a new age very soon. It was easy to equate this hope, as Bacon did, with the idea of dominating nature: humanity *ought* to have complete dominion over it, and one day would. In this way it was possible to believe that the task of establishing control was a limited one: once we had achieved it, there would be no need for further developments.

Progress, then, would consist of accumulating knowledge and learning how to manipulate nature. These ideas lie behind the constitutions of most modern universities. The assumption is that they are all allies, engaged on a worldwide task of generating ever more publicly available knowledge. The more knowledge we have, the better we will be able to control the world. All knowledge should be 'value free'; researchers look for it simply for the sake of building up the total amount of knowledge we have.

In Chapter 6 I described how eighteenth century theories reduced humanity to being part of the physical order, and no more. This gave rise to elitist programmes of social control. Each programme borrowed the idea of humanity controlling nature in order to improve the conditions of human life, and extended it to the idea of 'us' controlling human society, again in order to improve human life.

One programme was to speed up evolution. Well before Darwin's time, theories of evolution explained how Africans had evolved out of baboons, or something like them, and Europeans had evolved further. Other races were somewhere in between. It could be assumed that progress would consist of learning the laws of evolution and then manipulating them to speed the process up. Imperialists could interpret Darwin's theory as scientific proof that killing off inferior races was all to the good.[1]

Another programme was utilitarianism. Jeremy Bentham's theory called upon governments to produce the greatest happiness for the greatest number, by studying the laws of human behaviour. He believed it should be possible to describe all happiness and unhappiness in terms of pain and pleasure, and measure it all on a single scale. The task of governments was to maximize pleasure and minimize pain. Because most people did not understand the principle, social reformers should create situations in which the unenlightened would be manipulated into doing what was in the general interest. The most well known of his programmes was in penal policy. Britain produced a draconian system of deterrents, far more severe than any other theory could justify. It seems ironic that a harsh system should be based on the principle of maximizing pleasure and minimizing pain, but according to the theory a stiff enough deterrent would produce the required behaviour. When it did not, the answer was to increase the deterrent.[2]

Perhaps the most influential social control programmes have been capitalism and communism. Just as Descartes reduced rationality to a simple process of deductions from first principles, and Bentham reduced happiness to a single pain-pleasure scale, so also the eighteenth and nineteenth century economists set out to reduce human well-being to wealth. The more wealth, the better. It was to be measured on a single scale of money. The economists were the experts who knew best how to do it. The rest of us should leave them to work out how we should be governed. Just as Lenin and Trotsky could appeal to the working classes to entrust leadership to those who understood Marxist analysis, the citizens of western democracies could be urged — right across the left-right spectrum — to vote for the party most likely to manage the economy in the general interest.

There have been many other grand programmes. I have already mentioned behaviourism. Among the influential ones we might add planning and education. What they all have in common is the idea of a united humanity trying to improve its environment. In the seventeenth century this environment was the natural order: in the eighteenth it was extended to include human nature. It was being improved by the experts for the benefit of all.

The decline of the grand programmes

These programmes made sense within a view of reality which was largely, but not entirely, neutralistic. The seventeenth century mechanists set about controlling nature because they believed it was God's purpose for humanity. They had a hierarchical view of reality.

(i) God lives in the spiritual world and provides humanity with values.

(ii) The human soul, or mind, lives in the spiritual world, receives values from God and applies them in the way it controls the body.

(iii) The human body is under the control of the mind and serves it by exercising dominion over the physical world.

(iv) The physical world has no value in itself, as it lies entirely outside the spiritual world, but God has created it to serve human needs.

Eighteenth century theories abolished the spiritual world. *God's* agenda for humanity became *the* agenda for humanity. The grand programmes continued, but the justification for them changed. This created a weakness. As I noted in Chapter 7, realist theories of value are difficult to justify. Even if there is an impersonal 'notice board in the sky', setting out the true purpose of human life and what we ought to do about it, why should those who feel oppressed by it obey it?

Universities still function on the basis that accumulating more and more knowledge is a worthwhile activity in itself. Many academics are content to think their work is justified in these terms. On the other hand there is no publicly available world knowledge-bank. Nor is there a universally agreed team of experts who can be entrusted to use the information for the benefit of all. Research grants are made available by those with particular axes to grind and the money to pay. Within universities, different departments are motivated by radically different value systems. There is no united humanity accumulating knowledge for the benefit of all.

Technology is still highly valued. Many people still believe that creating new technologies must be a good thing in itself, but the old reasons no longer convince. The hope for a new age, with complete knowledge and control over nature, has been abandoned. To most of us the thought of it sounds more like a nightmare than a vision, because we know all too well that nobody can be trusted with that much power. Even the greatest enthusiasts for science and technology do not envisage it.

What do they offer us instead? The images now presented by mass markets characteristically look forward to more and more, without limit, for its own sake. For example, if we ask 'When will the design of cars be good enough, so that there will be no need to produce new designs?' it is car enthusiasts who will characteristically answer 'Never!' There is no shortage of people thrilled by the thought that science and technology will carry on, producing more and more novelties, without limit. If we insist on asking what is the purpose of all this novelty, the usual answer is that it will make the human experience of life better and better. Cynics are regaled with catalogues of the dreadful conditions in which people were forced to live, in the bad old days before modern technology. Flushing toilets... penicillin... television... microwaves... mobile phones... how did they manage without them? Life must have been *dreadful!*

These answers are a neutralistic alternative to Bacon's theory of the fall: the natural order, without technology, is unpleasant because we live in a God-free zone and this is just the way things happen to be. Only our technology makes life pleasant. In other words, Bacon's reason for dominating nature has been replaced by appeals to self-interest. Just as God's purposes have been turned into *the* purposes, *the* purposes have been turned into *our* purposes. Science and technology benefit us, so we should support governments which invest in them.

In practice, then, the realist justifications for the grand programmes have collapsed into social construct justifications. They are there because the state creates them, and the state creates them in the nation's interests. The focus shifts from humanity's well-being to society's well-being. There is much internationalism left, but it is bound to decline when a sense of a united humanity, faced with a common task, is replaced by appeals to self-interest.

The economic programmes have adapted as well as any: it becomes the state's task to maximize wealth for the nation, and other nations become 'our competitors'. If any social goal can be said to dominate the affluent west today, it must surely be the determination to increase the nation's wealth. Of the many theories which, in one way or another, over-simplified reality in order to set about controlling it, the one which remains most popular today is the economic one: that human well-being can be measured by amounts of money. Since the Second World War, the Gross National Product — which adds up the total amounts of money we all spend and receive — has become the main way of judging the wealth of a country. A great deal of public debate presupposes that the bigger it is, the better off we are.

It is at this stage of modernity's development, when the grand programmes are understood as social constructs, that modern neutralism compares most closely with the ancient Babylonian religion I described in Chapter 1. The way things are is fundamentally impersonal and chaotic and has no intrinsic value. Out of it have evolved beings which are capable of acting on it and changing it. For the Babylonians, these are the gods; for us, the laws of nature. These powers conflict with each other and none of them has complete control. One power happens to dominate at present: in one case Marduk, in the other the economy, or perhaps an alliance of the economy with technology. The economy, like Marduk, has created order out of chaos and banished its grandmother — religion, or perhaps ignorance — to the edges of reality. Within this order it has created a situation where human life is acceptable.

This provides the context for our lives. We are completely dependent on an order created by one of many conflicting powers. Just as the Babylonians described the original chaos as completely inhospitable, modern society loves to describe past ages as though they all languished in miserable poverty. It is our good fortune to live 'in this day and age'. On the other hand the creator remains in conflict with other powers, so the present order cannot be taken for granted. There is always the possibility that it may return to the original chaos. From the human point of view, this is the worst thing that could ever happen. Therefore the most important thing for humans to do — the agenda which overrides every other human activity — is to obey the instructions of the economy, like Marduk, down to every last detail. We are free to do other things as well, but only if they do no harm to the economy.

Because we cannot speak directly to the economy, any more than they could to Marduk, we depend on a class of experts who understand what we must do for it. However poor we are, we must keep 'tightening our belts' whenever they tell us to. If their calculations reveal that they should pay themselves twenty times as much as a hospital nurse, we accept their judgement. They are worth every penny. As each crisis strikes — recession, inflation, unemployment, balance of payments deficits — we are reminded again how important it is to 'get the economy right'. When economic theories fail, left blames right and right blames left. Few recognize that the main problems are caused by what left and right have in common, not what divides them.

As I described in Chapter 7, social construct theories lose their credibility when people stop trusting the experts. If the purpose of the grand programmes is to serve the interests of the people, we can judge for ourselves whether our interests are being served. Why should we accept higher taxes, or noisy lorries past our front door, or laws forbidding us to do whatever we want to do? If the answers — a growing economy, or a law-abiding society, or whatever — are nothing but the preferences of the governing elite, others may have different priorities. Even if the government's calculations are correct — even if, for example, lorries past front doors really are a necessary price to pay for a growing economy — it is perfectly legitimate to decide that I would rather do without a growing economy at that price, or I would welcome it on condition that the lorries do not go past *my* front door. Once society's grand programmes are revealed as social constructs, these are legitimate responses, and we can no longer expect support for any programme of social improvement, except from those who will personally benefit.

Thus the grand programmes, once they have declined from *the* purposes of life to *our* purposes, are bound to decline still further, into alliances of self-interest. If there is no real, objective, truth about what we ought to be doing, we can decide for ourselves what to do, and there is no presumption in favour of improving the order of nature.

This, I have argued, is the inevitable result of neutralism. There is no supreme authority to give our lives direction or tell us what would be worth doing. It is up to us, as individuals, to set our own agenda. Whatever agenda we set, the only reason for it is that we have set it. Once neutralism has taken its full course, as I argued in Chapter 7, the only meaningful reasons for doing anything at all are that our hormones make us feel like it, or that we have chosen it at random, or that it will gratify our desires.

In the long run, neutralism produces that attitude to life which has become all too prevalent in the affluent west. Life consists of two processes: getting what gratifies our desires, and gratifying them. We go to school to get a job. We go to work to get money. At work, we do whatever we are told, for the money. When off work, we have no obligation to society, nothing to strive for: we simply do what we like. The only vestige of an agenda is to maximize the amount of time we spend gratifying our desires. Life offers nothing better than to go to work, come home, sit down and passively receive meaningless entertainment from a box in the living room.

Neutralist religion

In Chapter 5 I described how the fourteenth century sceptics divided reality into the separate worlds of 'faith' and 'reason', so that religious doctrines tell us nothing about the material world. Modern neutralism takes the theory further: since there is nothing outside the material world, religious beliefs cannot tell us about anything at all.

Thoroughgoing neutralism has no use for religion. However, I think many beliefs and practices in modern western religion are best understood as ways of continuing to believe in 'the other world' within a generally neutralist understanding of reality. Because the world we live in can be fully understood without religion, religious commitment is a voluntary activity, for those who are interested in it. It therefore functions as *membership of a voluntary club*. Evangelism is a membership drive: it cannot tell people that they ought to go to church, but it can appeal to their religious sentiments.

The key to understanding neutralistic religion, then, is the idea that the world is godless and valueless, but religion provides symbols of a separate, religious world and the means to make contact with it. Good symbols maintain the distance between the two worlds.

The symbols

Perhaps the most obvious symbol is the church building. Optimists and pessimists expect it to be used for a purpose: they may want to heat it or add an office or toilet. Neutralists generally oppose all changes: what is important about the building is not what happens in it but that it should be *seen*. The older it is, the better. Many of our churches were gutted and refurnished in the nineteenth century but in the twentieth have been zealously preserved unchanged. Feelings can be extremely strong. When the opponents of change are able to express their reasons, they often appeal to a gut feeling that any change is *blasphemy*: there is a moral duty to preserve the building as it is.

Another symbol is the minister. This character, like the building, ought to seem different from others. Neutralists like their clergy to wear distinctive clothes. Lifestyle should be different too. Stereotypes describe them as morally upright, upholding standards which others fail to achieve. This lays them open to the accusation of hypocrisy. When a vicar elopes with a neighbour's wife, it is not just one more affair: a symbol of distant holiness has been shattered, and the sense of outrage is increased accordingly.

Like the building, the most important function of the clergy is to be seen. For some, the vicar should appear at every public function and speak to everybody without ever addressing a controversial issue. There is a common gut feeling that to be visited in one's home by the vicar is to be *blessed*. Conversely, neutralists are often fascinated by the clergyman who enjoys a pint of beer or plays football.

To attend a service is to perform a religious act and the purpose, if there is any, is to receive a sort of 'spiritual uplift' or 'recharge our spiritual batteries'. These common phrases imply that spiritual strength cannot be found outside the symbols of holiness: the outside world is spiritually draining and the church renews the strength to cope with it.

Worship is not expected to explain or change anything. It is a source of spiritual power in itself, and the power is imparted to the *individual*. Once again, what counts is that it should be different. If the language, music and ceremonial create an aura of a bygone age, so much the better.

The bible, too, is often a symbol of God or a holy thing in its own right, rather than a source of information. It is neutralists who insist that the Authorized Version is the 'proper' Bible, admire the beauty of its language and give copies of it to their grandchildren as Confirmation presents — in tiny print but with attractive leather covers.

For many, the individual's inner *feeling* of the presence of God is the most important symbol. Many sects define true Christians in terms of 'conversion experience' or 'knowing Jesus in your heart'. This idea is also common among pessimists, but pessimists expect the inner experience to make an outward difference. For neutralists what is important about it is that, like the vicar and the building, it is just *there*.

Authority and doctrine

Since the nature of reality is fully explained in secular terms, the function of religious doctrines is to tell us about its own sphere of expertise. This, characteristically, consists of the other world, life after death, prayer and the conduct of worship.

Neutralists often inherit the content of doctrines from pessimism or optimism, but change their significance. Many are happy to believe that they simply do not matter at all. They may attend church services throughout their lives without developing any interest in religious doctrines. The most interesting thing about the sermon will be how long it is. In academic circles, neutralists of this type may think of theological education as just one more academic discipline: the Christian botany lecturer treats theology, just like engineering, as one more subject of somebody else's expertise.

Since this idea empties doctrine of all significance, it does not satisfy all neutralists. Perhaps the most common way of making doctrines important without letting them loose on the secular world is the idea that people will go to heaven after they die, provided they believe the right doctrines. We are to believe what we are told, not because knowing it helps make sense of our lives, but because the knowledge is needed *for salvation*. In an age when many young people are obliged to learn information they do not need to know, and are then tested on it, religious faith easily degenerates into a kind of revising for an exam.

Because doctrines have no practical significance, we do not need to understand them. It is enough to believe that they are true. As a result, a high degree of mystification becomes acceptable. Mediocre teachers can tell critics that the received doctrine is the truth and just has to be accepted as it is. Doubts, instead of being part of a creative learning process, merely indicate lack of faith. Mystification hides nonsense and is explained as mystery.

Mystification has another use too. Since religion is not about this world, it does not need to share a common language with this-worldly matters. Just as neutralists are more impressed when religious language and music are different from secular language and music, so also with theological explanation. If it operates on a holier plane, barely visible through the incense, so much the better. We do not need to understand it: we only need to accept it. This is why the people who object most strongly to 'clergymen who interfere in politics' are often the keenest on the Virgin Birth and the Resurrection. These other-worldly events from a dim and distant past belong to a package of information provided by religious authority and can safely be affirmed because they are quite irrelevant to their own lives.

Ethics

Neutralist religion faces a dilemma in the role of ethics. On the one hand churches are better than other institutions at upholding moral systems, so neutralists expect religious leaders to affirm moral standards. They criticize them for not taking a strong enough stand against drug-taking, homosexuality, or whatever they consider important. To this extent, they expect the churches to defend society's norms.

On the other hand neutralists also expect religious leaders to confine themselves to their own sphere of influence, the world of religion. If they speak out on other issues, they are 'interfering'. So *which* issues count as the church's responsibility? The only issues which fit within neutralism are ones which have no this-worldly implications at all. This would imply that the church should not uphold any moral standards at all. Within the terms of neutralism, there is no solution to this dilemma.

To summarize, neutralistic religion is best understood as a way of carving out a space for religious values within a neutralistic view of reality as a whole. In practice it is often socially conservative. In principle, however, it avoids all engagement with the secular world. Inasmuch as it does avoid engagement, it is quite literally irrelevant to people's lives. The cult of symbols, the fund-raising for the church roof, the debates about the Virgin Birth and who can administer the chalice, the prayers for the sick, the memorials to the dead, the safe moral condemnations of things which nobody publicly defends, between them make up a sub-culture which finds plenty to do while obsequiously leaving secular society untouched. Like the bowling club, it provides a social centre and a set of activities for anybody who would like to join. It is a small step from being a neutralist Christian to being a lapsed Christian.

Conclusion

This completes my account of neutralism, as illustrated by the mechanistic paradigm developed in modern Europe. In Part 1, I distinguished between optimistic and pessimistic theology. In Part 2, I distinguished between these two on the one hand and neutralism on the other. Again, the cosmology informs the evaluation and the evaluation informs the agenda. The key distinction is that there is no higher authority which establishes the truth about value and gives us a reason for responding to it. Realists argue that things called 'values' really exist, whether humans recognize them or not, but as non-realists point out there is no good reason why we should pay attention to them. Non-realists argue that we create our own values and our own reasons for relating to them, but as realists point out they deprive themselves of any justified reason for doing so. We are left with the conflicting desires of individuals, and no way to resolve the conflicts. Conflict is as inescapable for neutralists as it is for pessimists.

Either we live without values, then, or we create our own. Values which are created by us are no more than constructions of our own imagination. Outside our dreams, the whole of reality is a valueless machine. This evaluation of the world leads in turn to its own characteristic agenda for human life, quite different from the optimistic and pessimistic agendas. If neutralism describes the true state of the world, then of all the many things which we could do, nothing needs to be done, or ought to be done, or would be a valuable thing to do. Reality, and our lives, are just *there*. We are like hikers whose map has been blown away by the wind: as we do not know which way to go, we carry on following the path we were on when we still had it, assuming that eventually something will turn up.

It should now be possible to make some generalizing observations which parallel the conclusions reached at the end of Chapter 4.

First, there is no tradition within modern western thought which accepts all the conclusions of neutralism. Anybody who was determined to do so would, like Nietzsche, be driven mad. Even the most determined philosophers find value in *something*. In practice all neutralists make compromises.

Second, there is a wide variety of possible compromises. Some approximate more nearly than others to extreme neutralism.

Third, every compromise position is flawed. The alternative cosmologies are mutually exclusive. Once the logic of neutralism is accepted, it is unstoppable: there are no true values, and creating our own values really consists of nothing more than expressing our desires.

Fourth, outside the specialist world of religion, western society is dominated by the neutralist evaluation of the world. Many of its judgements are widely taken for granted as 'common sense'. Even within religious circles, it has immense influence. Of course, most of the people who accept neutralist attitudes are not philosophers and do not think of themselves in these terms. but it is those who do in fact presuppose a neutralistic understanding of reality who will most strongly feel that its logical implications make sense.

It is hardly surprising that so many of the people who reflect on the state of western society conclude that we have reached a crisis. We cannot carry on as we are. We need a new mood, a change of direction. But what will it consist of, and where will it take us? In Part 3 I shall make some positive proposals.

1   M Banton, *Race Relations*, pp. 45-7.
2   W Moberly, *Ethics of Punishment*, pp. 43-52.

PART 3

Chapter 9

Faith: trusting the transcendent

S O FAR IN this book I have analysed value judgements about the world, and have categorized them into three types: the world is good, evil or neutral. These evaluations depend on cosmologies. When scientists tell us that the hole in the ozone layer is larger than ever, some say 'It is a criminal destruction of a wonderful, healthy world'; others, 'This world is riddled with evil and destined for the fires of hell anyway'; others again, 'The world happens to be here by chance; it is not designed to be a healthy environment, and we shall just have to add anti-cancer skin creams to our medicine cupboards'. Our cosmology tells us how to evaluate it, and our evaluation of it tells us what kinds of responses to make.

In Part 3 I aim to be more constructive. I hope to show how it makes sense to believe that the world is objectively good, and set out the practical implications. The ingredients of my account are taken from optimistic theology; my contribution will be to put them together in a way which avoids compromise with pessimism and neutralism.

The need for trust

I shall begin by assuming as little as possible. In Chapter 6 I described how the mechanistic philosophers tried to establish how we could know things with certainty, so that we did not need to trust in anything uncertain. Despite their efforts, the logic of their arguments led to the opposite extreme, that we cannot know anything at all. In real life this does not help. In order to get on with our affairs we need to be confident that we are in tune with reality, and that when we relate to other people they have minds like ours and belong to the same reality. Even if it was theoretically possible to establish certainty, we cannot wait until somebody does. We have no option but to *trust* that there are things which really exist even though philosophers and scientists have failed to prove them.

On this point the mechanistic paradigm is clearly wrong. There is something else, essential to all human activities and more fundamental than either observation or rationality, which underpins them: *trust*. It is more fundamental for two reasons. Firstly, every theory of knowledge includes an essential element of trust. Rationalism cannot lead to any truths until after we have accepted on trust the axioms of rationality. Empiricism depends on trust that our senses are reliable. Coherentism and inductivism explicitly accept the need to trust what has not been proved. Even pessimistic theology calls for trust that the bible, or whatever else, is divinely revealed. Secondly, we cannot first gain the knowledge we need for life and only then start living; we have to trust what we think we know, and develop our knowledge *as* we live.

Contrary to mechanists, then, I suggest that no account of knowledge can be of value unless it gives a central and permanent place to the act of trust. To trust is to go beyond what can be rationally deduced. This is what scientists have been doing throughout the modern period, despite the theories of philosophers. By using induction, they generalize from what they have observed in order to create hypotheses about what they have not observed. I shall use their method. Like scientists, we need to trust that there is something more to reality, beyond what philosophers have been able to prove.

So which acts of trust do we need to make? Are they consistent with each other? What problems do they generate and what solutions can we find? What theory of rationality results? These are the questions I shall explore in this chapter.

I shall begin with the unsolved dilemmas of modern philosophy. Mechanism believes that reality consists of impersonal matter and laws of nature, and anything which cannot be reduced to them does not exist. As we have seen, it does not work. It ends up denying the existence of anything at all. We can be confident, then, that reality does *not* reduce to matter and laws of nature. There is more to it. What else do we need to trust in? At the minimum, if I am to accept the existence of anything at all, I need to trust the following:

- that I have a thinking mind;
- that there is an external reality;
- that my mind accesses external reality well enough for normal purposes.

Social control theorists at their most reductionist have attributed this much to their subjects. If they credit themselves with no more than this, there is no reason to believe in their own theories. In order to feel we understand what is going on in our lives and the world around us, we must also trust:

- that there is order and coherence in reality;
- that events take place through relationships of cause and effect;
- that my rationality represents this true order and coherence, and understands relationships of cause and effect, well enough for normal purposes.

Only by these six acts of trust can we accept the existence of matter and order, and the human ability to perceive them and rationalize about them, well enough to engage in ordinary daily activities like shopping and cooking, and understand what we are doing. That 'well enough for normal purposes' is significant: we need to be able to trust not only that our observations and rationality can represent reality, but also that there is a rational explanation of error. The explanation of error must be of a kind which does not undermine our understanding in general.

If we trust no more than these six we are in the position at which logical positivism collapsed. I exist, the external world exists, and I can understand the basic functions of the external world. There is still no reason to assume that other people have similar minds and feelings. In order to accept that other people are like us, we must make two more acts of trust:

- that my mind can combine the information provided by my reason and sense impressions, to produce additional information which they cannot produce on their own;
- that other people have minds like mine.

We have now reached the stage at which we can recognize other people as other people and accept things like mathematical formulae and scientific laws. In other ways the mechanistic paradigm still stands. My mind, and these musings, may still be determined effects of prior causes, like all else that exists. People who really do have no sense of freedom, purpose, morality or value are rarely found outside psychiatric hospitals. The rest of us put our trust in yet more unproven propositions:

- that we have free will;
- that our life has a purpose;
- that there is a possibility of progress towards the fulfilment of that purpose;
- that our actions have moral significance;
- that life and the world have value.

I have now listed thirteen features of reality which we all need to accept on trust if we are to live anything remotely resembling normal lives. In order not to presume more than necessary at this stage, I shall refer to them blandly as 'the constituents of reality'.

My hypothesis needs to explain how we can account for them. We must not do this with a nod and a wink, knowingly agreed that we are not really committing ourselves but it might help social stability if we can persuade other people. We must move outside the culture of social control, and enter the culture of the scientist, genuinely wanting to know the truth about reality.

The source of reality

I propose, then, that we treat the existence of these thirteen as a hypothesis. Where does this leave us? On its own it puts us back into the kind of neutralistic realism which fills the sky with invisible entities: these thirteen, like the Babylonian gods, all impact on us in some way or other, but we have no account of how they relate to each other.

In addition to accepting their existence, we also need to trust that they are consistent with each other. For example, if the same thing has caused both the existence of the material world and our five senses, this may provide a reason for believing that our senses are designed to perceive the material world. Or if freedom and morality have the same source, this may provide a reason for using our freedom in a moral way. It may not, of course: before we can take this possibility seriously we will need to know more about the common source and how it functions. However, if the constituents of reality have no common source we have no reason to suppose there is any coherent relationship between them.

If we are to have any handle on reality, we must therefore add another detail to the hypothesis; that the constituents of reality have a common source. What can we say about this source? If we can describe it in a way which is internally consistent and meets our requirements, the hypothesis will pass its first test.

The most reductionist theory would be that the universe has been caused by an impersonal, determined process which can be traced back to the Big Bang, and its fundamental elements are impersonal matter and laws of nature. Could it be that all the constituents of reality have developed out of these? This would mean, for example, that freedom has developed, in a determined way, out of determined processes, and value has developed out of valueless processes. However, as we saw in Part 2, neutralists have questioned the existence of the constituents of reality precisely because they *cannot* be reduced to matter and laws of nature.

In Chapter 7 I argued that when we deny the existence of objective values we deprive ourselves of any good reason for creating our own. Since 'good' is a value, nothing can be good until *after* values have been created. Even the idea of creating our own values presupposes that there are pre-existent values.

The function of values is to set an authoritative standard for our lives. Values are meaningless unless they can transcend our impulses. They must be able to tell us what we should do even when we do not want to do it. Values which we create ourselves can never do this. If, today, I create my own values by committing myself to a lifetime of sexual abstinence, they are only my values because I choose to make them such. I have no more authority over my own values today than I will have tomorrow, and tomorrow I can change them. If values are to have any authority over our lives, without being changed every time we change our moods, they must tell us what to do with an authority which stands above our own decisions.

In practice, values are hierarchical. Whenever we justify any particular value, we do so by setting it within the context of greater and more authoritative value. The child asks the teacher, 'Why can't we play outside?' The teacher replies, 'Because the head teacher says so'. The child asks the head teacher the same question; but if the head teacher says 'Because your teacher says so', it will seem that somebody is passing the buck. If the head teacher says 'Because it's pouring with rain', this would be acceptable. The fact that it is raining provides an overall context, which explains both why the children should not play outside and why the head instructed the teacher accordingly.

In the same way, let us say that I enjoy learning to play the piano so I apply to take an exam in it. I then practise for the exam. Taking the exam has only one purpose, and that is to give a framework to the practising which I enjoy. If I get bored with the piano before I take the exam, the exam loses its purpose and there is no longer any reason to practise. What would legitimately keep me practising, even when I do not feel like it, is a different purpose which is independent of my feelings of enjoyment and has authority over my day-to-day decisions. For example, I might need a qualification in order to get a job.

This hierarchical structure is the only way we can explain or justify our values. All our valuings are rooted in greater and more authoritative value. If the universe really does have purpose and value, over and above human beliefs about them, they cannot have developed by impersonal and determined processes out of purposeless and valueless matter. Purpose and value are not the kinds of things which can just 'turn up' in a purposeless and valueless world. If they exist at all, they have been there all along.

If we are to avoid the absurdities of extreme neutralism, then, we must believe that the constituents of reality come from something which is itself a source of purpose and value. It gives purpose and value to the universe, whether we recognize them or not. Purpose and value are just as much basic constituents of reality as are matter and the laws of nature.

The source of the constituents of reality is, then, purposive and evaluating. It is difficult to imagine what this might mean, unless it also possesses a mind, rationality, freedom and in fact all the other constituents of reality.

What I have done so far is to stand the mechanistic paradigm on its head. Mechanism believes that everything can be reduced to impersonal matter and deterministic laws of nature, but when we follow its logic we find that it cannot account for all the constituents of reality. I have altered the theory in order to correct its weakness. I am already in deep water: if the source of reality is not, after all, impersonal and determined, but possesses the higher values right from the start, it is the kind of entity we would normally describe as God rather than an impersonal force. Does my proposal boil down to an argument for the existence of God?

Most of the modern arguments for the existence of God have attempted deductive proofs. In this sense Descartes has set the tone, even if the details of the arguments date back to Anselm and Aquinas. My proposal is far too modest to claim any such proof; it does not add up to anything remotely resembling the certainty which moderns have demanded.

On the other hand, why all this special pleading? Philosophers have shown that absolutely nothing at all can be established with deductive certainty: why does God require stricter proof than everything else? I offer no certainties; instead, like a scientist, I use induction to propose what seems the best available hypothesis. The hypothesis that everything boils down to impersonal matter and determined laws of nature does not work, because it cannot account for reality as we experience it. I am suggesting an adaptation which reintroduces God.

I see my proposal as a version of the design argument, much the same as Paley's 'watchmaker'. Like Paley, I suggest that the higher qualities, like purpose and value, are essential ingredients of reality, and no account of the universe is complete without them. The only satisfactory way of accounting for them is that the causal force, which makes the universe the way it is, has an intending, purposeful and evaluating mind.

Much has changed since Paley's time. Then, there were two main objections to the design argument. One was that science would soon produce a complete account of reality with no room for any inference to God. The other was that arguments for God's existence should produce strict deductive certainty. Neither objection can be justified now.

I am not, therefore, proposing a new argument for the existence of God, merely claiming that a very old argument is good enough once we abandon the unrealistic theories of certain knowledge and mechanistic reality. In order to account for reality, the best hypothesis leads to positing a divine being rather than impersonal causes. Like all inferences to the best hypothesis, it is open to challenge. I am not appealing to a divine revelation which stands aloof from reason. If my argument can be disproved, disproved it will be.

I suspect that my theory expresses why the majority of people believe there must be a divine being. It lies behind the common claim that 'There must be a God up there because if there wasn't...' and the sentence continues by describing some quality of life which cannot otherwise be explained. Throughout the modern period there have been theologians willing to defend it. Many have discredited it by arguing too hastily that the God they are positing must be the God of their own religious tradition.

It is an easy temptation. The God whom my argument proposes does not necessarily have anything to do with the bible or the Quran or the Christian Church.

However, there are some things I do need to claim. I have already noted that, if the constituents of reality derive from a single source, this makes it possible for them to relate to each other in a coherent way. I now wish to elaborate the point. In order to make any sense of our lives we need to believe not only that the constituents of reality exist but that they are consistent with each other. It will not help us in the least to believe that our minds exist and external reality exists, if the two do not relate to each other; we need to believe that the design of our minds includes the capacity to perceive reality. Freedom to choose between right and wrong is meaningless unless we have some way of knowing what is right and what is wrong. Similarly for all the constituents of reality: they need to relate to each other in such a way that they produce a unified picture. God must be self-consistent and harmonious.

Secondly, my hypothesis of God will not work unless it incorporates everything which exists. Suppose, for example, that as well as the constituents of reality which I have listed, there are other independent realities of which we know nothing. If these other realities do not affect us in any way, they do not threaten the hypothesis; but if they have the power to undermine any of the constituents of reality or the harmonious relationship between them, the initial act of trust will be unjustified. Anything might happen, and as far as we know we will have no power to do anything about it. If we are to have any reason for trusting that the natural order will continue as it is, we must assume that God has complete power over everything which exists, observed and unobserved alike, and complete knowledge of what everything can and cannot do.

Thirdly, there remains an outstanding problem with regard to the higher constituents of reality. In Chapter 7, when discussing purpose, morality and value, I argued that realist theories face two problems. The first is 'How do we know that these things exist?' I have now answered it: we do not know that they exist, but I am proposing their existence as the best available hypothesis. The second is: even if they do exist, why should we respect them?

In order to answer this question I need to affirm that God's creative processes are of such a type that we would be well advised to respond positively to them. Of course, it will not do to claim that it is always in everybody's personal self-interest to do what God wants. The reason why moral issues are so thorny is that one person's interests so often conflict with another's. What we need to believe is that, in the long run and from an overall point of view, there is good reason to accept God's evaluations, even when it does not suit our immediate interests and even though we do not know why. We need to be confident that, if we could understand everything, God would turn out to be fundamentally *on our side*. We need to evaluate God positively, and believe that God evaluates us positively.

In other words, God must be self-consistent, omnipotent, omniscient and good. All these characteristics need to be absolute: any compromise at all undermines the hypothesis. These are the characteristics of optimistic theology as I defined it in Chapter 2. It is no coincidence: the reason why we need to believe in a God like this today is the reason why the writers of Genesis needed to believe it then.

Reality as God's creation

The constituents of reality, then, have been deliberately created by a self-consistent, good, omnipotent and omniscient God. The fact that the same God created them all unifies them into a harmonious scheme, designed both for our well-being and the well-being of the whole. This means we can say more about them, from the perspective of optimistic theology.

Matter

Pessimism easily sets us against the material world. It often describes it as hostile to us, full of hidden spiritual entities which make life insecure. Neutralists reject hostile and hidden entities and instead describe matter as determined, simple and observable. Optimism welcomes the fact that matter cannot be explained deterministically, is extremely complex and contains many unobservables. We do not need to know everything or control nature: the world is precisely what we need as it is.

The laws of nature

Pessimism includes an element of chaos in reality, through the limitations of the gods. This leads to a sense of ignorance and helplessness in the face of whatever might happen next, and makes us fear the natural order. Neutralists go to the other extreme, that the world is altogether governed by regularities which can be observed and measured. This leads to the view that the future is determined and predictable, but our own lives are trapped in determinism and predictability too. Optimism takes a moderate position between the extremes. There are regularities, but not everything is governed by them. If there was no order, we would not be able to make any plans, but too much order would take away our freedom and creativity. The interplay between order and openness, which we naturally attribute to the world around us, really does exist and has been created by a good God to be just what we need. We will never be able to predict the future with certainty, let alone establish complete control over nature, but we do not need to. The world is ordered to the extent that it is good for it to be ordered.

It is the balance between the extremes which makes life enjoyable. When we buy a new car, most of us do not expect to know how all the parts work. If we did we would prefer simpler cars rather than more complex ones. As it is, most drivers prefer cars with a greater number of useful features; if the new one is so much more complex than the old one that it will take months to master the additional features, this is a thought we characteristically *enjoy*. Similarly, optimism welcomes the fact that the natural order is far richer than we will ever understand, because we are confident that it contains the regularities we need.

Minds

Pessimists may exalt our minds at the expense of our bodies or our bodies at the expense of our minds. In either case the relationship between them can easily become a problem. Neutralism leads to the conclusion that the mind is nothing but a way of talking about brain activity. Optimism claims that mind and body are deliberately designed to complement each other. Whatever the neurological processes, mental activity is real and meaningful, as part of a bodily life.

Rationality

Pessimistic theologies are wary of our natural reasoning powers; they may have been deliberately created to deceive us, and even if they have not, we cannot be sure that they are reliable. Modern neutralism goes to the other extreme, exalting reason to the point at which it is capable of producing deductive certainty. However, certainty has not been forth-coming. Optimism begins with trust: we trust God, and because God is good we trust our reasoning powers. Sometimes we make mistakes. God has not made us capable of perfect reasoning on all matters, but we have enough rationality for the purposes for which we have been made.

Empiricism

Many pessimists, influenced by eastern or Platonist traditions, have believed that the physical world is not real. Modern empiricists have often gone to the other extreme and denied that anything exists except what can be publicly observed and measured. As more and more theories explain observables in terms of unobservables, this has led to a contradiction. Optimism accepts that the world really does exist, as created by God, and is accessed by our senses. When our minds develop pictures of the world outside, we are doing what we normally think we are doing: observing a reality which is objectively there whether we observe it or not. There may be any number of unobservables. Our senses have been designed to perceive what we need to perceive, but not everything. The same is true of every animal, bird and fish. If dogs are colour blind but can hear a higher range of sounds, we need not agonize over what exists and for whom: God has enabled dogs to perceive what they need to perceive, and us likewise.

Understanding

Once we accept rationality and empiricism as sources of knowledge, we can build upon them the laws of logic, mathematics and science. Pessimism challenges the assumption that we can access truth in this way: at any stage in the process there may be conflicting principles, or pure chaos, to limit our understanding. Neutralism tears itself apart by trying to move in opposite directions at once: it sets out to build a complete and certain account of reality, but undermines rationalism and empiricism themselves. Optimism affirms that God has designed our faculties in such a way that we can check our theories against our observations and our observations against our theories, gradually building up systems of logic, mathematics and science. By doing so we make sense of what we do, and look back on the past and forward to the future with the expectation of continuity. We can discover patterns of agriculture, or the properties of electrical currents, which enrich our lives and can be expected to enrich the lives of our descendants too.

Speculation

As well as relating our sense perceptions and rationality to each other, we are capable of going beyond both to reflect on what else may exist as well. Characteristically, the more we examine and speculate on physical things, the more they lead us beyond the physical. We develop theories not only about scientific and mathematical laws, but about causation, freedom, beauty, God and many other things. Pessimists warn us that the more we trust our natural capacities the more we are likely to be led into error. Neutralists have reason to deny the existence of anything metaphysical. Optimism has no reason to hold back. By reflecting on the observable we are led to the unobservable. We are still prone to error; but the environment we have been designed to relate to may well contain many things which do not become accessible to us until after we have acquired a thorough understanding of more accessible things. In the case of causation, for example, we can agree with Hume that we never really see one thing causing another, but if causation is the best hypothesis, all we need to affirm is that the processes we describe as 'cause and effect' are some of the regularities God has imposed on the world.

Freedom

Neutralists have difficulty accounting for freedom at all: in a deterministic universe everything must be caused. Pessimists generally accept the reality of freedom, but vary in their evaluation of it or how they think it should be used. Optimism believes it is really there, and adds to the goodness of the created order because it enables us not only to do good but to choose it. This leaves open the question of *how* free will works, but we can accept its existence, like the existence of everything else, without needing a complete scientific account of it.

Other minds

Neutralism leads to doubting the existence of other people's minds. Pessimists generally affirm their existence, though some theories make a sharp distinction between those who know the revealed truths of their religion and those who do not. Optimists accept that there is no deductive proof of the existence of other minds, but we learn in other ways that other people's minds are like ours. As toddlers, for example, we notice that when we poke our fingers into other children's eyes they behave just as we behave when somebody does it to us. Later, when we come across people who are mentally handicapped, this does not destroy our trust that other people's minds are generally like ours; it simply indicates the limits to equality and reminds us that our own mind has imperfections too.

Sources of knowledge

I propose, then, that if we are to understand reality in a way which does justice to our experience, the best available hypothesis is that there is a God who is self-consistent, omnipotent, omniscient and good. God creates the things we need to believe in, in such a way that they complement each other. Because the universe has been created like this, it has an underlying unity. There are three immediate implications.

Firstly, each of the constituents of reality must be consistent with the others. For example, it cannot be the case that true progress is inconsistent with realizing the purpose of life, or that our natural rationality necessarily misleads us about the nature of God or matter. Evolutionism has led to many conflict-based theories of social progress;[1] optimism expects an underlying harmony.

Secondly, each constituent of reality must relate to different people in a consistent way. For example, the world I perceive through my senses is consistent with the one you perceive through yours; we may see different bits of it, and interpret it in different ways, but it is the same world. The purpose of my life is consistent with the purpose of your life; it cannot be the purpose of your life to kill me and the purpose of my life to kill you. Because God is self-consistent and harmonious, reality is self-consistent and harmonious.

Thirdly, the unknown aspects of each constituent of reality must be consistent with its known aspects. This is an essential presupposition of all science. Whereas modern science justifies it on the basis that the laws of nature are eternal and unchanging, I, like Basil, justify it on the basis that God is consistent and good.

Trust underpins knowledge. Only God is infallible. We must abandon the attempt to secure complete and certain knowledge, and instead aim for the humbler objective of knowing what we need to know, with enough assurance for legitimate purposes.

Once we have accepted the principle of trusting what cannot be proved, we may as well admit that we get information not only from reason but from a variety of other sources which we have learned to trust. Each source in its own way cooperates with reason, shows reason where its limits are and provides information which is unavailable to reason. The goodness of the world is richer than it would be if we only had one source of truth.

What are these other sources? The most obvious are *the five senses*, which produce empirical information. Another is *instinct*. Like all animals, we can be instinctively aware of what is going on in particular situations, even when we cannot explain it in words. Often we cannot distinguish in practice between our instincts and *subconsciously learned information*. Our rationality enables us to override them, but we still depend on them a great deal. A common experience is that the answer to a problem lies in a subconscious awareness, and after a while it works its way to consciousness and manifests itself as an intuitive leap, or a dream, or even voices in the sky. Different traditions interpret these experiences in different ways. Many interpretations are pessimistic, but in principle optimism can welcome the idea that, as well as our rationality, we share with other animals a faculty of instinct and the ability to learn things subconsciously.

Reason, observation, subconscious learning and instinct all belong to the individual. Other methods of gaining knowledge are social. A society can arrange for some of its members to develop *specialist skills*. *Tradition* can over time develop an understanding which is not accessible to a generation which starts from scratch. The corollary is that, for people who live in a society with low educational standards, the best hope for discovering truth may, after all, be to accept the wisdom of past ages. The ideas that 'we can learn from the past' and 'we can learn from other societies', far from being anti-rational, are a necessary defence against arrogance.

We can therefore affirm the value not only of reason but also of observation, instinct, specialist skills, tradition and inter-cultural exchange. We might add to the list, but my point should now be clear: reason, like all the other faculties, is not an absolute authority. It is the range of faculties between them which is adequate to human needs, but no one is infallible. There are no trumps.

My account of knowledge, then, is coherentist rather than foundationalist. There is no single self-evident starting point from which we deduce everything else with certainty. Instead we trust God, and God gives us a variety of faculties. Between them these faculties enable us to know what we need to know, and check each other for error. As with induction, we use what is known to develop theories about what is not known. With its fuzzy edges and its interplay between different sources of information, the process of gaining knowledge allows for new possibilities to emerge.

At its simplest, the process is empirical. When we look at a stationary football, we only see one side of it. We assume there is another side, of the same colour. Non-realists may debate the point, but if football players have their doubts they will score no goals.

Just as we make inferences from the observed to the unobserved, we also make inferences from the observable to the unobservable. When we see someone kick the football, and the football flying into the air, we assume a relationship of causation. In the same way, we take still bigger steps: we choose to do things for our own purposes, and by reflecting on our purposes we are led to believe that our life as a whole has a purpose. By reflecting on the purpose of our own life we are led to believe that the universe has a purpose. By reflecting on goodness, creativity, causation and design in the world around us, we are led to believe in a good Creator, First Cause and Designer.

These new insights are not deduced. They depend on trust, just as everything else does. The type of trust is the type I have described as necessary: gingerly, like a scientist with a new hypothesis, we are led from our reflections on the familiar to propose theories about the unfamiliar. Each time we develop a hypothesis about a new dimension of reality, we explore what reality must be like if the hypothesis is true. If our explorations are successful, we become more confident, and eventually the time comes when the new hypothesis becomes old, and serves as the foundation stone for the next one.

When pessimists affirm the existence of higher realities, they characteristically emphasize them at the expense of more accessible and ordinary things. They may, for example, contemplate the spiritual realm because they despise the physical. Optimism affirms the higher, but not at the expense of the lower. It is by building on our understanding of the observed that we are led to understand the unobserved. This is clear enough in the case of empirical knowledge: the reason why scientists believe in black holes and subatomic particles is that they help us make *more* sense of the things we observe directly. Similarly, when we reflect on the goodness of human life as we experience it, it becomes possible to speculate about a greater goodness which we have not yet experienced, and develop visions of a better society. These visions do not downgrade our present experience but complement it, giving it a new meaning by setting it within a larger moral context. The same applies to freedom, value and all the qualities which enrich our life.

In practice I believe this is how religious traditions characteristically develop over time, even though pessimistic theologies usually deny it. The overall aim is to explain the nature of reality, so that we know what to do. As in science, good theories comprise the best understanding so far of the subject matter, and practice reflects theory. Over time new developments in theory and experience lead to adaptations. It is true that most religious hypotheses cannot be tested under controlled conditions, but many respectable scientific hypotheses cannot either. Many religious traditions teach that there are certain truths which we cannot perceive until our spiritual development has progressed to a certain stage, and my theory allows for this possibility; this too has plenty of parallels in science.

This means there is no simple rule for settling disputes. Disagreements about religious authority often arise because reason and tradition reach different conclusions. By denying that either takes automatic precedence, I deny that a solution can be found by simple appeal to one or the other. There is nothing unusual in this. In any developing science, new arguments challenge old traditions and the issue has to be considered on its merits.

Conclusion

The central argument of this chapter has been that all human knowledge incorporates acts of trust. Rather than try to produce an expurgated knowledge, we should clarify what we need to trust and what reality must be like if we are right to trust it. This has led to reaffirming a traditional argument for the existence of God, and suggesting reasons why believing in God helps us to understand reality.

The negative side of trust is that certainty and control, which mechanists have sought for themselves, must be left to God. The positive side is that the act of trust does not leave us insecure. We do not need to know everything, because God enables us to know what we need to. When we trust that God has given us the opportunity to live good lives in a good world, we can have enough confidence to get on with it.

Christianity has generally referred to this attitude as 'faith'. In the New Testament there is a key word which is usually translated 'faith' but can equally well be translated 'trust'. The significance of this concept is easily overlooked by Christians because the word 'faith' has been borrowed to apply to different things. Sometimes 'the faith' has been a body of doctrinal statements which Christians are expected to believe. Sometimes faith has been thought of as a thing the believer 'possesses'. In the New Testament, the word is rooted in the idea of trusting God because God is good.[2] This, I believe, is the kind of faith we need to rediscover today. As long as we feel dissatisfied with the world around us, we shall feel the need to change it. As long as we feel the need to change it, we shall carry on messing it up. We are now making such a mess of it that we are right to feel dissatisfied with it. We shall never be masters of the universe. We do not need to be. What we need is have the right kind of faith: confidence in the goodness of what God has given us.

1   For example, Huxley. See S L Jaki, *The Purpose of It All*, p. 46.
2   A Walker and A Davison, 'Belief and Faith in a Religiously Plural Society', *Modern Believing*, July 94, p. 25.

Chapter 10

Hope: aspiring to higher values

IN ORDER TO make sense of our lives we need to believe in a number of realities which we cannot prove. In the last chapter I discussed what they are. Among them are value, purpose and goodness. If they exist, we need to answer two questions about them: how do we know they exist, and why should we pay any attention to them? I believe that only optimistic theology can give a satisfactory answer to both. The answer to the first is that they are the standards by which God has designed us to live. The answer to the second is that God has complete knowledge and power, created us to be the way we are and cares for our well-being even more than we care for ourselves. When we value the wrong things, we end up doing the wrong things and destroying the value of life. When our values are in tune with God's values, we shall naturally want to do the things which lead to true fulfilment, both for ourselves and for others.

If I am right, what do value, purpose and goodness come to? What light does optimistic theory shed on them? In this chapter I shall discuss the structure of value and purpose, and how they relate to our lives. In addition I shall consider that closely related concept, progress. In the next chapter I shall explore their implications for practical moral issues. I shall concentrate on the way they function at their best, and leave till Chapter 12 the question of what happens when things go wrong.

Value

The simplest theories of value are neutralistic. One describes value in terms of what people want, another in terms of how much money they are willing to pay. These answers reduce value to the valueless. I have argued that value cannot be reduced in this way. God's act of imbuing things with value achieves what humans cannot achieve: it gives things a quality which we cannot even describe, let alone reduce.

In Chapter 9 I described three implications of my theory for the constituents of reality, and these can be applied to value. Firstly, each constituent of reality must be consistent with the others. Our values must be consistent with respecting the goodness of all God's creation. Secondly, what each constituent of reality means for one person must be consistent with what it means for everybody else. Whatever is of value in my life must be consistent with what is of value in your life. Thirdly, the unknown aspects of it must be consistent with its known aspects. Let us consider some implications.

What we value must be consistent with the goodness of all God's creation

God, the creator of human beings, is also the creator of everything which exists, so the kinds of things which increase the value of human life must be consistent with the kinds of things which increase the value of the world as a whole. Any activity which destroys its life-creating powers must be against God's purposes and therefore ultimately — although we may not be able to see the link — contrary to human fulfilment.

This raises the question of anthropocentrism, a major theme of western thought. Pessimists often emphasize the value of the human soul, or spirit, or rationality, on the ground that it is quite different from the physical world, and opposed to it. Neutralists argue that only humans can evaluate anything, and therefore values can only operate from a human point of view. Optimists reject both these reasons for anthropocentrism. All value is rooted in God's valuing, and the value of every part is consistent with the value of every other part. Therefore the value of humanity is not to be contrasted with the value of other things, but cooperates with them and reinforces them. Our evaluations are limited by our human perspective, but this limitation does no harm as long as we recognize that the value of our lives is only part of the value of the whole.

Let us take an example. When a sheep eats grass, the farmer values the process because of its economic benefits. To the farmer, the sheep are more valuable than the grass because they produce wool; the value of the grass lies in being food for the sheep. The sheep have a different perspective: to them, the grass is directly valuable as food. The grass has no brain and cannot evaluate anything, but it does have an interest, and from its perspective the sheep are valuable because of the urine and droppings they provide.

So when we ask 'What is valuable about the grass-eating process?' we can answer it in different ways according to the different perspectives. To the perspectives of farmer, sheep and grass we can add the perspective of the ecosystem as a whole. Like the grass, it does not have a mind of its own but does have interests. The value judgments of farmer, sheep and grass are legitimate in themselves, but in addition they contribute to the total value of the ecosystem, which includes worms and woollen jumpers. While there is harmony between farmer, sheep and grass, the ecosystem affirms and increases the value of their interactions by including all the parts in a wider valuable process.

Within the constraints of this example, I suggest that we can think of God's perspective along the lines of the ecosystem's perspective, though God really is capable of evaluating. God sees and values the whole process, the farmer only a segment of it. When the value judgements are in harmony, this difference does not cause problems. In principle, there is nothing wrong with farmers calculating how they can get the most benefit from their farms, just as there is nothing wrong with sheep deciding — if they do — how much grass to eat. We do not expect even the most ecologically minded farmer to go home at the end of the day and say to his wife 'I am so glad for the sake of the grass that the sheep are urinating on it'. What the farmer fails to do, sheep and grass do. Problems only arise when one of the participants adopts different value judgements, which create conflict with the others and therefore cannot be incorporated by the ecosystem into a harmonious whole. If the grass were to demand more droppings from the sheep in return for less grass, the sheep would suffer and in time the whole process would collapse. Fortunately, grass does not do such things. But humans do.

Human valuing, then, is legitimate within limits, and the limits are provided by the wider picture, God's perspective. The wider picture tells us that the goodness of the ecosystem depends on a huge variety of different creatures taking what they need and returning it in a form suitable for other forms of life. Within this system, human activity can play a positive part.

We should not, then, think of humans as being the only valuable beings, or even as being at the apex of a pyramid. A better image is to think of ourselves as part of a very complex network. One thing is of value to another, which in turn is of value to something else. We cannot describe the value of any one thing by only talking about the thing itself: everything is of value as a part of the whole. The complexity of the ecosystem enhances the value of our lives, and the existence of humanity can — if we do not cause destruction — be one more form of life to enrich the value of the ecosystem as a whole. The complete interlocking network is so complex that it is well beyond the power of scientists to describe it, let alone measure it.

This leaves open the question of uniqueness. Even if the rest of the ecosystem has value, is the value of humans unique? There are many things which only we can do, and this does seem to give us a unique value. This much can be said of every species: we could equally conclude that frogs and oaks have unique value. So are there unique features of humanity which raise us to a quality of life which is not shared by other forms of life? I am inclined to answer 'yes', and locate the special features in the usual places: free will, self-consciousness and rationality. Even this, however, does not justify the anthropocentrism which has dominated western thought. We have become defensive about being the only possessors of these higher faculties. If whales have rationality and self-consciousness too, good!

There is no justification for the sharp distinction, so common in western thought, between the value of humanity and the rest of the ecosystem. For thousands of years the despisers of physical matter, whether pessimists or neutralists, have exhorted people to transcend their 'lower nature' and aspire to higher things like spiritual and intellectual pursuits. All too often they have ignored the fact that these higher faculties of ours are only possible because we are animals, and we share with other animals a wide range of more basic faculties. There is nothing wrong with the material, and no reason for supposing that our minds would be any the better if we could detach them from our bodies. Whatever God or angels may do, humans cannot pray or reason unless we also eat and excrete.

A minority of deep greens go to the other extreme, that the most valuable actions are the most earthy ones, in which we play a natural part in the ecosystem just like any other animal. From this point of view, enjoying our food is more in tune with eco-spirituality than thinking about metaphysical things. This theory, I believe, reduces the value of human life unnecessarily. Every species has its own unique features, and if humanity has features which others do not have, we can welcome them and use them without thereby setting ourselves against other forms of life. A world in which humans do not pray and rationalize is a good world, but even better is a world in which we do. If we and we alone can relate to God, our relating to God is part of the richness of our earthy life, not a reaction against it.

If humans are not the only locus of value, how do we compare the value of natural things with artificial things? If plums are of value to wasps as well as humans, what of cars?

To pessimists, the natural order is positively hostile. To neutralists, it is valueless. In either case positive value only begins when God or humans do something to change things. To optimists, the natural order is full of value even without human intervention. Our actions have value when we enhance the value of the ecosystem as a whole, and have disvalue when we destroy it. It cannot be wrong for humanity to play its own natural part within the ecosystem.

This leads green theorists to a wide range of proposals. Some model 'natural' human behaviour on what the higher animals do. Like them, we should value our most basic functions like eating and sleeping, and avoid whatever can be called artificial. This is the 'going back to living in mud huts' argument. At the other extreme, some argue that every species pursues its own self-interest, without reflecting on the needs of others. If baboons could drive cars, they would. We can, and it suits us, so it would be unnatural not to. My account rejects both extremes. Part of the value of human life consists of doing the same activities as other animals. Another part consists of doing what only humans can do. We are unique in being able to drive cars, and if it is a legitimate thing to do it does not set us apart from nature, but simply gives us one of our unique functions within it. Yet another aspect of our uniqueness is our ability to debate whether we ought to drive them and reflect on value in a way which — as far as we know — other animals cannot do.

This does not tell us whether we may drive cars or genetically engineer plum trees. But it gives us a reason to avoid the extremes of either automatically rejecting, or automatically accepting, every new artifice which suits our self-interest. We should consider each one on its merits as an addition to a God-given ecosystem which is already rich and admirable.

As source of value, then, God has a unifying function. What gives value to me as I eat, sleep and write books also gives value to the distant planet as it hurtles through space and designs the nettle to attract butterflies. When we understand correctly the truth about value, we seek to live in harmony with the whole of God's creation.

What is valuable for one person is consistent with what is valuable for other people

Because God is self-consistent, we expect that as we discover what it means to enhance the value of our own lives, it will turn out to be consistent with enhancing the value of other people's lives.

This raises an issue for physical resources. We need them to provide for our needs. Modern neutralism often treats them as a source of conflict because they are in limited supply. Many pessimists despise their bodily needs, or even deny the value of physical things altogether. Optimism affirms the real value of physical resources, while denying that there is any need for conflict over them. The way to do this is clear enough, as it is a common theme in the ethics of the world's major religions. It is a question of *balance*. To have enough of what we need is valuable; to have more than enough is not necessarily better, and is certainly worse if it deprives others.

An obvious example is eating. If we are hungry, to eat food is valuable. Once we are full up, to eat more does not increase value: overeating causes illness and reduces the value of life. The edges are fuzzy; we can eat more than the minimum necessary for good health without necessarily getting fat, and some people need more food than others. Even so, we all know that too much, like too little, is harmful. God has given us enough for our legitimate needs. Hungry people are right to seek more food, until they have enough. Once they have enough they will achieve further increases in the value of their lives, not by seeking more and more food, but by doing other things.

I suggest that the principle of balance is an important part of recognizing value. When we have enough of one thing, to increase the value of our life will mean not getting more of it, but turning our attention to another dimension of life.

By exploring the nature of value as it is most familiar to us, we are led to discover its less familiar characteristics

I have argued that we cannot define value in terms of other concepts, because this would reduce it to the valueless. We cannot, then, begin with a definition of value and examine the things around us to see what fits the definition. Instead we discover it by experience. When we begin life we discover value in a few things, like milk and warmth. At their most basic, our evaluations simply respond to our senses. Gradually we learn to make wider connections and evaluate things which do not have an immediate impact, like being told about a future event. Over time we learn to check our evaluations for consistency with each other and with other people's evaluations.

When it comes to *justifying* our evaluations, we tend to explain our more immediate and local judgements by locating them within the context of something wider and more valuable. We value the pocket calculator because it helps us do our sums more quickly. We value doing sums more quickly because they contribute to the success of the firm. We value the success of the firm because we think it is helping society. At each stage, the only acceptable answers to the question 'Why do you value *this*?' are of the type 'Because I value *that*'.

In other words, our awareness of value at any given level depends on presupposing a greater value at a higher level. The logic of our valuing always presupposes that there is more to value, just as there is more to matter and order, than we have yet appreciated.

Thus, although we learn about value from the bottom up, it has a 'top-down' structure. Logically, God's valuing of the world comes first. The value of society is derived from the value of the world, the value of the firm from the value of society, the value of the accountant's work from the value of the firm, and so on. As long as these objects of value are consistent with each other, they enhance the value of the whole.

Neutralist accounts of value often describe it in static terms: a thing either has, or does not have, value. My account is more dynamic: as we explore value, we find higher and higher qualities in it. When we think about the things we value, we realize that we are presupposing higher and more general values; and when we think about the higher and more general values, we realize that they presuppose other values again, which are higher and more general still.

When we do a valuable act, we increase value and prepare the ground for doing acts of even greater value. When farmer, sheep and grass interact harmoniously, the benefit they provide each other makes it possible for other activities to take place, involving other forms of life and other parts of human society. In the same way a person who is suffering from starvation is quite right to put a top priority on looking for food. Part of the value of having enough food is that it becomes possible to turn one's attention away from food and start thinking about other things which will enhance the value of life in other ways. People who have all the material necessities can stop getting things for themselves and help provide for the needs of others. Thereby they are directly enhancing the value of other people's lives and the community; but at the same time they are also enhancing the value of their own lives in a different and higher way, by developing the practice of caring for others. As in emergence theory, higher levels of value develop out of lower levels when the lower level has reached a certain stage of development.

This leads us to wonder whether there is an ultimate value, hidden in the mind of God. As I am not God, I do not understand it. If we did have a complete account of it, so that we could map it all the way from the concept in God's mind to our day-to-day judgements, it might seem that we then had control over it and could decide for ourselves whether to accept it. We do not. Part of what it means to be human is that we cannot live without values, and values direct our attention to that which is greater than ourselves.

Within religious traditions many people have speculated about it. Naturally, the idea is closely related to the being of God, and is best expressed — though only imperfectly — by our highest values. In the Christian tradition perhaps the word which most commonly relates to this concept is 'glory'. God's glory is beyond our understanding; we are called to share it, and we come closest to it when we live in a way which expresses our highest values.

Purpose

My account of purpose follows the same lines as value. Again, a full account of it is beyond our present understanding, but we should expect the same principles to apply. Firstly, realizing the purpose of our lives is consistent with affirming the goodness of the rest of God's creation. Secondly, the true purpose of each person's life does not conflict with the purpose of other people's lives. Thirdly, although we cannot perceive the more distant purposes of our lives, they are consistent with the purposes we can perceive.

These principles are enough to rule out some highly influential theories.

It cannot be God's purpose for our lives that we should replace the natural environment with an artificial one, or produce and consume ever-increasing quantities of manufactured goods. In one way or another, the grand improvement schemes I discussed in Chapter 8 all set one element of God's creation against another. Instead we must affirm and build on the harmony which underlies all reality.

In ordinary life we are familiar with a distinction between two types of achievement, those which bring a process to an end and those which lead on to another. The purpose of a war is achieved when it has been won. There are no more battles to be fought and we look forward to peace. When we reach the top of a mountain there is no more uphill climb. But human objectives are often more like the earlier stages of climbing a mountain: time after time we see a peak ahead of us which looks like the very top, but when we get to it we see a higher peak beyond it, still waiting to be climbed. If we are looking forward to a good long rest, we feel disappointed, but if we are enjoying the walk we are pleased to see another challenge, and look forward to climbing it. In many situations the value of each achievement is *increased* by the fact that yet more can be built on it. The child with her first bicycle looks forward to endless hours developing cycling skills. If it were possible to become an expert cyclist in one day, cycling would be less fun and in two or three days it would become boring. The same is true of God's purpose for our lives: if we welcome the challenge to climb the peaks God sets in our path, it will delight us to think there are even higher peaks beyond the horizon.

Because we cannot see everything that lies before us, we trust that the purpose towards which God is beckoning us now will turn out to be a necessary stage on the journey towards more distant purposes. Were we to achieve our present purpose, only to discover that the next stage is to retrace our steps and go off in a different direction altogether, this would mean that something had gone wrong. Whatever the setting, we can expect that, because God is consistent, the more distant and ambitious purposes will be in keeping with the purposes towards which we should strive today. They will be more like the way we live when we are at our best, only more so. They will build on all that is good in our lives so far and develop them further in ways we cannot yet perceive.

For this reason we do not need to ask whether the purpose of human life is to be achieved in this world or the next, as though the two were alternatives. We can believe in life after death, provided that it affirms and develops what is good about this life.

What, then, is the purpose of life? Which actions express it? According to my theory, I cannot give a complete account of it because I am not God, but I should be able to describe as much of it as I have been aware of so far.

As with value, we cannot deduce purpose from rational principles. Instead God has made us able to recognize quite naturally which activities are in keeping with the purpose of our lives. We can do this most easily, and are least likely to fall into error, at an immediate and local level, when considering what we ourselves should do in familiar situations. Others can always question our judgements, but in practice we cannot live without making them, and there is so much agreement on the most basic purposes that even the most hard-nosed neutralists accept them in their own lives. For example, the purpose of parenting is expressed by feeding healthy food to our children, not by turning them into drug addicts. The purpose of social relationships is expressed by doing things which our neighbours will appreciate and not deliberately annoying them. We do not have a method for deducing what true purpose consists of; instead, we naturally recognize that purpose is expressed in some ways and not in others.

As with value, our understanding of purpose begins with natural, instinctive ideas. In order to build on them, we need to do two things: direct our lives in accordance with them, and reflect on them. Theory and practice inform each other as we develop a deeper understanding of God's purposes for our lives. There is always the possibility of error. We have freedom too, and self-interest can distort our understanding; but at each stage God enables us to perceive the direction our lives should be taking.

We begin, then, by naturally recognizing immediate and local purposes and seeing what we can build on them. So what are these purposes, apart from feeding babies and being nice to neighbours? If we do not accept the pessimist's escape from the evil world, or the modernist's drive for ever-increasing economic growth, what kinds of activity *do* express the purpose of our lives?

The answer is clear enough. None! There are *no* characteristic activities which fit the bill. Instead there is a countless variety of *different* activities. Nothing is more characteristic of purposeful, valued human activity than diversity and innovation. In this respect our actions echo the rest of the ecosystem, where nothing is more regular than the startlingly new and nothing is more to be expected than the unexpected surprise.

Both pessimists and neutralists have been far too taken with the idea of '*the* purpose of life' and have tried to fit diverse people into standard moulds. By contrast I suggest that although there is an objective truth about the purpose of our lives, it works out in practice in diversity and creativity, not uniformity. We must reject all theories which describe the purpose of life as a specific thing — to fight for our country, or to work for the firm or the economy, or to marry a young man and bear him children. Any theory which states a single purpose sets itself in conflict with the diversity which is God's gift to us. Nor will it do to replace a single purpose with a limited list: the diversity keeps developing in unforeseen ways.

I suggest, then, that the nearest we can get to describing the purpose of life is that we should all develop in our own different ways, creating ideas, skills and lifestyles which have not been laid down for us in advance. If we add to this my argument that the purpose of life must be consistent with affirming and valuing the created order, there is no better way to describe it than to say that God has created us to *celebrate*, *explore* and *do what we like*. The purpose of life is to enjoy ourselves!

Many Christians today believe that God has planned everybody's life down to the smallest detail, and if we are to fulfil our purpose we should pray for guidance every time we have a decision to make. This view is more appropriate to pessimists, with their anxiety to avoid evil. When the salvation bus comes, they must jump on it. My view is the opposite: far from being a petty autocrat, God is more like the father who takes his children to the adventure playground. He says 'Off you go!' and watches them with amusement as they enjoy themselves. He does not expect them to keep returning, after every turn on the slide, asking 'What shall I do now?'

There are limits. Some activities are contrary to the purpose of life. There are characteristic types of activity which we recognize as normally consistent or inconsistent with it. However, these characteristic types are to be found within an overall picture of diversity.

What is the ultimate purpose of human life, the final objective towards which God is calling us? Religious traditions have explored the question. According to my account we would expect it to be closely related to God and true value, and to affirm the goodness of creation as a whole and our past achievements. The best examples, to my mind, are those which have described the purpose of human life in terms of becoming like God, or becoming divine. This was a common theme in early Christianity. In the second century, Irenaeus wrote that Christ 'became what we are in order to enable us to become what he is'.[1] The idea became common in the east; according to Athanasius, writing in the fourth century, 'The Word became flesh in order both to offer this sacrifice and that we, participating in his Spirit, might be deified'.[2] It continued to be a standard feature of eastern Christian theology; a thousand years later, Gregory Palamas could write

> Adam of old was deceived:
> Wanting to be God he failed to be God.
> God becomes man,
> So that he may make Adam God.[3]

This, of course, is speculation. Like value, purpose is beyond definition, but our lives really do have a purpose, and this purpose is given to us by God whether we recognize it or not. Because God is self-consistent, omnipotent, omniscient and good, it is the best way to live. We can reject it if we wish, but if we do we shall be at odds with the way we have been designed to flourish.

Progress

Once we accept that our lives have a purpose, we have something to strive towards, and this makes progress possible. As with value and purpose, we do not see the whole course of future progress spread out in front of us like a map. What we understand is what it means in our immediate and local situation, and by exploring it, in theory and practice, we are led to speculate about its more long-term and universal dimensions.

Let us return to the child with her first bicycle. She admires it with excitement, and even before she has a chance to sit on the saddle she imagines herself pedalling away like her big brother. When she does ride it, she begins a long process of developing her cycling skills. At first she wobbles and falls off. Each time she falls off she gets on again, determined to do better next time. Part of the excitement lies in the thought that her skills will gradually improve with practice. As the years pass she learns to negotiate the traffic. Each bicycle lasts a few years and is then replaced by a bigger one. One day she gets a job which involves cycling to work every day. By now she has an adult sized bicycle. On her first morning, she opens the garage door to fetch it. Her eye catches that very first bicycle, hanging from a joist in the garage ceiling, gathering cobwebs. She remembers her first attempts to ride it, and laughs. Now, it looks so small. Still, she does not despise those first attempts: she is only too pleased that she learned to ride when she did, because now she can cycle to work.

We can see here three elements of progress. There is a starting point, an objective and a process of development from one to the other. The objective of our lives is their purpose, which I have already discussed. The starting point and the process of development need further comment.

The starting point

Progress must begin with a creative situation, from which gradual development is possible. It needs to be valued positively. The child values the gift of her first bicycle, as she looks forward to endless fun riding it. Historians often describe an era of cultural progress as beginning after the end of a devastating war, when a peace treaty established a fruitful order. Even in situations where progress cannot begin without radical change, we can distinguish the radical change from the progress.

For this reason progress is different from reaction, revolution or intervention. Reaction takes place when we reject the immediate past and turn back to something more distant. Revolution is when we try to start from scratch. Intervention is when a completely new system ignores and overrides what was there before, as when a society is invaded by foreigners and a completely different culture is suddenly imposed on it. In these cases, even if we believe the new situation is better than the old one, we would not describe it as progress, because the change is too abrupt. Progress takes place when there is gradual change from a valued starting point.

In some situations changes which are reactionary, revolutionary or interventionist make progress possible. Before the young girl was given her first bicycle, her cycling skills could not develop. From her perspective the gift of the bicycle was not progress but an unexpected surprise; in the terms of the last paragraph, it would count as intervention. A community being besieged in time of war may be so completely occupied in surviving and defending itself that there is no meaningful progress; but once the siege is relieved by the unexpected arrival of a friendly army, the war comes to an end and progress becomes possible again. In these cases progress only becomes possible after a sudden event which was not itself progressive.

However what is reactionary, revolutionary or interventionist from one perspective may be progressive from another. From the child's perspective the gift of a bicycle was an unexpected surprise; but her parents had already been discussing her progress and had decided that her fifth birthday would be a good time to buy her a bicycle. The general supervising the war effort had planned the relief of the city, and to him it was not a bolt out of the blue but one more step in the army's progress towards victory. The wider the perspective, the fewer the unexpected events. From God's perspective, there are no unexpected events.

For this reason we may say that although people often find themselves in situations where progress is not possible, *hope* is always possible. It is always the case that from a wider perspective — even if only God's — there is the possibility that something good will happen. It is not that reaction, revolution and intervention are good things in themselves. As permanent states they do not work. I have suggested situations in which they make progress possible, and sometimes they are the only source of hope, but it is the progress which is desired, not the sudden changes for their own sakes.

The process of development

Progress takes place when each achievement prepares the ground for the next. It is characteristically gradual. The child first of all learns to ride a bicycle with both hands on the handlebars, and only when competent at that level does she practise hand signals. From the earliest use of writing to the Shakespeare play, a new generation learns old skills and builds new skills upon them. What we praise at one stage we take for granted at a later stage. Any particular story of progress will include occasions of going two steps forward and one step back, but the overall picture is of gradual improvement.

If we are to think of our lives as part of a story of progress, we need to value not only the starting point but also the achievements already made. This means it must be possible to say of one stage in our past that it had progressed further than another, without despising the earlier stage. Scientists value the contributions of Copernicus and Newton, even though others have improved on their theories. Sometimes changes will turn out to have been regress, or change with no future, even though they seemed at the time to be progress, but if we are to believe that progress is taking place we must be able to tell some success stories. These stories will describe how we developed what was good in the old situation, to produce something new. Similarly, if progress is to continue in the future, we need to believe that further achievements can still be made.

Human progress must be part of the progress of the universe as a whole. Immediately after the Big Bang, reality consisted of a small number of different gases. As they interacted more gases developed, and interacted in more diverse ways. Those gases still exist, but some of the matter which formed them has now been developed in more complex ways. When carbon was formed, and this planet with its atmosphere came into being, most of the things and processes which already existed continued to exist, but there was greater diversity. As plants, insects, animals and humans developed, each new process used what was already there and built on it to produce something new and yet more complex.

Most people today believe humanity developed along these lines. There was a higher mammal — a 'missing link' or whatever — and some of them became more complex, in such a way as to fit the description of 'human'. In some ways we can think of our continuing mental and social development as part of this ongoing process.

For present purposes it does not matter whether the first humans appeared gradually or suddenly. What matters more is that there have been changes in what it means to be human. Perhaps we first thought about how to create tools, then thought about other people, then noticed that we were thinking, then noticed that we could choose between alternative courses of action. We do not know whether this is the right order, but whether it is or not, there is one sense in which human progress is a continuation of natural progress: that is, that the new develops out of the old, depends on it and discovers within it the potential for greater complexity and diversity.

Within its human context, then, we might describe progress as follows. Just as a universe with planets and living systems is better than a universe of nothing but swirling gases, so a universe with thinking beings is better than one without them. Every step forward increases the value of the whole: freedom is better than being determined and freely choosing to do good is better than pursuing self-interest without caring about others.

Human progress, then, involves valuing the natural order — including our own bodies and minds — and discovering within it the potential for realizing ever greater value. This is similar to the scientific concept of emergence, with its higher levels emerging out of lower levels.

Because I have included the idea of future progress yet to be achieved, it must go beyond the emergent processes which are already publicly accepted. Secular theorists often imagine that they themselves are the highest possible form of life into which anything could emerge. There is no justification for such arrogance. If there are higher levels than we ourselves have reached, we should expect that the limits to our own progress will stop us understanding what they are like. We are like dogs, with no concept of the use of writing, wondering why our owners spend so much time looking at white paper with black marks on it. There are two alternatives: either to trust that there is something about newspapers which dogs simply cannot understand, or to laugh at humans for attributing to newspapers a significance which is not there. A sceptical dog with a degree in chemistry would be well qualified to assure other dogs that newspapers consist of nothing but paper and ink.

We too will always have the option of refusing to believe that others have progressed further than us. Their theories will sound to us like nonsense or superstition, and when we ask them to explain them in terms which make sense to us, they will be unable to. If, however, we accept that there are levels of progress higher than our own, we must also accept that we can only see them from the underside. If we know of particular people who, we believe, have progressed significantly further than us, we will expect them to understand things which we ourselves do not understand.

Contrary to many nineteenth century theories of progress, my account does not make it inevitable. We have been given free will. We may stop believing in progress, stagnate, and thereby bring it to an end. Or we may make valiant efforts towards a mistaken purpose which in the long run turns out to be regress. Western mechanistic society, with its commitment to endless economic growth and technological development, is a highly successful attempt to do the wrong things.

Can we be confident that God's purposes will ever be achieved? Is progress inevitable in the long run? Or has God withdrawn from control so much that this too is an open question? Either answer seems compatible with my theory, but if, as it suggests, moral progress in a society makes it easier for its members to behave morally well, what seems most likely is that progress can reach a stage at which it develops a momentum of its own and becomes less likely to be stopped except by intervention from outside. In this case, God's purposes seem certain to be achieved given a long enough time scale, but our good and evil actions will respectively reduce and increase the time it takes.

Conclusion

Value, purpose and progress, then, really do exist. This is to say that some things and actions really are valuable, over and above whether we value them; our lives have a purpose, whether we recognize it or not; and we may or may not progress towards it. Value is based in a God who is self-consistent, omnipotent, omniscient and good. If value, purpose and progress really do derive from a God of this type, we can say more about them. They must be consistent with the rest of God's creation, they must be consistent between people, and their higher levels must be consistent with their basic levels. These principles are quite enough to discredit the value systems which dominate modern society and to demand more positive, life-affirming alternatives. Rightly understood, value, purpose and progress affirm harmony rather than conflict, complexity rather than simplicity and openness to higher levels of reality rather than reducing everything to its lowest level.

In practice life is not so straightforward. Because there is so much evil in the world, our values and our understanding of purpose and progress often enough contradict each other and cause us to do the wrong things. People often find themselves trapped in situations where progress is impossible and all that is left is hope. I shall discuss the existence of evil in Chapter 12. I have described value, purpose and progress as they are in themselves before relating them to evil, because they would still exist even if there was no evil in the world: indeed, they would flourish all the more. The higher values are without doubt essential tools in the struggle against evil, but that is their secondary role. Primarily they are a matter of directing us towards God, building on what is good, using our God-given faculties.

God's good provision makes it possible for value, purpose and progress to work together in harmony and lead us to fulfilment beyond what we can see or even imagine at present. Our lives have a direction — something to *achieve*. When young children open their Christmas presents, things which are to be put on the mantelpiece and only looked at are rarely the favourites: they like things which present them with something to *do*. So it is too with God's gift of life to us. What this means in practice, I shall explore further in the next chapter.

1   *Against the Heresies* 5, preface.
2   *De Decret.* 14.
3   *Doxastikon at the Praises, Feast of the Annunciation,* quoted in G I Mantzaridis, *The Deification of Man,* p. 13.

Chapter 11

Love: responding to God in action

'THIS FOOTBALL PITCH is tiny.'

'It isn't a football pitch, it's a croquet lawn.'

'It's all very well calling it a croquet lawn, but where are the goal-posts? Somebody could trip over those hoops.'

'You're not supposed to score goals. You're supposed to hit the balls through the hoops.'

'Speaking of the ball, it's wooden. Let's hope there are no injuries.'

So also with the world: when we misunderstand what it is for, we try to do the wrong things with it, and when it fails to work the way we want it to, we decide that it is no good and set about changing it.

In this book I have described two ways of misunderstanding the nature of reality. Pessimists believe there is inescapable and tragic evil in the world. The agenda for human life therefore becomes a matter of resisting it. Neutralists believe there are no objective values and therefore we can do what we like with our own lives and the world around us. By contrast with these, optimists believe the world has been designed to be the way it is, and the agenda is to make the most of it and discover fulfilment within it. The difference between the three is a bit like three possible responses to a new computer game. The optimist plays it and tries to win. The pessimist thinks it does not work properly and asks the manufacturer to repair it. The neutralist only sees a piece of plastic with a label stuck onto it and breaks it open to see whether there is anything inside.

In this chapter I shall describe what moral goodness means from an optimistic point of view. At its best, moral debate has a positive function. If progress means getting towards the purpose of life, morality is about which acts contribute towards progress and which do not. We should expect it to focus not on a few well rehearsed issues but on countless decisions which need to be made, by both individuals and communities. Most will be of comparatively small importance.

The last two chapters provide some general principles. We do not decide for ourselves which actions are to count as right and wrong, because there is an objective truth about them. In a different sense, we can speak about one thing being right for me and another being right for you. The truth about moral goodness is as complicated as the world we live in. Each of us is a unique person in a unique situation. It will not be surprising if the best way to make progress is to do something unique. Within this diversity we find that certain types of activity usually help and other types usually hinder. Stealing and murder usually hinder. So we generalize, and lay down rules against them. But every student of ethics can dream up exceptional situations in which they would seem good things to do. The exceptions remind us that the rules are only generalizations, not moral authorities in their own right.

Every society engages in lively debates about moral issues. At their best, the initiative is taken by those who have a practical decision to make, whether individuals or communities. The purpose of the debate is to decide what to do. At their worst they are vehicles of hatred, through which some people condemn the actions of others.

Let us take an example of constructive moral debate. A mother and father are discussing how much time to let their children spend watching videos. Subjectively we might think that 'a good video is one which grips its audience with excitement', and this is what the children say. If, however, goodness is about helping us to progress towards the purpose of our lives, does the purpose of life include being gripped with excitement? The parents decide that fantasy and entertainment are legitimate in themselves, as a rest from school homework, and some videos have educational value; but they can also become addictive, or occupy so much time that the children do nothing else. They decide to permit some video-watching, but only between certain hours and only after all homework has been done.

Whether or not this is the right answer, it is the right approach, and it is a moral issue because it is concerned about the children's progress. However, the parents cannot debate questions like this without some presuppositions about the purpose of their children's lives. They may only be hazily aware that they are presupposing anything at all. If somebody asks them what the purpose of their children's lives is, they may be quite at a loss for an answer. Even so they may feel quite sure that it is not the purpose of life to be addicted to videos, and that the purpose, whatever it is, will be better served by a wider range of activities and by educational videos rather than pornographic ones. Even if it has never crossed their minds, their judgements derive from presuppositions they already hold about value, purpose and progress.

This is the way we normally make moral judgements. When faced with a practical decision, we do not begin by analysing our theory about the ultimate purpose of life and then make deductions from it. Instead, we concentrate on the immediate issue, but as we do so we reveal more general presuppositions. It then becomes possible, and sometimes necessary, to clarify the presuppositions. Sometimes this leads us to change our moral judgements.

The proper use of moral debate, then, is to consider what we should do in order to progress. I think about whether I should continue to see my girl friend, and seek advice from friends. The parish council discusses what to do about the dangerous corner in the road. The nation openly debates government policies. United Nations committees discuss how to improve relationships between governments. These discussions are all aimed towards making the best use of life and are therefore proper uses of moral debate. The better they understand the true nature of value, purpose and progress, the more likely they are to reach the right conclusions.

Which kinds of activity, then, count as good or bad? Which generalizations does my account produce? As in the last chapter, I shall depend on the theory that God is self-consistent, omnipotent, omniscient and good. For this reason, moral goodness is consistent with the goodness of the rest of God's creation; what it means for one person is consistent with what it means for everybody else; and as we grow in goodness, the higher levels are consistent with the lower levels. The practical examples I offer in this chapter will be more specific than heretofore. This, I appreciate, opens me up to criticism. Some of my examples may be undermined, if the scientific evidence changes. Each one deserves a book of its own, not a mere paragraph. I accept these shortcomings because I am concerned to show that my optimistic account of reality is not just of theoretical interest. It demands major changes of priorities in modern western society.

Caring for the world

To get our relationship with the world right, we need to affirm and celebrate that it is God's creation and therefore good. The planet, the
atmosphere, the ecosystem with all its plants and animals, our own bodies,
our appetites, our interests, were all designed to find fulfilment in harmony
with each other. The natural is of value in itself. Like the natural theologians of the English Enlightenment, we wonder at the beauty and
complexity of the created order and, through it, learn to wonder at the
Creator. It is not that the world is the highest value or the highest
authority. Only God has that status; but because of what God is like, we
affirm the goodness of the world as God's creation.

Valuing the natural order, then, must be fundamental to moral theory.
We should so organize our lives that we work with the grain of nature, not
against it. This immediately sets us against that dominant assumption of
modern neutralism, that only the results of human work have value. Based
on this neutralism are countless patterns of activity which in some way or
other harm the ecosystem. We are all so tied up in anti-ecological
lifestyles that it is difficult to see where to start developing a more acceptable pattern of living, and where it would lead if we did start. Is it enough
to use unleaded petrol? Or should we minimize car use? Or not have a car?
Or refuse to use all petrol-based transport? Is it enough to take our used
paper to the recycling skip? Or should we minimize our use of paper? Or
only buy paper from ecologically sustainable sources? Most of us have
made ourselves so dependent on environment-destroying practices that we
do not know what it would be like to avoid them all. It all seems far too
complicated, and if we take the matter seriously we may well become
afraid of the thought.

Some green philosophies compound the problem by insisting that there
is only one alternative to continuing on the present course of mutual
destruction, and that is to return to some rural past, perhaps based on self-
sufficient smallholdings. Hardly surprisingly, most people are not prepared
even to countenance the thought. Short of a justified alternative, they
settle for carrying on as we are and turning a blind eye to the damage we
are doing.

I believe my theory can fill the gap. With its account of the nature of
reality and the purpose of life, it can explain why some activities are legit-

imate and others are not. It provides a middle way between abandoning all modern technology and carrying on along the path to destruction.

Strictly, my theory only tells us not to destroy nature, not that we should positively care for it. It is a theory of *affirmation* rather than stewardship. Nevertheless, within the context of western society, with the huge amount of damage it does every day, the principle of not harming it means rushing to its defence. So what should we defend? What is it about life on earth which is valuable and needs to be protected? As in the last chapter, I shall begin with the characteristics which we naturally observe and value, and draw out their implications. Of course, when we reflect on the natural ecosystem, we also see many things we dislike. Much seems cruel, wasteful and conflictual. I shall consider these points in the next chapter. At present I am concerned to ask: what is it about the natural order — about the world as God has created it — which we naturally recognize as good? I suggest five principles which fit the bill: diversity, creativity, interdependence, inclusiveness and balance. They have all appeared in the last chapter in one form or another. I do not claim that they are exhaustive, or that this is the only way to categorize nature's goodness; but I do think they are essential principles of the ecosystem and that humanity instinctively values them.

Diversity

Nature is full of variety. Every species has its own unique place in the ecosystem and goes about its own unique affairs. If we value the natural order we will add to its diversity, not destroy it. In fact we often do add to it. There is no need to set culture against nature, as western thinkers have so often done. By valuing what humans do, we do not deny the value of what nature does; instead, we see what humans do as *part of* nature's diversity. By valuing our rationality, we do not deny the value of our physical bodies; our rationality is *part of* the value of having a human body. By valuing our ability to adapt our environment, we do not deny the value of the natural order; our power to use and adapt is *part of* the glorious excitement of living in a bountiful world.

Because we value nature's diversity, we must oppose activities which destroy it. There is no shortage of them at present. The most publicized are destructions of tropical rain forests, but there are many others. These destructions are motivated by neutralist value judgements, which value non-human forms of life only when humans put a price on them. We need to recognize that a world in which many species have been made extinct by human destructiveness is a poorer world, regardless of how much money they would have fetched on the open market.

This is not to say that every form of life must always be preserved. Extinctions of species sometimes happen naturally. Nature lovers have often agonized over the 'right to life' of the cancer cell or the AIDS virus. We do not need to maintain a specific list of species in existence. What we need to maintain — or rather, avoid destroying — is the diversity of the ecosystem as a whole, from its simplest to its most complex forms.

Creativity

Nature keeps doing new things. Circumstances change and different forms of life keep developing new, often unique, ways of responding to them.

We too can be part of this creativity. We know the difference between a good painting which simply hangs on the wall and one which we painted ourselves. The fact that we did it is part of its value. Similarly, God offers us a part in the work of creation. The fact that we have recently been doing more destroying than creating need not drive us to complete inaction. If true progress values the achievements of the past and builds on them, we should do the things which affirm the goodness of nature as it is, and build on it, rather than undermining it.

We rightly use our creativity to develop new technologies, when we draw out the potential in the created order without harming it. However, because neutralism tells us to ignore the value of the natural order, we exaggerate the value of our technology. All too often, students of botany, biology or even psychology are encouraged to think of their subjects mechanistically — as determined, simple and observable — while the Department's new X-ray machine or computer programme is eulogized as wonderfully complex, valuable and exciting. The fact that no computer programme is anywhere near as complex as an average leaf on a tree is easily overlooked.

My theory accepts the distinction between the natural and the artificial, but evaluates them differently. The natural is God-given and designed to be consistent with our well-being. Sometimes, instead of benefiting us, it harms us; but when it does, we rightly ask what has gone wrong, or whether we are using it in the wrong way. I shall return to this point in the next chapter. When it comes to the artificial, the fact that it has been created by humans does not tell us whether it is valuable. Things are created for different purposes.

(i) Some things are created for purposes which are opposed to God's purposes. They are unlikely to help anybody at all towards their true fulfilment and are likely to be a hindrance. Opinions may vary about the candidates for this category — nuclear bombs, torture equipment and cigarettes are likely ones — but at present I only wish to note that the category exists.

(ii) Some things are created simply as a result of practising skills. God invites us to explore the world; we do not need to feel that everything we do is morally significant. Some of the things we create may turn out to be of value to some, or of disvalue to others, or both, in unforeseen ways.

(iii) Some things are created for morally good reasons — to achieve aims which accord with God's purposes for our lives. Like natural things, we can describe them as fundamentally good, though they can still be misused. Because they are the result of human goodness, not God's goodness, they are also part of a story of moral progress.

Creativity, then, is a gift which we rightly value and use. When we value the wrong things, as we often do, we create the wrong things. This should not stop us being creative: when we learn to value the right things, we can put our creativity to good purposes.

Interdependence

Every form of life depends on its environment, and humans are no exception. We do not do ourselves any favours when we pretend that our real nature, or humanness, is distinct from our physical bodies with their needs.

It has happened often enough. Pessimists often urge us to think of ourselves as spiritual beings who happen to have bodies. Neutralists tell us that the natural order results from impersonal processes and it is up to us to create for ourselves whatever environment we choose. To take an example, the main causes of global warming are power stations, industry, motor transport and central heating systems. Public discussions usually assume that these things are necessities. They are not: they are all recent arrivals in the history of humanity. They are only treated as necessities because public discourse, based on neutralism, overvalues the results of human work and undervalues God's work. Optimism is far more realistic. The right balance of gases in the atmosphere *is* a necessity, but we could live without those recent inventions, however useful they are. We need to take seriously our own dependence on the natural order and make sure our technologies do not damage it.

In practice, this means finding out which technologies are harmful and which are not. If we successfully use our God-given scientific faculties to create new technologies, we are also capable of using them to make sure our technologies do no harm. We can affirm the value of science and technology but still put them, like everything else, within moral constraints.

The more realistic we are about our dependence, the less we will like the idea of running risks with the ecosystem. Of course there may be some strokes of fortune, when one act of destruction counteracts another. For example, as global warming continues, it may be that the damage done by rising sea levels and changing weather patterns is partly compensated by greater fertility in northern Russia and Canada. To a neutralist, the new situation may seem just as good as the old one. To the optimist the atmosphere as it used to be was given by a good and reliable God to be just what we needed; if our technology accidentally turns it into something different, it is hardly likely that the new situation will be as good as the old.

Therefore we should abandon the programme of changing the natural order into something else more to our liking. The physical order and the ecosystem do not need to be organized by us. The modern determination to blame nature for humanity's shortcomings, and to develop technologies to make it fit our preferences, has harmed nature without benefiting us. I have already argued that there is a proper place for technology; but all too often we have been developing the wrong kinds of technology, based on the conviction that the natural order has no intrinsic value until it has been 'developed'.

Inclusiveness

All forms of life use and adapt their environment. Plants take chemicals, use them, and return them to the earth, changed but equally valuable to some other form of life. In the same way animals take plants, use them, and give back something which another form of life will use. In nature, nothing is wasted. Everything is included. We too are part of the ecosystem, with our own unique place in it, like all other forms of life. We may take what we need, and even use it in a way in which no other animal does, but when we have finished with it we must return it in a form which some other species can use.

For city dwellers, used to an artificial environment, it may be hard to appreciate the point. On a country footpath it is easy enough to believe that the empty yoghurt carton is more offensive to nature than the pile of dog dirt. On a city pavement the dog dirt seems more offensive. It is not. Nature has a way of dealing with one but not the other.

A more significant example is the discharge of radioactive waste into the Irish Sea. It is not the case that, if the discharges are kept to a low level, nature will be able to use them. There are no fish which benefit from high levels of radioactivity or neutralize its toxic effects. At any significant level, it is harmful. The most we can claim is that, at a low enough level, humanity will not be affected; but if the well-being of humanity is of a piece with the well-being of the Irish Sea, by hurting the sea we are hurting ourselves too.

In the context of the current public debate, this is an extreme view, so it may be worth clarifying why I think it is important. Let us imagine the most extreme position of the case for radioactive emissions: either we emit, or the entire nation goes without electricity. Our first response is immediate self-interest: the fish may prefer clean water, but the humans prefer electricity. This response is neutralistic: we are thinking about humans-as-distinct-from-the-ecosystem, not humans-as-part-of-the-ecosystem. We are taking for granted that our true interests conflict with the interests of other forms of life. I have already argued that this assumption cannot be correct: when our interests seem to conflict with the needs of the ecosystem, it is a sure sign that we have misunderstood what human life is for.

To state my position like this may seem so extreme as to be hopelessly unrealistic. This is only because our neutralistic society has turned reality on its head. Let us spell out the truth which is as unpopular as it is obvious. The overwhelming majority of the world's population, even today, let alone in past ages, has managed without electricity. Nobody can manage without clean water and radiation-free sources of food. We can welcome electricity when it respects the value and complexity of the ecosystem and makes its own contribution to it, but we should not accept it at that cost.

Nor should we weigh amounts of electricity against amounts of radiation; *any* attempt to compare the value of electricity with the disvalue of emitting radioactive waste is only possible for people who have already renounced their role as part of the ecosystem and have set themselves against it.

Balance

The ecosystem sets limits to creativity. It maintains its complexity through a balance of processes, like eating and being eaten. Each form of life uses others and is in turn used by something else. There is a huge number of feedback mechanisms which stop any one process becoming too dominant. Every animal needs its particular kinds of food; but if it takes too much and depletes the population of its prey, there will be a shortage in the future. The overall effect of each species taking and being taken is to maintain a rough, though changing, equilibrium.

We too should take no more than we need. Because we are taking far too much, we are preparing ourselves for a future shortage. Behind our determination to take more than we need lies a neutralistic theory of value. Instead of seeing our lives as part of a larger, balanced whole, we overvalue human activities and undervalue other forms of life. This leads to two errors. Firstly, we look for value in a limited list of *things* which we can possess and control, while failing to recognize the value of other things. We are like over-neat gardeners who expect every flower to look exactly the same as the next one in the row, and define everything we have not planted ourselves as a weed. Secondly, we set about getting as many as possible of the things we value, without limit and without regard for the effects on other things. To produce and consume more each year than the previous year is persistently counted as better, even though we are already producing and consuming far too much. Like puppies on a lead, we find nature's limitations frustrating, but instead of respecting them we pull as hard as we can, determined to defy them.

Until we accept that the demand for more and more is out of place in the real world, all other attempts to solve ecological problems will be piecemeal and inadequate. We need to recognize value in balanced and healthy relationships. We need to rediscover the idea of *enough*.

I argued that the discharge of radioactive wastes should not be permitted at all. Other environmental problems are a matter of balance, because they are caused by substances which only harm the ecosystem at artificially high concentrations. Carbon dioxide, for example, is a necessary gas, but industrial emissions are increasing its concentration and causing global warming. In this case the problem is created not by discharge of a toxic substance but by imbalance. Again, if we are clever enough to produce the technology, we are clever enough to examine its effects, if we have the motivation. We can learn about the nature of each particular balance by observing how it functions naturally. Carbon dioxide is part of the interplay between plants and animals: we breathe it out, trees breathe it in. The reason why we can get away with some artificial emissions, in addition to what we emit naturally, is that there is some flexibility in the system. The exact answer to the question 'How much carbon dioxide may we emit artificially?' depends on exactly how much flexibility there is. We should not exceed it.

I suggest, then, that we can see in our natural environment five processes which enhance its value: diversity, creativity, interdependence, inclusiveness and balance. When we get our value judgements right, we affirm all five and avoid destroying them. When we do not destroy them, we naturally add to them, just as every other form of life does.

Relations with other people

All human affairs are rooted in the natural order. We are physical, bodily people, dependent on our environment. Theories about morality must be developed within this context. Many of the pressing issues which face us today are not directly related to specific environmental issues, but they are all related to what being a human being means — and to be a human being is to be a bodily creature, rooted in the earth. For this reason my discussion of morality has begun by considering how we relate to the natural order. It does not end there; whatever issues we discuss — abortion, homosexuality, economic exploitation, war, politics — we are talking about what they mean for real human beings, beings who depend on the natural order and enjoy well-being through the natural interplay of diversity, creativity, interdependence, inclusiveness and balance. As we value these principles and build on them, we learn their implications for every moral issue.

Diversity

The ecosystem, when it is healthy, expresses and develops diversity, both between and within species. The human species is no exception. Left to ourselves, when nobody is telling us what to do, we do things differently. Moral progress, then, characteristically produces diversity. We should be suspicious of attempts to impose uniformity.

At present there is a wide range of attempts to impose uniformity. Governments impose lists of what must be taught in every school. The European Union standardizes weights and measures. Television makes it possible for everybody to be fed the same value judgements and encouraged to follow the same fashions and buy the same products. Behind all these uniformities lies the neutralist's programme of 'improving' life in ways which can be measured. For those who believe that the purpose of life can be described in terms of efficiency and profits, it would make life easier if everybody spoke the same language and used the same currency, every town centre had the same shops selling the same things. As the twentieth century draws to a close, there is no shortage of political leaders assuring us that greater uniformity will increase efficiency and economic success, and most of us believe them. Few of us like it.

We are right not to like it. A healthy society is a diverse society. For jetsetters who speak English, French or German and who often travel from airport to airport on business matters, it would be nice not to have to learn a few words of Greek or Portuguese for the occasions when they visit Athens or Lisbon, and it would help not to have another currency to handle. But people who are rooted in a local area take pride in its unique culture and traditions. When they travel, what makes other places interesting is precisely the differences.

When we value diversity, decisions are best made on the most local level possible, so that they can vary from one place to another. This slows down certain types of activity, like foreign travel and international business. By so doing it contributes to the principle of balance: activities like these are not wrong in themselves, but they should not take place too much.

Creativity

Just as we value the creativity of the natural order, we also value our own ability to innovate and experiment. We like to believe our lives are not determined. We can think up new ideas and try them out. Creativity means we make mistakes, but even the mistakes are an important part of life's fun. A healthy tradition allows for innovation and change within it.

Creativity is often suppressed when there is an imbalance of power, and the powerful can express their own creativity at the expense of other people's. Things go wrong, and we dislike it, when we are told exactly what to do — by our parents, employers, civil servants or governments.

The principle of creativity, then, opposes laws and theories of morality which present us with lists of permitted activities and try to confine everybody's behaviour within them. Two examples spring to mind. One is totalitarian governments, which expect all their citizens to work together for an overriding objective, whether it be communism, fascism or whatever. The other is the tragic history of sexual ethics within the Christian tradition. Since the second century sexuality in general has been treated with suspicion, and despite some liberalization the controlling model continues to be a tightly limited list of permitted activities.

Interdependence

In nature each form of life depends on others. In the same way, human beings depend not only on other species but on each other. It is a mistake to think our problems would be solved if we could avoid depending on our neighbours.

Modern social theories often describe humans as basically self-sufficient, independent individuals. Many of them describe all obligations in terms of freely chosen contracts, and refuse to recognize obligations which cannot be fitted into this scheme. From this cult of independence it follows that to have our own washing machine, lawn mower and car is better than borrowing somebody else's, even if we could easily share. Theories of this type are not true to reality. By the time we are old enough to assert our independence, we owe more to others than we shall ever repay. To repudiate these relationships in the name of an absolute right to self-determination is to repudiate what it means to be human. In practice, everybody belongs to networks of interdependence.

Nineteenth century evolution theory led to the idea that the way to make progress was to allow weaker people to die off. In practice, we all begin life totally dependent on our parents. Some suffer ill-health or handicap and depend heavily on others throughout their lives. Some are very dependent in some respects but make outstanding contributions in others

— perhaps they have weak constitutions but are gifted scientists or musicians. There is no equality of dependence and there is no way of measuring who owes how much to whom. There is no reason to suppose that humanity as a whole would be better off without its more dependent members. Nor should we treat them as inferior, or deny them a share of society's luxuries on the ground that they cannot partake in paid employment.

Inclusiveness

In nature, living things take what they need from their environment and give back what they do not need in a form which others can use. Similarly with humans: it is right to provide for our needs through our interactions with others, but we should do so in ways which affirm their role in society.

Economic theories based on individualism tend to assume that a customer who buys something in a shop has no further obligations to the shopkeeper after paying the price. This may seem a normal attitude in a city where customers only relate to shopkeepers when they want to buy something, but it excuses the rich for not caring about the poor and leads to extremes of wealth and poverty. As trade becomes more and more international, the gap between rich and poor gets bigger.

In a small village, where there are only one or two shops, it is often a different matter. Customers are likely to be more conscious of the fact that they value the shop's existence. They are likely to be more aware of the shopkeeper's circumstances and needs. The success of many village shops depends on social interactions and networks of caring which cannot be expressed in economic terms. The village situation is healthier; when people relate to each other in more than one way, there are more checks and balances to ensure that everybody's needs are taken into account. Economic activity should always balance legitimate self-interest with a concern for everybody involved.

The principle of inclusiveness applies in the same way to all social groupings — our relationships with members of our families, or within the institutions where we work or take our recreation. Just as we should accept responsibility for our unwanted products, and not just throw away things which cannot be used by other forms of life, so also we should accept responsibility for the way our actions affect other people, and not just ignore them when we have no further use for them.

Balance

Nature maintains a balance between its many processes. It uses feedback mechanisms to prevent any one process becoming too dominant. Humans, too, are designed to live balanced lives. Whereas our society is right to innovate and make changes, it must recognize limits. Whatever changes we make, we must stop when we have done enough.

The principle of balance, then, opposes all programmes of activity which set out to do more and more of the same thing without limit. On an individual level, we might think of a number of examples: to drink as much alcohol as possible, to accumulate as much money as possible and to have as much power as possible. They all have an addictive quality and easily lead to tragedy. On a public level, the most heavily promoted limitless objectives are economic growth and technological development. There are circumstances in which a society would benefit from these things, but there are limits. When we have enough of any one thing, we can stop trying to produce more and turn our attention to the next stage in our progress.

This, perhaps more than anywhere else, is where modern western society goes wrong. Because of its neutralism it cannot provide a defensible account of value or purpose. It therefore hangs on to the values and purposes it has inherited from its past, and sets them up as objectives to be pursued without limit, even though the need for them has long since passed. The demand for more and more, without a satisfactory account of enough, is bound to cause conflict. Characteristically, each nation would like more oil, more gold, more land — as much as possible of everything which is classified as an economic resource. Resources are limited, but the amount wanted is not. States grab for themselves as much as they can of whatever is valued, regardless of how much they need, and thereby create real shortages. Inevitably, they come to see each other as competitors.

When economists and politicians tell us that the economy, or productivity, or exports, need to grow, we must ask them how much they need to grow. At what size will the economy be big enough, so that it can stop growing? When will productivity be enough for the population? How fast is fast enough to travel twenty miles? If they have no account of enough, they are ignoring the real constraints of human life and at the same time chaining us to an endless treadmill.

For the sake of world peace and justice, we need to be much more aware that we are sharing the world's resources with the rest of humanity and should not take more than we need. We know only too well that present patterns of consumption in the affluent west are already unsustainable, and if the rest of the world's population were to imitate us, the environment would very rapidly be destroyed. As long as we do not have enough, it is legitimate to seek more. When we do have enough, we should be satisfied. Those who consume more than their share are not increasing value, despite what economists say. They are destroying it. They are being anti-ecological by making too many demands on the ecosystem and anti-social by privileging themselves at the expense of others.

Of course, people who now take more than their share will not lightly give it up. However, I have argued that our well-being is *increased* by learning how to live in harmony with other people and the ecosystem. If we stopped doing the things we do not need to do, we would find that there is enough for everybody, and we could all live better lives.

We should therefore oppose the high levels of consumption which the affluent west has developed. I do not oppose it for the same reasons as pessimists. Whereas pessimists tend to deny the value of worldly things and disapprove of physical pleasures simply because they are physical, I affirm their value to the extent that they are properly used. One criterion of proper use is that others can do the same. To have enough is valuable. To have more than enough is not necessarily valuable at all, and to have so much as to deprive others is positively harmful.

I suggest, then, that the principles of diversity, creativity, interdependence, inclusiveness and balance show us how we can discover fulfilment by living in harmony with each other as well as nature. These principles are useful because they describe features of life which are inescapable and which we are right to value. Theories which oppose them destroy life's value. When we affirm them we can build on them and develop them in ways which are appropriate to humanity or to particular human societies.

Between them the five principles, particularly creativity and balance, provide a response to the left-right debate of twentieth century politics. Both capitalism and communism derive from nineteenth century reform programmes, with a great deal in common. Both were developed as social control programmes, committed to the view that the elite who understood the laws of nature would improve society by manipulating human behaviour. Both accepted Bacon's view that nature was something alien to be conquered. Much remains of these beliefs: that progress is unstoppable, that there is no limit to the amount of economic growth which is possible and desirable, and that human life will become more pleasant as more and more technological artefacts are created.

Left wing theories have emphasized balance at the expense of creativity. The balance they have sought — avoiding extremes of wealth and poverty — has generally been motivated by single-minded theories of the purpose of life and has been imposed on large scales by central bureaucracies. The result has usually been oppressive uniformity rather than complex balances between complementary activities. Right wing theories have emphasized creativity at the expense of balance. The creativity they have sought has also been motivated by single-minded theories of the purpose of life — usually, increasing wealth — and all too often means nothing more than maximizing profits.

Most of us do not like either extreme. We would not like either a uniform society which suppressed the real differences between people, or a society with extremes of wealth and poverty and no fairness. Most people support a position somewhere between the extremes on the left-right spectrum, and most of the larger political parties in the western democracies describe themselves in these terms. According to my account, however, this will not do. What is wrong with the extreme positions is not what divides them, but what they have in common: the attempts to dominate nature and manipulate human behaviour in the interests of a nationally imposed objective.

We should therefore reject not only the extremes of political left and right, but all stations in between on that spectrum. In terms of modern politics, I am advocating a position which is even more extreme; but in another sense I am arguing for a moderate, middle-of-the-road view. My account affirms both creativity and balance, and by taking its cue from nature, defines them in such a way that they reinforce each other rather than conflicting with each other. It explains the limits to both, and at the same time explains why those limits are for the well-being of humanity.

This may make my theory seem contradictory. How can it stand for the normal and moderate and at the same time denounce all our society's values? The answer is, by drawing attention to the contradictions within our society. In practice we function according to conflicting sets of values. I am proposing that we affirm one set at the expense of another. In our everyday lives we base most of our decisions on our natural instincts and rationality and ignore what the nation's leaders tell us. We like a balance between work and leisure, regardless of the effects on the economy. Teenagers spend time meeting the opposite sex, despite all the warnings that they should spend all day revising for exams. We enjoy giving things to people we like, without analysing the economic impact of the gift. Our natural, God-given faculties usually make us want the things which God has designed to be good for us.

On the other hand, the neutralist values which dominate public life are quite different. The harder people work, the better for the economy — without limit. Higher grades in Mathematics exams will help students in the future; better skills at relating to boy friends do not lead to exam results and therefore do not count, even if they produce more successful marriages. When government statisticians tell us that we were 2.3% better off last year than the year before, we all too easily fall into the trap and imagine that they know about our lives better than we know ourselves. These neutralist values set us against our natural faculties, but they are so deeply ingrained in our society that we have learned to think of them as 'obvious' or 'common sense'. My theory opposes them. It therefore rejects the entire left-right spectrum of western politics today and affirms those other, God-given values instead.

When we want the wrong things, whether we get them or not we are dissatisfied. At any one time, what we ought to want is strongly desired by many people, because God has designed us to want it; but our theories make it seem the wrong thing to want, or society is set up in such a way that achieving it would have adverse side-effects. As a result it often happens that the correct objective is something which political moderates might support — like, for example, wanting everybody to have enough money to live on — but the correct way to achieve it is to reject the whole of neutralist theory and practice, and to most people this seems far too radical to be taken seriously.

My theory, then, is an unusual mixture of extremity and moderation. This, I believe, is the kind of judgement which needs to be made on modern society. Our natural instincts and feelings are a better guide to the way we ought to live than the theories which dominate our public life. We shall be dissatisfied until we want what we were designed to want; and we can discover what that is by reflecting on the way God has made us.

Conclusion

My account of morality is a natural theology. It does not bypass the natural order and seek an unworldly divine revelation. Instead, it observes the way God has made things to function naturally, and fits in, using publicly available knowledge to fill in the details. It accepts that the way to work out exactly what we may do with which chemicals is by depending on the scientific evidence, not by squeezing ever more inventive interpretations out of biblical texts; but it also accepts that, however many scientific facts we know, there remains the question of which principles we apply. Our principles come from evaluating the world positively. We perceive around us the ways in which God creates value, we affirm them, and we take our pleasure in sharing God's creative work.

This moral goodness can never be reduced to a set of commands. It is far too varied, far too dependent on circumstances, far too exciting. Tomorrow it will mean doing something we have not yet thought of, let alone legislated about. What is *always* morally right is to respond to God's call to progress towards the true purpose of our lives. A large part of the moral task, then, is to maintain our vision of God's purposes. Instead of interpreting the way things are from our own self-interested perspective, we need to pay attention to a wider perspective, God's, which sees our own experiences as part of a wider whole. The better we are attuned to a God's-eye-view, the greater our chance of understanding which actions would count as true progress.

Moral progress therefore involves reflecting on God's perspective, so that we may think the way God thinks, want the things God wants and do what God would have us do. When we get it right, the things we do are too diverse to categorize under a simple moral rule. What unifies them is the commitment to sharing God's perspective and cooperating with God's work of blessing the whole creation with goodness. It means being on God's side, being on the side of the fundamental value of all things. This attitude of positive evaluation is justified by a cosmology which trusts the perfect goodness of a creator God, and it leads to an agenda of practical concern. It develops as it grows. It cannot be fully described because it cannot be reduced to lower level terms. In the Christian tradition, the nearest we get to describing it is the word 'love'.

This, I believe, is the way to discover the fundamental truths about reality. It needs to be affirmed in the face of all the world's evil. We cannot understand what has gone wrong with the world until after we have clarified what it would be like for things to go right.

Why, though, have so many things gone wrong? Why, if God is so good and powerful, is there any evil at all? This is the question I shall discuss in the next chapter.

Chapter 12

Evil in God's good world

IN THE LAST three chapters I have explained why I believe that the world has been created by a God who is self-consistent, omnipotent, omniscient and good. I have developed the details in my own way, but the theory is very old. The biggest problem with it has been recognized at least since the books of Genesis and Job were written over two thousand years ago: if the world has been made like this, why is there any evil in it?

People who defend this kind of theology usually appeal to free will. This is what Genesis and Irenaeus did, as we saw in Chapter 2. Within the Christian tradition others have done the same. A recent example is John Hick.[1] God could have retained complete control over the universe, so that everything operated exactly as planned. A universe like that would be perfect within its own limitations, but since we would not have free will, we would not be able to be morally good. To make moral goodness possible, we need freedom.

Pessimists have often argued that this does not provide a strong enough account of evil. Many neutralists are determinists, so the free will defence cuts no ice with them.[2] In order to reconcile evil with a good God, we need to take freedom seriously. But even if we are free to do wrong, why do we? How can we account for misfortunes which are not caused by human actions? This chapter responds to these questions in three sections. The first considers why there is any evil at all, the second why there is so much and the third why there is natural evil.

The origin of evil

In Chapter 3 I described the Christian doctrine of the fall. At first there was an original righteousness, but then things went wrong. Genesis and Irenaeus, on the other hand, tell us that the first sin followed a state of amoral innocence, not moral perfection. This not only makes the problem easier to solve on a theoretical level; it fits better with the way individuals develop moral awareness, and with evolution theory.

A young boy, for example, is being weaned off milk. He learns how to use his hands to put things into his mouth. There are many things around the house which he would like to try sucking. At first his mother makes sure that anything potentially harmful is put on a shelf out of reach. Gradually he learns to move around the house and reach more things. He also learns about obedience. When he is allowed to toddle around the living room, he often sees something he would like to suck and crawls towards it. One of his parents jumps up, shouts 'No!' and removes it. At a later stage again, he can see that the object is within reach and neither parent is looking; but he understands that if he picks it up his parents will be angry. One day temptation gets the better of him; he knows his parents will be angry but he picks it up anyway. He has done wrong.

This process, I suggest, is typical of the way moral good and evil originate. First of all we have an instinctive desire to do certain things. Later we become conscious that we are doing one action rather than an alternative, and this consciousness leads us to evaluate the action and consider the possibility of doing something else instead. Only when we have reached the stage of thinking about what to do, and freely deciding, do our actions become morally good or bad.

We must assume that a similar process of moral development has taken place on a social level. If we evolved out of animals, there must have been a time when our ancestors lived by instinct, just like other animals. They had no sense of the freedom to choose between alternative actions. They had no awareness of their own capacity to think. They did not think about the effects their actions had on their environment and other people. There were therefore no publicly discussed rules of behaviour and no sense of moral right and wrong. Now, we have all these things. There must have been a stage when they developed for the first time. We do not know the historical details; no doubt they varied from place to place. Whether the changes happened before or after the transition to a human body, makes no difference. We can describe some stages on the way.

(i) The bird sees the worm, dives down and eats it. Moral concepts have not arisen at all: there is no room for discussion about whether the bird has a right to the worm, or the worm has a right to life, or it should have been left for a different bird. The action is part of the world's goodness as God's creation. I shall reply to worm-lovers later in this chapter: at present I am considering *moral* evil and the bird's action is morally neither good nor evil.

(ii) Many animals have territorial instincts. They mark out territory and defend it against competitors. They growl and fight, and learn when to give in and when to stand their ground. To minimize unnecessary fighting, they develop an instinctive sense of when not to enter another's territory. Like (i), they still spot food and grab it while it is there, but in addition social systems have developed. There is still no freedom or morality.

(iii) At some stage there arose a further development within human society: they became *aware* that they were about to do a particular thing. When this awareness first developed, it was a new departure within a life which was otherwise governed by instinct. People could think to themselves, for example, 'Here I am, a fighter, putting my life at risk for the sake of the tribe'.

(iv) Once we become aware of our actions, the next stage is to reflect that we might have been doing something else. By saying to ourselves, 'Here I am, a fighter, putting my life at risk for the sake of the tribe', we pave the way to the thought 'I am terrified! I would much rather run away'. The next thought is 'Why don't I run away?' Once people can reflect on their choice of action before they make it, they can decide which action to take.

For this reason we should not think of immorality as a limited set of acts and ask whether there was once a time when nobody committed them; rather, we do acts which at one stage did not count as immoral, but do now. At first there are only instinctive actions; then people become aware that they are doing one action and declining to do another; then they become aware that the alternative would suit them better; then they make a free decision independently of their instincts. Each new stage counts as progress, even though immorality only exists at the end of it. Each stage is a necessary step on the road to a human society which is both free and morally good.

Neither individuals nor societies begin their moral lives with a blank sheet. We are never in a situation where we have a full understanding of moral rights and wrongs and are also completely free of habits, desires, prejudices and influences. By the time we know the difference between right and wrong, we are already in the habit of doing some acts rather than others, and we feel strong desires.

I am not suggesting that these are the only situations in which evil originates. Another might be the man who enjoys a bar of Nestlé chocolate, but one day is told about the Baby Milk Campaign and the Nestlé boycott. Once he knows about it, it would be a morally significant act to stop buying the chocolate. To carry on buying it would also be morally signif-icant: it would be a *decision*, either to disagree with the campaign or not to care.

Changing circumstances often create new possibilities for morality or immorality. For example, a stone age society which has neither money nor any means to store food is likely to be comparatively poor and egalitarian, simply because there is no way to store up surpluses. If it then develops more efficient ways of storing food, there will be more to go round in times of shortage, but it may be under the control of only a few people. Still, there is a limit to how much any one person can eat, and storing unneeded food will be costly. Introduce money into this society and it becomes easier to store up greater and greater wealth. Greater debts become possible too. Now add in the vast range of financial services avail-able today, and the potential to maximize surplus wealth without regard for the effects on other people is magnified still further. With each new development, it is possible to benefit everybody but it is also possible to gratify the greed of some at the expense of others. In this way, a new devel-opment in technology often needs a new development in morality if it is to do more good than harm.

This account of evil's origin is not just an alternative version of pessimism. At no stage in it does God incorporate any act or process which is intrinsically evil. Nor is it a divine trick, as though God was getting evil in by the back door so as not to seem responsible for it. God permits evil, but does not oblige anybody to do it.

Let us take the example of our young boy, and suppose he eats a paper clip. Whether we blame him depends on his stage of development. There is an early stage when he is too young. The blame lies with his parents for leaving it within reach. By the age of seven he should know better than to eat it and we would not blame the parents at all. To get from one stage to the other, the parents watch how his sense of responsibility develops. At first they are very protective and give him little freedom of choice. Gradually, he internalizes messages about the things he is not allowed to do. When they are confident that he would not eat a paper clip even if he could, they relax their oversight. From the boy's point of view, his first opportunity to eat one takes place when his sense of its wrongness is stronger than his sense of freedom, and he does not seriously consider the possibility. Later he becomes more aware of his freedom to choose, and asks questions about what would happen if he ate one. What makes the rule against eating paper clips a *moral* rule, as opposed to a parentally imposed discipline, is precisely the physical freedom, combined with the mental capacity, to consider either option and make a free decision. Once this stage is reached, he is responsible for his decision.

This, I suggest, is the way moral development works. I have defined morality in terms of progress towards God's purposes for our lives. To develop freedom is to become able to choose between alternative actions. The choice is morally relevant whenever it has a bearing on progress. The moral significance is there, not as an extra process which links freedom to progress, but simply by definition: morality *means* comparing what free people do with what progress invites them to do.

To those who like to apportion blame, this may leave the edges too fuzzy. But in practice any satisfactory account of morality must allow for fuzzy edges. The boy's awareness of freedom develops gradually. If he eats a paper clip on his second birthday, who is to blame? By then we would normally expect him to have passed the stage of wanting to put everything in his mouth, but if he does, his parents will feel that they should have been more careful. They may well blame both themselves and him. In ordinary life, it is unrealistic to turn all moral judgements into simple verdicts of guilty or not guilty. The freedom-and-responsibility combination does not arrive one day as a complete package; it develops a little each day, through our relationships with each other and the world around us.

If this is how evil originates, there is nothing surprising about it. Every time somebody does something wrong, they could have avoided doing it, but it would have been most surprising if everybody had acted with perfection from the start. There is no place for the God of wrath who is horrified by every sin.

The spread of evil

So far I have described how evil originates in a situation which was previously free of it. We might define it as failure to make moral progress when the opportunity arises. Yet why is there such a huge quantity of evil, and why does it become so intense? I do not think all evil can be explained as failure to make moral progress. Once it originates, it spreads and takes new forms, and we experience not just failure to progress, but real regress.

A child from a deprived subculture comes to new foster parents. To the child, lying and stealing are essential and normal parts of life, and at first he carries on behaving as before. The wise foster parents recognize that it will take a long time for these habits to be unlearned, and instead of condemning every dishonesty they praise and encourage any signs of developing honesty. They expect quite different standards from their own son. The son, however, sees it differently. He knows that stealing and lying are wrong, and when his own possessions begin to disappear from his bedroom, he complains loudly and expects the foster child to be given the same punishments as he would have been given himself.

Among these characters we can see three stages of moral development. The foster child has not yet learned to tell the truth and desist from stealing. The parents have learned to forgive his misdeeds and respond in a positive way which will enable future progress. Between the two is the son, who knows that lying and stealing are wrong but has not yet learned to forgive. As he suffers the lies and thefts of the foster child, he finds life to be a worse experience than it was. He feels more and more bitter, and takes it out on the foster child by stealing from him in return. When he does this — as opposed to when the foster child does it — it is not mere failure to progress. It is real regress.

Another example might be the economic situation of a society which is rapidly getting poorer. Let us say the cause is a war. Resources are scarce and there is competition for basic necessities. Many are forced into theft or prostitution to avoid starvation. The younger ones, growing up in this situation, come to believe that this is what life is normally like. Because they think of it as normal, they develop a poor view of human nature. The women dismiss the men as thieves and the men dismiss the women as prostitutes. It becomes difficult to believe the world was made by a good God. Because of the high crime rate, they come to believe that oppressive governments are the only hope for security. They develop strong racist feelings against the enemy nation which has caused them so much suffering. Eventually the time comes when they cease to be oppressed. Living standards rise. By this time enough evil has been done. There is a well established conflictual culture, convinced that the only way of securing prosperity for itself is at the expense of other nations. The racism born in oppression becomes a justification for oppressing others in turn. The high number of prostitutes becomes a political embarrassment and vicious laws are enacted against them. By now there are large numbers of girls who have been brought up in brothels, know of no other lifestyle and cannot understand why they are being victimized.

Usually, the spread of evil happens in mundane ways. The person subjected to harsh criticism becomes defensive, and more likely to find fault in others. The person who is overcharged in a tax bill and has no means of redress bears a grudge against the taxation system, and feels more positive about the thought of illegally evading a tax next time the opportunity arises. The person who is mugged on the street loses confidence in human nature and becomes more likely to support a repressive government. In countless tiny ways, and some big ones, people suffer evil and, unless they have morally progressed far enough to absorb it into themselves, they pass it on to others in turn. Evil, like good, multiplies with its own momentum. Usually, the result is the level of evil we have grown used to. Occasionally it coalesces round a particular programme and millions are sent to the gas chambers.

As it develops, evil produces other features of life, like conflict, error, injustice and blame, which would not otherwise have existed.

Conflicts of interest

In the last three chapters I have argued that, fundamentally, the interests of each person are in harmony with the interests of other people and the whole of God's creation. Fundamentally, it cannot be the case that the natural environment is bad for us, or that meeting the needs of our bodies conflicts with other people meeting the needs of their bodies. My account needs to insist on this claim, because otherwise it will collapse into pessimism.

On the other hand, evil creates real conflicts of interest. Evil actions characteristically produce situations where it really is in the interests of one person to act counter to the interests of another — for example, because there is conflict over resources. People find they have to either starve or steal, kill or be killed. Or their instincts tell them to do one thing, but their rationality tells them to do another. Or the well-being of the individual conflicts with the well-being of society. In these situations it is no use theorizing about the fundamental unity of everything, as I have been doing: what is needed is to decide between real conflicting interests. What, then, is left of the fundamental God-given harmony I have been describing, in the real world full of conflict?

This is a crucial question for my theory. If there is nothing left of the fundamental harmony, the existence of evil has overcome the goodness of God's creating and my theory collapses into another version of pessimism. I believe it can withstand the challenge. Even when we take into account the huge amount of conflict, the way it relates to God and to human potential remains quite different from the way it relates in pessimistic theories. There are three points of distinction.

(i) God remains firmly in control. All evil has been positively permitted, for the sake of the greater good. Contrary to pessimistic theories, in which evil is an unmitigated tragedy with no redeeming features, the reason why God allows it still stands.

(ii) All evil has been caused by human beings and at any stage can be stopped by human beings. The more evil there is, the harder it is to overcome it; but it is always possible to overcome it. The world we live in is still the world made by a good God and there is always room for hope.

(iii) Although there are real conflicts of interest in particular circumstances, there still is a way to harmonize the interests of the whole world, and that is by overcoming evil and directing our lives towards God's purposes.

We recognize this relationship between harmony and conflict often enough in ordinary life. For example, a teenage boy is upset when he is sacked from a job and is taunted by his insensitive father. The result is a major row, after which the boy leaves home, steals a car, drives it away and is caught by the police. The car's owners are furious and will not hear a good word said for the boy: the act was inexcusably wrong and he deserves to be locked away. His mother takes a different view. Given the situation, she had feared violence between the boy and his father, and is greatly relieved that no serious harm resulted. Maybe father will learn to be more measured with his words, and maybe the son will learn to be more patient with life's trials. There is hope. In this example God's perspective comes closest to that of the mother, who sees each evil act in a wider context and notices the good things as well as the bad.

Similarly, in the example of the foster parents, a situation was thoroughly evil from a particular narrow perspective — the son's — but from a wider perspective it had its place within a story of progress. Both perspectives were true within their own terms, but the wider perspective is a more inclusive statement about reality.

On the one hand, conflicts of interest are real. On the other, they only arise within a world which at its most fundamental level is characterized by harmony. Evil and conflict have not usurped its position. They only take place where God, for good reason, permits them: within the sphere of human actions and their effects and inside the story of an all-encompassing goodness. Whenever evil takes place, it is always possible for good to take place instead.

Error

In Chapter 9 I argued that for God's creation to be good, we must have been designed to know what we need to know. I described various sources of knowledge, such as rationality, observation, instinct and tradition. None of them is infallible, but God has designed them so that when we take them together we know what we need to know. How, then, are mistakes possible?

(i) Conflicts of interest create situations where we cannot recognize the fundamental harmony of reality. It is easier to recognize it when we are lucky enough to have few anxieties, or when we have learned the discipline of setting aside our personal concerns to contemplate reality as a whole. Only then do we set our own problems within a wider perspective, perceive them as part of a more hopeful story and find it easier to reach the kinds of conclusions I drew in the last three chapters. At other times, to the oppressed and their oppressors alike, my theory will seem like idealistic nonsense: life seems too tied up in conflict. Far from perceiving other people's wrongdoings from a God's-eye-view, most of us only pay attention when we ourselves are hurt, and then we respond on the level of retaliation. This limits our understanding. The evil we see is real enough, but by failing to adopt a wider perspective we fail to see how conflicts of interest can be reconciled at a higher level.

(ii) Evil can create situations in which our sources of knowledge mislead us. When somebody deliberately tricks us, our faculty of observation misleads us. Similarly, what seems to us to be 'common sense' or 'justice' is influenced by our vested interests and the information which others have chosen to feed us, and this affects our rationality.

(iii) We are not designed to know everything. Some evil influences, such as the mechanistic paradigm, motivate us to seek knowledge which we have not been designed to need, and this too creates error.

Injustice

Collectively we get what we deserve, but many individuals suffer far more than they deserve. Even though suffering is allowed for the sake of freedom, God is still allowing it. Does this make God unjust?

God's policy can be vindicated, provided we accept on trust that the ultimate purposes are worth it. We are still left with many people who are not prepared to make this act of trust and have just cause for complaint. They were brought into the world without prior consultation — as far as we know — and subjected to undeserved suffering at the hands of others. Are they not entitled to say that, whatever God's ultimate purposes, they would prefer not to pay the price? Why should they not opt out? I believe this question should be taken seriously. When people endure great suffering, their response to it must be respected. When they commit suicide to escape it, we should not lightly condemn them. The complaint is legitimate.

Is it fair, though, to direct it against God? Suppose you give your son a motor-bike. Your heart is in your mouth because you are afraid he will drive dangerously, but he is old enough and needs transport. You cannot protect him from danger for the rest of his life; he has to develop into maturity his own way. He accepts it with delight, and within a few days has killed a young child. How do you feel now? Perhaps full of regret, saying to yourself, 'If only I had not let him have it...' Nevertheless, when you reason with yourself you feel you did what seemed right at the time.

The parents of the child feel angry. When they hear that it was a new motor-bike and you had only just given it to him, they tell you that a dangerous youngster like him should not have been allowed on the roads with it. They blame not only him but you. They are not interested in your prior deliberations because they are not interested in your son's process of growing up and maturing. 'Lucky him', they will say, 'because of what he has done, our child will never grow up!'

The parents of the victim have suffered a great evil which would not have happened if the boy had not been given the motor-bike. Nevertheless, when young people grow up they need freedom. The parents of the victim are too distressed to see the whole context, and only see it from their perspective. Those who do not belong to either family can see it from both points of view, and put them together in the context of dangerous roads, the transport needs of teenagers and all the other considerations. In effect, society has created a situation of conflict by setting the needs of teenagers against the safety of others. Much of the responsibility lies with society for accepting road accidents as a price worth paying for its transport system. Both families are part of this society and may or may not have already been concerned about the dangers on the roads.

In the wider context, suffering can have a positive role. Earlier I argued that people who are obliged to endure undeserved suffering often react in anger or hatred and pass on the evil, multiplied, to others. The converse is that those who can simply endure it, without passing it on to others, are performing a positive act of helping to reduce the amount of evil in the world.

When people endure suffering, then, from their own perspective it may not only seem, but be, quite unjust. From the widest perspective — God's perspective — it may positively contribute to the greater good. If we can trust God's fundamental goodness, we are more likely to believe that undeserved suffering is not an unmitigated tragedy.

Blame

I have set out to explain why evil exists in a good world. To be credible, my explanation must really *explain*, without taking free will away, and the explanation must be so sympathetic that we can see why people do evil. Here another problem arises: *any* account of evil which meets these criteria will be unacceptable to some people because it will seem too sympathetic to evildoers: by explaining evil, it will seem to explain it *away*. If thieves do their thieving because they have not had opportunities to progress beyond a thieving lifestyle, or because society has imposed regress on their community, it seems that they are only partly to blame and that a vague, unspecified number of others are also partly to blame. Are we not in danger of becoming wishy-washy liberals, unable to give a clear account of who is to blame?

This criticism really arises from a debate between pessimists and neutralists. Characteristically, it is pessimists who are keenest on blaming others. To blame is to locate evil in others and set oneself in an attitude of conflict with them. The question 'How could anyone bring themselves to do such a thing?' is repeatedly asked but rarely answered, because any answer would invite sympathy. The characteristic statement of blame begins 'What I don't understand is…' By contrast, neutralists are characteristically deterministic: nobody is to blame for anything because our actions were caused by our circumstances. There is an explanation for everything. The debate between these two theories continues in penal policy today. Should we take freedom seriously and impose heavy punishments, or should we accept that people's actions are caused by their nature and nurture, and be lenient?

I have agreed with pessimists that we have free will and often do evil, but I have also agreed with neutralists that every wrong act has an explanation. When we are sympathetic enough to the wrongdoer, we may respond to the explanation by saying 'Ah yes, if I were in your situation I would have done the same'. This does not make it any less wrong. Wrongdoers really are responsible for their deeds, but there are also reasons why they do them. As we become better people, we spend less time noticing and condemning the faults of others and more time trying to make changes for the better. On this point I side with the wishy-washy liberals.

Feelings of blaming, and the associated senses of anger and frustration, tend to make a hurtful situation far more hurtful than it needs to be. A common situation is where a house has been burgled but nothing of great value stolen. Some victims respond in a practical way, checking what has been broken and what needs to be replaced. For others, the very fact that the house has been burgled at all has a significance of its own, producing anger and hatred which would not have arisen if the same goods had been lost by accident. Those who know how to forgive are spared an extra burden.

Natural suffering

As well as *moral* evil, various natural events cause pain and suffering, and are often cited as arguments against a good creator. Optimistic theory insists that what God creates is good. Everything which we experience as evil, then, is either the result of human sin or is not really evil at all.

Death

Death is often treated as a great evil, perhaps the greatest evil of all.[3] However, it is clearly part of the natural order, so we must take it that, in itself, it is good. In particular circumstances it may well be evil, but the evil is caused by the particular circumstances rather than death itself. God has created us in such a way that we will die, and if we respond positively to God's good provision we will accept death as part of it, not as an enemy to fight against.

Animal suffering

If God's creation is good, why do animals cause so much suffering to each other and eat each other? Since the nineteenth century evolution debates, the idea of 'nature red in tooth and claw' has become a common argument against a good creator.

To clarify the issue we must first dispose of excessive claims. The idea of the 'survival of the fittest' has tended to treat all life as though it was a never-ending struggle for survival against competitors. The implication for humanity is that we should spend our lives fighting for our own interests at the expense of others. Many racists and capitalists welcome this conclusion. As an account of the way plants and animals live, it is no longer as convincing as it seemed in the nineteenth century. Some competition often helps redress imbalances, but competition does not dominate all life. There is also much cooperation. The idea that animals spend all their lives in fierce struggle for survival is no more realistic than the idea that all birds are idyllically happy and sing for the benefit of humans.

The real issue is animal suffering. Here we are faced with a problem of understanding. Directly, the only suffering we experience is our own. From our personal experiences we generalize to other people's suffering. In the same way, and equally naturally, we generalize to the suffering of higher animals. If other people are hurt when we kick them, so is the dog. This assumption is reinforced by the dog's response when it scowls and runs away. If dogs can suffer, where do we draw the line? What about worms? Cabbages? Bacteria?

Major issues are at stake. Vivisection and factory farming impose on animals what many people take to be suffering. As we have no language to find out exactly what it is like for them, we can never be sure; all we can do is infer from their body language that the way they feel is similar to the way we would feel. In reply, defenders of vivisection and factory farming point out the huge amount of suffering animals endure in the wild. Is a hen in a cage really worse off than it would be in the wild, three feet in front of a fox?

The extreme positions seem most logical. One extreme is Descartes' theory that animals do not have souls and therefore do not suffer. This view has dominated the modern period and is still widely used to justify factory farming and vivisection. At the other extreme, some people believe all living beings can suffer. Every time we walk along the road we tread on countless insects and make them suffer. Some supporters of animal rights make this their starting point. It generally leads to the conclusion that we should minimize the amount of suffering we cause but cannot stop causing it altogether.[4]

These two extremes are, respectively, neutralistic and pessimistic. Animal suffering is dismissed as unobservable by one and treated as a cause of inescapable conflict by the other. Is there a middle way between them? The tidiest answer is to draw the line somewhere — perhaps at the larger animals, or maybe the larger fishes as well. We can then count those above the line as capable of suffering and stop worrying about those below it. This solution works well on a practical level, because it is possible to care about a limited number of animals. Hunt saboteurs can defend foxes and seal cull protesters can defend seals, while rats go unloved. However, this argument lacks evidence. It *may* be that foxes suffer but rats do not; but it is only a guess. The weakness arises wherever we draw the line. There is no justified place to draw it.

Optimistic theory, on the other hand, argues for an intermediate position and thereby sheds light on the practical issues. It follows the same reasoning as my account of freedom and moral responsibility. It is not the case that the only kind of capacity to suffer is the human kind and every animal either has it or does not have it. Instead, it develops, presumably through evolution, to the extent that it is useful to each form of life. Cabbages, worms and horses may all be able to suffer in some way or other, but what suffering consists of is different in each case.

Evolution theory would lead us to expect that each animal endures the types of pain and suffering which are useful in its natural environment, and no more. An optimistic account of creation would agree, as we would not expect God to impose unnecessary suffering on animals. When we see on our television screens a lion catching and eating an antelope, or watch our cat play with a mouse before killing and eating it, we may identify with the victim and feel that nature is cruel, but antelope and mouse are both designed to cope with being eaten. It is a normal part of animal experience, and from an evolutionary point of view there is no point in making the experience unpleasant once death is certain. Analogies with humans point in this direction too. According to research into near-death experiences, it seems that when death is certain and the body gives up trying to survive, the unpleasantness of suffering stops quickly.[5] Furthermore, children's stories all over the world show that the most fascinating way to die is by being eaten. If human children, who are rarely eaten, find the idea exciting, it seems that we still have instincts which enable us to cope with it. It is reasonable to infer that animals which do get eaten have these instincts even more strongly than we do.

This account does two things. Firstly, it solves the problem of where to draw the line. Different animals suffer in different ways and larger animals generally suffer more than smaller ones. Pulling the legs off a dog hurts it more than pulling the legs off a fly. It is a mistake to deny that animals suffer at all, but it is equally a mistake to think that every animal suffers in the same kind of way, and to the same intensity, as we would in the same situation. We do not know exactly what it is like for any other animal to suffer, but we can generally tell whether or not it likes what we are doing to it, and that should be enough to guide our behaviour. At the same time, we do not need to feel guilty about stepping on ants and cutting cabbages.

Secondly, my account suggests that natural suffering is quite different from artificial suffering. Hens have evolved to cope with being eaten by foxes, but not being kept in tiny cages. Rats have evolved to cope with being killed by cats, but not with vivisection. Painful experiments on animals cannot be excused on the ground that animals suffer in the wild.

Natural disasters

Earthquakes, volcanoes, floods and droughts have been cited as evidence of evil gods all through history. If there are no evil gods, why do they happen?

Increasingly, they are caused by human actions. More and more droughts and floods, for example, are caused by deforestation. Environmental destruction can now be recognized as a major cause of what we experience as 'natural' disasters.

Similarly, people often run risks with their lifestyles, or do things which spoil their health. An example would be living in a place which is not an ideal habitat. There is a range of possible places to live, not all of them suited to humans. The Canary Islands are, but the North Pole is not. Between the two extremes are countless borderline cases which are not as inhospitable as the North Pole but are only habitable when certain conditions are met; the community depends on a particular type of trade, or a government subsidy, or whatever. When the conditions cease to be met, the people suffer, but we cannot blame God for the suffering: somebody decided to move there, with all the risks involved.

Many natural disasters do not result from human actions. Perhaps the most obvious examples are earthquakes and volcanic eruptions. Even in these cases, however, it is not the events themselves, but the suffering they cause, which is the problem. Areas which are prone to them are well known, and the answer is to live elsewhere or to make sure the houses are better built. Often, of course, the victims have no choice but to live where they do, but this is because of poverty or political boundaries, both of which result from human behaviour, not nature.

Pain and illness

Another argument against the goodness of human life is the amount of pain and illness we suffer. Could not a good God have arranged things differently?

Pain has a positive function as the body's warning system. We have been designed to be capable of a limited range of activities, within a limited range of conditions, for a limited period of time. When we exceed these limits, our bodies tell us to rest, sleep, stop eating, or whatever. The more we persist in exceeding them, the more intensely our bodies tell us to stop. As critics of the mechanistic paradigm point out, western culture tends to treat human bodies too much like machines, and as a result we do not care for them as well as we might. In the affluent west the average amount spent per person on health care is very high. If we had to spend as much on the health of our dogs, we would not keep them. Even so, we spend much larger amounts still on things to make us ill: tobacco, alcohol, sweets, food additives, too much food, air pollutants. Lifestyles are often unsuitable for a healthy body. Many people are forced by economic circumstances to live or work in unhealthy conditions.

If we all accepted that our bodies have been designed to function well in harmony with the natural order, and lived accordingly, there would be much less pain and illness. How much would be left we do not know; until we reach that stage we cannot foresee what problems would remain and whether they would still make it difficult to believe in a good God.

Could God not reduce the intensity of suffering? Why are there not stricter limits on what people have to endure? The usual reply is that limits do exist. Beyond a certain amount of suffering, our nerves cease to function properly, or we go mad, or we die. God could no doubt have created us in such a way that the limitations came into play much sooner, to save us from the deepest suffering. But, whatever limitations there were, the same question could still be asked, and would be just as legitimate, as long as there was any pain at all. If pain is to play any part in our lives, for all we know God has set it at the best possible level of intensity.

Epidemics are a special case. They combine features of illness and natural disasters. Perhaps we can think of them as one of nature's last resorts. Killer epidemics tend to develop when population density is high and resistance to disease is low, usually because of poor nutrition. In these circumstances, they have the effect of restoring nature's balance. They are a cruel way of doing so, but there is a case for arguing that they are only triggered after nature's more benign balancing processes have been overridden.[6]

It is possible to argue, then, that pain and illness are consistent with the theory that God has created us to live pleasant and healthy lives. Within the design of our lives a certain amount of pain is made possible, to provide warning systems. When we do evil we can increase its frequency and intensity, for ourselves and others.

Whether the cause of pain is personal or social, then, our main response should be to accept it as a judgement. Something is wrong, with our personal lifestyles or our national culture or our local community, or a combination, and it needs to be put right. There is also a place for technological cures,[7] but western society tends to overvalue technological intervention into people's bodies, while it refuses to face up to the damage it is doing to a healthy environment. Prevention would be better than cure. Rather than trying to find more and more cures for the illnesses we cause, we should stop causing them. Then we would be able to see the rightful place technology has in keeping our bodies healthy.

Conclusion

The existence of evil has been debated for thousands of years. I have appealed to an explanation which is generally considered a difficult one to defend. It is criticized for many reasons and I cannot produce an adequate defence in one short chapter. Nevertheless I hope to have shown the kinds of responses which can be made. Moral evil becomes possible, together with moral good, at the time when people become aware of freedom. Both good and evil can arise through everyday situations and grow by the force of their own momentum. For widespread good to be possible, widespread evil must also be possible, and since God invites us to share in glories which are so great as to be beyond our imagination, very serious evil has to be possible too.

Although I cannot hope to solve a problem which has defied the best human minds for thousands of years, I do hope that I have shown the kind of response which fits optimistic theory. In the process, I hope to have shown that it has some force. One of its strengths is that it explains its own unpopularity. Because evil causes error, situations of great evil make it harder to believe the truth about God. This effect of evil has many dimensions, but three are worth noting. Firstly, when we ask the question 'Why is there so much evil in the world?' we naturally illustrate it by thinking of particularly great evils. Much of the writing on the subject in the second half of the twentieth century has focused on the holocaust. How could God allow the Nazis to do such evil acts to so many Jews?[8] Massive evils like this really do present a case against God's goodness and make it harder to believe. Although it is a legitimate procedure to theorize in a way which emphasizes events like these, by so doing we stack the odds against a good God.

Secondly, popular newspapers and television programmes provide more than enough evidence that most people actually *like* to hear about, and condemn, evil acts committed by other people. That we like to hear the evil side of other people is part of the evil within ourselves and gives us an unbalanced impression of the relationship between good and evil. We notice more of the evil than the good and therefore find it harder to believe in a good God.

Thirdly, people who condemn evildoers often imagine that they themselves would never have descended to such evil acts if they had been in the same situation. Our self-righteousness deceives us. In order to distance ourselves from evildoers, we demonize them and fail to appreciate the similarities between their behaviour and ours. As Richard Rubenstein remarked in a discussion of the holocaust, 'Until ethical theorists and theologians are prepared to face without sentimentality the kind of action it is possible freely to perpetrate under conditions of utter respectability in an advanced, contemporary society, none of their assertions about the existence of moral norms will have much credibility'.[9] If we were as patient with other people's misdeeds as we are with our own, the moral state of the world would not seem so horrifyingly inexcusable. Alternatively, if we were as impatient with our own misdeeds as we are with other people's, we would spend less time complaining about the world's evil and more time doing something to overcome it.

Thus my account can explain why the problem of evil seems more difficult than it should. I am still a long way from claiming to have solved it. What I do claim is that I am offering the best available hypothesis. In Chapter 9 I described my theory as a hypothesis which must be open to challenge. The existence of evil is its greatest challenge. I cannot hope to have refuted every criticism, but I do believe that it makes more sense of reality than the alternatives. The point becomes clear when we consider what the alternatives are.

I have offered an account of evil which fits optimistic theology. Perhaps there is room for variation in the details, but the general structure is the one which optimism must affirm. God has created a good world, and the freedom to do good or evil is part of its goodness. Nobody is obliged to do evil, but it exists because of the way we humans use our freedom. There is no evil which is inescapable or unredeemable, since it all takes place within a wider context of goodness and harmony. Faith, hope and love become harder in situations of greater evil, but no amount of evil can blot them out altogether. God remains in control, beckoning us towards a glory greater than we have yet imagined.

In other words, evil is a very serious matter, but it is contained within strict limits. Alternative theories of evil can disagree in two ways: either by denying the limits, or by denying the importance of evil. Stronger theories characteristically claim that evil is not encompassed within a fundamental goodness, but is just as much a fundamental part of reality as goodness is. It will follow that evil cannot be explained entirely by human misuse of free will; whatever we do, we are trapped in it. Evil will not be part of an overall plan, but be real tragedy, so that there is nothing good to be said about it.

Weaker theories deny that evil is as real as I have claimed. If we create our own values, evil only exists because we choose to disvalue some of our experiences. If we do not have free will, 'right' and 'wrong' are merely concepts which we have been conditioned to invent.

In other words, those who do not accept an optimistic account of evil are faced with the choice between pessimistic and neutralistic accounts of it. There is no fourth possibility: only these three exist. While recognizing that the optimistic theory has been subjected to much criticism, it is fair to ask whether the alternatives fare any better.

Pessimistic theories affirm the reality of evil, but explain its existence by locating it in some metaphysical reality over and above the evil humans do. This metaphysical reality may be one or more evil gods, or it may be an impersonal feature of 'the way things are'.[10] In this way they avoid having to answer the question 'Why does a good God allow evil?' I argued in Chapter 3 that although they seem to explain the origin of evil more easily, in fact they merely relocate it in the heavens, where it is even harder to explain.

Neutralistic theories explain evil by abolishing it. We create our own values, and evil is just as much a value as good. The way to live without it is simply to evaluate our experiences differently. This account of evil is even less satisfactory than the pessimistic one. However much we try, we cannot convince ourselves that evil is nothing but an invention of our minds. We experience many things as really, objectively, evil, just as we experience many things as really, objectively, good.

Despite the immense difficulties, then, I believe the optimistic account of evil is easier to justify than the alternatives. It is the best one we have. Like any good hypothesis it does not solve every difficulty at a stroke, but it leaves open the possibility that they will be solved in the future as we improve our understanding of the evil which we and other people commit.

Pessimistic and neutralistic theories both claim that what we experience as evil is inescapable. It cannot be entirely overcome. My theory, on the other hand, argues that it can be. There is a right answer to the question 'How can we make the world a better place?' Harmony really is possible, and if we do the right things we really can achieve it. If optimistic theology stands as the best available hypothesis on a theoretical level, on a practical level it is the only one which can offer humanity any hope.

1   *Evil and the God of Love.*
2   Other neutralists believe freedom does exist, but in such a weak form that it cannot justify evil. For example, J. Mackie's argument in 'Evil and omnipotence', M M and R M Adams, Ed, *The Problem of Evil*, pp. 25-37.
3   1 Cor 15:26 indicates that Paul shared this view with the Apocalyptists.
4   A Linzey, *Animal Theology*, Chapter 1.
5   P Badham, *Death-Bed Visions and the Christian Hope.*
6   C Merchant, *The Death of Nature*, pp. 42-50, describes the Black Death in these terms.
7   My account of progress allows a positive role for them. Without some theory of progress, of course, there would be no role for technology in a green theology.
8   See John Roth's contribution to S T Davis, Ed., *Encountering Evil.*
9   S T Davis, Ed., *Encountering Evil*, pp. 11-12.
10 For a modern example, see Griffin's contribution to S T Davis, Ed., *Encountering Evil.*

Chapter 13

Green theology: celebrating God's goodness

I BEGAN THIS BOOK by referring to the range of crises facing our society today. The technical details are often discussed, but technical solutions are not enough. The main problem is that we think about the world in the wrong way, and this makes us do the wrong things to it.

To understand what is wrong with the way we think, we need to notice our presuppositions, and ask why we have them and what the alternatives might be. This takes us into the realms of philosophy and theology. It is our philosophies and theologies which tell us what reality consists of and how to evaluate it. Our evaluations, in turn, give direction to our lives by telling us what we ought to do and not do.

In Parts 1 and 2, I described three ways of evaluating the world. In our society, and in our minds, these three are jumbled up together and produce contradictions. By analysing each one, it is possible to see its strengths and weaknesses, and also to see why compromises are bound to produce contradictions. I argued that pessimism dominates modern western religion, while neutralism dominates the society around it.

In Part 3 I argued for an optimistic account of reality and described it in greater detail. The universe has been created by a God who is self-consistent, omnipotent, omniscient and good. Nothing at all takes place without God's permission. Nothing God does ever goes wrong. Everything which exists fits together within a harmonious scheme, designed so that we and others may find fulfilment in life and realize God's greater purposes.

Within the western tradition there is plenty of support for optimistic theory. Wherever it appears, though, it tends to be joined in uneasy combination with pessimistic or neutralistic theories. My contribution has been not to devise new doctrines but to bring some of the old ones into a coherent scheme and clarify how and why they differ from the alternatives. It is now time to consider my theory as a whole and ask what status it has and what claims can be made for it.

I have offered a *theology*. It is a specific kind of theology, the kind which starts with our ordinary lives and the world around us. By being concerned about what is going on around us, we reflect about it and are led to deeper truths. It is a *natural* theology.

I have also argued the other way. After accepting that there must be a God, and that God must have certain characteristics, I have argued that we ought to understand and evaluate the world in a way which is consistent with that sort of God. It is a *rational* theology.

There is nothing unusual about arguing in both directions at once. Scientists do it all the time, and call it induction. They begin with experiences, construct theories to account for them and from the theories derive conclusions which can be tested. Following the same pattern, I began in Chapter 9 with the elements of reality which we need to trust, and proposed that the best way of accounting for them is by positing a creator God. In subsequent chapters I developed the theory, arguing that if my account of God is correct, the world and our lives should have certain characteristics. I have avoided claiming any special sources of authority; every element is open to challenge and must stand on its own merits.

I have included much *philosophy*. Two questions are at the centre of modern philosophy: what exists? and, what can we know? I have offered theological answers: the world we experience has been designed by God to match our needs, and what we can know about it is what we need to know if we are to fulfil God's purposes for us. Answers of this type are unpopular among western academic philosophers. Many believe that God's existence has been disproved, and of those who do not, many insist that theology cannot answer any of philosophy's problems. I have tried to show that it can.

My analysis has used material from the ancient near east, western Christianity and modern European philosophy. Not only is it a natural theology, but it reflects the problems of a mainly Christian tradition, puzzling over how it should relate to the world around us. Some questions arise about the status of my theory as natural theology, as Christian theology and as this-worldly theology.

Natural theology

Natural theologies are often criticized for being too quick to support the status quo in their own society. Throughout history, time and time again governments have appealed to God's natural order to justify their hold on the reins of power, leaving the poor and oppressed to find consolation in pessimistic theologies. Perhaps the most famous example is the verse from C F Alexander's hymn:

> The rich man in his castle,
> The poor man at the gate,
> He made them high and lowly
> And ordered their estate.[1]

Is my theology one more justification of the established political order? I believe not. Natural theology encourages us to observe what happens naturally and extrapolate from it to the way God has ordered the world. This does not mean that whatever actually happens must be God's will. I have made a sharp distinction between God's creativity and human creativity. God's is always good. The way plants and animals behave in the wild must be the way God made them to behave. We, by contrast, have been given freedom and can use our free will for good or ill. Every human society is affected by the decisions of its members. There is not a single government or constitution which can claim to represent a God-given order free of human vested interests.

Christian theology

I write from within the Christian tradition and have often appealed to Christian theologians, but I have not made exclusive claims for Christianity. I would like to think that Muslims, Buddhists and others could apply my analysis to their own traditions with similar results, though not being a Muslim or Buddhist myself I have no business to do it for them.

To many Christians my theology may not seem Christian at all, because it has shown no interest in the uniqueness of Christ. It does not deny his uniqueness, but it does deny pessimistic theories about it, and there is nothing in it which leads to the conclusion that Jesus of Nazareth has a central place in the divine system.

The uniqueness argument gives Christianity a black-and-white character. It means Christianity is by definition the only true religion. This is what gives it its reputation for intolerance and encourages that sense of arrogant superiority which the victims of evangelism so often complain about. It is proclaimed loudly and often, but in my view it only shows that western Christianity is in a pessimistic phase. New Testament scholars have long recognized that, within New Testament times, the early church changed its attitude to Jesus. According to Matthew, Mark and Luke he did not teach about himself. The first Christians responded to his message rather than speculating about his status. Later, Jesus became the message rather than the messenger. What the uniqueness argument claims is that the later theology, rather than the earlier one, is the only legitimate basis for being a Christian today.

This argument has two serious weaknesses. One is that the New Testament itself does little to support it. True, Paul wrote of Christians being 'in Christ', and John told his readers that Jesus had been sent by the Father, but when they did so they were referring to a real person who had lived quite recently. Their sayings about Christ can hardly have been intended to stand on their own without reference to that man whom first century Christians had heard about, with his arguments, parables and healings. To ignore the content of Jesus' teaching is a strange way of affirming his unique importance.

The other weakness is the obvious logical one. If a group of people believed that the psychologist Sigmund Freud was the unique Son of God and co-creator of the universe, but completely disagreed with his writings, would they be Freudians? We would probably laugh at the idea. A Freudian is a person who thinks Freud was right, or at least stands in Freud's tradition. Similarly, we should expect a Christian to be a person who thinks Christ was right, or at least stands in Christ's tradition.

I suggest, then, that my theory can describe itself as Christian if it stands in the tradition of what Jesus taught. Whether it does is a matter of debate among scholars, as I indicated in Chapter 2. If, in the future, scholars agree that his message was quite different, my theology will have to give up its claim. It will still be *biblical*, as I showed in Chapter 2, and it will still be Christian in the broader sense that it expresses what many Christians have believed throughout Christian history; but it will not express what Jesus taught. So be it. I accept the risk. The truth about reality is more important than defending my right to fit within a definition.

This-worldly theology

My theology begins with the way we experience the world around us and our own lives. It also leads on to beliefs about God, but a God who affirms our world and its value, not one who turns our attention away from it. To affirm this world is not to deny life after death. Rather, life after death gives this life greater value by setting it within a larger context: whatever happens after we die will continue our progress beyond the stages we can now see. God acted wisely in not telling us what life after death is like: we are to live one life at a time, value it and trust God for the rest.

Part of the goodness of the world is the potential to progress towards greater goodness. We have been given freedom to develop into moral goodness, if we so choose. My theology, then, is *ethical*. It is more as well: it believes in the importance of morally significant choices, but it also values our opportunities to be creative even when our choices are not morally significant. It is not only ethical, but more generally a 'hands on' theology. Theologians might refer to it as *engaged* theology.

The kind of theology which is this-worldly and engaged, and welcomes the creativity and fulfilment which life offers, has many supporters today. They are often less interested in institutional churches than pessimists are. Like the eighteenth century natural theologians, they can think of more important things to do than persuading others to attend church services. They are more likely to donate money to a charity than to their local church. In debates about homosexuality or divorce, they are likely to care more about loving relationships than the exact meaning of biblical texts. They are more afraid of nuclear weapons than of hell. They would rather help decorate an elderly woman's house than convert her. They are more likely to be found on the streets campaigning for a political party, than in church praying that whoever wins the election may be guided by Christian principles. As a result, the churches they support are usually short of money and their views are poorly represented by religious hierarchies. Despite this, I believe that by and large it is they who are passing judgement on inward-looking church institutions, not the other way round.

Green theology

Socially concerned theologies usually end up being identified with a particular cultural or political movement. They 'mix religion with politics'. There is nothing surprising in this: if the same logic which produces one also produces the other, they will naturally fit. My theology is no exception; because it argues for particular attitudes to reality, it affirms particular programmes of action. Which parts of our culture come closest to it?

It is not a 'back to nature' theology. It does not oppose everything new and artificial, or seek to rediscover an original rural idyll. It values human creativity and looks forward to continued progress in it. Nor does it despise the past and the natural: it affirms their value and expects the new and artificial to build on them. Because it affirms a nature which is dynamic, to be for nature does not mean being against history, or culture, or technology, or change. It sees all these other things, not as opposed to nature, but as part of it. By aiming to bring them together in harmony, it sets a standard by which to judge whether we are doing the right things or the wrong things.

By taking this view, it opposes many of the attitudes which dominate modern society. By affirming the value of nature, it opposes all programmes of suppressing it or replacing it with an artificial alternative. It opposes the idea that nature only has value as a resource for human use. As I argued in Chapter 11, the political implications are sharp. The mechanistic paradigm, with its programme of imposing its own regime on the natural order, treating everything natural as a valueless and free resource until somebody puts a price on it, 'developing' parts of the world which are 'undeveloped' and measuring success in terms of ever-increasing production and consumption, has provided the agenda for political debate today right across the left-right spectrum. The disagreements between left and right are disagreements about the most efficient way to do the wrong things.

Despite all this, it is not against modern western culture as a whole. There is much good in it too. It would be a mistake to try to re-create the Middle Ages. I have painted a more moderate picture: progress often involves going two steps forward and one step back, and when a particular change turns out to have been a backward step we review directions and decide what to do next.

The movement in western culture today which comes closest to my critique is, of course, the green movement. This is hardly surprising, in view of my determination to value nature positively. I think my theology can justifiably call itself 'green theology'.

The most popular expressions of green concern are, of course, very superficial. Many people think that 'being green' goes no deeper than a list of practical activities like taking paper and glass to recycling skips. My interest is in deeper green challenges to modern society, which in many ways are similar to mine. The main points of contact are these:

(i) Greens respect the ecosystem as valuable in its own right, not merely as a means to satisfying human desires. What is of most value is given, not created by human labour. Because capitalism and socialism calculate value only in relation to human desires and labour, green politicians characteristically treat these political theories as two sides of the same coin, just as I have done.

(ii) Greens treat human life as being rightfully involved in the natural order, in a natural manner. Human bodies are designed to function properly within their natural setting. All animals use nature, and that includes adapting the immediate environment; but if we set out to reshape it or dominate it, we shall do harm to ourselves, let alone other forms of life. True human value, purpose and morality are rooted in, and developed by, our physical life as part of the ecosystem. Green theories of health care encourage people to accept responsibility for their bodies. When they are ill, the first thing to do is to look for the root causes rather than suppressing symptoms. Usually this means trying changes in diet and lifestyle before resorting to artificial drugs.

(iii) To greens, human minds are designed to serve human bodies in their natural setting. There is no need for any fundamental tension between mind and body, or soul and body. Intellect, spirit and culture develop within our natural setting, not outside it. Green educational theories expect that the interests which people develop naturally are a good guide to what they need to learn at each stage of life.

The term 'green theology' sounds analogous to a range of greeneries: green consumerism, green politics, green philosophy. By analogy with these, it could refer to one of many elements of green thought, namely the one which thinks about theological questions. This is not what I mean by it. The kind of theology I have proposed is not the kind which lives in a spiritual world of its own. It is the kind which describes the whole of reality. It therefore claims a wider significance. To those who are committed to the ideas of the green movement, it offers a way to make sense of the whole green agenda, by providing a single, unifying justification for its vast variety of concerns.

It is much needed. One of the ways the green movement contrasts with modern society is by respecting the spiritual dimension to everything, not putting spirituality to one side while discussing material things. The green movement therefore recognizes that it needs a spirituality to underpin its activities. In Europe and North America, many of the most committed greens, hardly surprisingly, react strongly against mainstream religions. The result is that they tend to look for spiritual nourishment in a ragbag of ideas and traditions which have nothing in common with each other except that they are 'alternative'. Yoga, Buddhism, astrology, magic, witchcraft, old Celtic paganism, meditation techniques and a wide range of therapies, are often to be found advertized on the same leaflet or offered at the same conference. The absence of a unifying justification tends to make the New Age movement individualistic; people choose what appeals to them personally, without being able to justify their choices to other people. The result is a range of single issue interest groups which are not good at combining forces. My theology explains how taking bottles to the bottle bank, signing petitions to save whales, and choosing not to have a car, fit together within a consistent theory of reality.

If green theology can make an important contribution to the green movement, I believe it can make an equally important contribution to theology. Again, 'green theology' can mean two things. Theologians sprout theologies: process theology, liberation theology, feminist theology. In their simpler meaning, they refer to theological reflection on a specific subject matter. In their more complex meaning, the specific subject produces a way of doing theology in general. Over the last generation, feminist theology has successfully moved from the simpler to the more complex. At first most academic theologians treated it as theology about feminist issues, or even theology about women. Over time the feminist case was accepted and it is now widely recognized that feminists have distinctive things to say on most theological issues, not just matters of gender. I am making the same claim for green theology. Although it is inspired by the natural environment, it is not primarily about the environment. Instead, it reflects on the whole range of theological issues and offers an approach to them which is derived from the conviction that we live in a good world created by a good God.

Green theology has implications for a wide range of current issues. In Chapter 11, I suggested some methods which might characterize my approach. Green theorists on a wide range of issues — politics, philosophy, economics, health, work, education, sex and many others — have already done a great deal of the work. This is not to say that I agree with the dominant green view on all these issues, but by and large the green way of approaching them will be along the same lines as mine.

It may seem odd to claim that one theory can inform a cultural movement and a theological tradition at the same time. Part of my argument has been that theology should never have allowed itself to be parked on a cul-de-sac, let alone left there for so long. Rightly understood, theology is relevant to ordinary people in their ordinary lives. It helps us to see what we ought to be doing.

By being relevant, it makes demands. It challenges the whole of our society to change its priorities. A growing number of people are already concerned about the mess we are making of the world, and wondering what can be done about it. I hope this book can help. I hope to have shown that there is a coherent account of reality which can justify our concern and show where we should go from here.

When we think of the world as evil, we set ourselves against it and become its enemies. We turn away from it and look elsewhere for fulfilment. When we think of it as valueless, we set ourselves above it and become its oppressors. We make ourselves the masters of it and when we look to it for fulfilment we find it has nothing to offer us because we have destroyed it. When we think of it as good, we set ourselves inside it and become its friends. We make our home in it and learn to delight in it. We take it as our partner, learn its steps and dance to its tune.

Fulfilment comes through living with the grain of nature, not against it. We delight in its diversity, creativity, interdependence, inclusiveness and balance, and imitate them in our own ways. As we use what nature has provided, we allow it to use us in turn, giving back to the earth only what can be used by other forms of life. As we seek to live within its limits, in a harmonious balance with the other forces of nature, we protect the balance for their sakes as well as ours. As we care for it and value it, it reveals to us ever greater value. Through it, we discover the value of our own bodies, human society and culture, and God's goodness beckoning us to ever greater glory.

It is precisely the God-given order of nature — the living and dying of plants, the movements and lifestyles of animals, the regularities and surprises in the weather, the atmosphere's many-layered task of giving us the right air, and among all these the observations, calculations, pleasures and desires of humans — it is all these which show us how we were designed to live and flourish. God could have put us somewhere else. But we have been put in this world, neighbours of these animals, able to eat these plants, breathe this air, reflect on these events, build our houses with these stones, and discover value in all these things and their Creator, so that these bodies of ours may love and celebrate.

1   *Ancient and Modern* 573.

Glossary

Animism. The belief that divine spirits are closely related to aspects of the environment.

Apocalyptic. A Jewish movement, dating roughly from the middle of the second century BC and suppressed by the Rabbinic movement at the end of the first century AD. It continued to be influential among Christians. Its best known examples are the biblical books of Daniel and Revelation.

Behaviourism. A school of psychology which concentrates on observable and measurable behaviour, leaving out mental processes. Leading behaviourists have usually denied that the mind has any significance apart from being a by-product of physical events.

Coherence theory. The theory that knowledge is not derived from self-evident and self-justifying foundations, but from a variety of beliefs which support each other, none of which is certain.

Constructivism. A form of non-realism, which believes that reality is in some way constructed by human minds.

Cosmology. The study of the nature and origin of the universe. The word is used both in theology, where it relates to the creative acts of God or the gods, and in physics where it relates to the physical processes by which the universe has been formed.

Demiurge. Greek word for a craftsman or maker. Following Plato, it is used for a divine creator of the universe whose powers were limited.

Determinism. The theory that each event is the inevitable result of prior causes. It denies freedom.

Dualism. The theory that the universe is constituted out of two different substances. There are different types of dualism, depending on what the principles are believed to be.

Emergence. The theory that not all the processes studied by scientists can be reduced to the processes of physics. When processes at one level reach a certain complexity, a new process emerges at a 'higher' level and needs another science to examine how it functions.

Empiricism. The theory that knowledge is derived from the experiences of the five senses. Usually contrasted with 'rationalism' and 'idealism'.

Eschatology. A theological term, describing the study of theories about what will happen at the end of history.

Form. According to Plato there exists a set of eternal and unchanging realities in the heavenly realm. The word he used is translated into English either as 'forms' or 'ideas'. Every material thing in the world is an imperfect expression of its form. Plato's disciple Aristotle did not believe that forms existed independently of their material expressions.

Foundationalism. The theory that knowledge is derived from a set of self-evident and self-justifying foundations.

Idealism. There have been various idealist theories. What they have in common is that the mind creates reality. Kant believed that certain judgements which people make are provided by the mind. Many idealists today believe that material reality is constructed by the mind.

Logical positivism. A philosophical movement developed in the 1920s, based on the Verification Principle, which states that the meaning of a statement is its method of verification.

Mechanistic paradigm. A theory of reality which describes the universe as like a machine, operating deterministically according to sequences of cause and effect, all its processes accessible to human observation.

Modern. The modern period of European history is usually dated from the seventeenth century, though sometimes from the Renaissance. In this book I have used it in the former sense.

Monism. The theory that the universe is constituted out of one substance, usually either matter or mind.

Monotheism. The theory that there is one, and only one, God.

Myth. I have used this word in its technical sense, to mean a story about God or the gods. Usually it illustrates a feature of life. It does not mean that the story is untrue.

Neutralism. I am using this word, in contrast to 'optimism' and 'pessimism', to refer to the theory that the world has no objective value.

Objective. I have used the word in its modern philosophical sense, to refer to that which is external to the human mind and exists independently of it. Opposite of 'subjective'.

Omnipotence. Possessing all power. Some theologies attribute it to God. Generally it is not taken to mean the ability to do the logically impossible.

Omniscience. Possessing all knowledge. Some theologies attribute it to God.

Optimism. I am using this word, in contrast to 'pessimism' and 'neutralism', to refer to the theory that the world has a positive objective value.

P. The 'Priestly writers' who edited parts of the Old Testament, including Genesis, around the fifth century BC.

Pantheon. A set of gods who are believed to live in relationship with each other.

Paradigm. A person's general theoretical framework, within which they understand the nature of reality. Sometimes referred to as a 'world-view'.

Pessimism. I am using this word, in contrast to 'neutralism' and 'optimism', to refer to the theory that the world contains inescapable objective evil.

Polytheism. The theory that there is more than one god.

Postmodern. Covers various reactions against modernism which have developed in the twentieth century. This book has been concerned with some of the issues in philosophy.

Rationalism. The theory that knowledge is derived from the exercise of reason. Usually contrasted with 'empiricism'.

Realism. To be a realist about a thing, or a quality, or a fact, is to believe that it exists independently of whether the human mind perceives it or believes it.

Reductionism. The theory that it is possible to get a complete understanding of a complex whole by splitting it into its component parts and learning about each part.

Solipsism. The belief that 'I, and only I, exist and have a mind'.

Subjective. That which exists in, or is derived from, the human mind, or expresses its contents.

Theodicy. The study of why a good creator God allows evil.

Bibliography

Adam, D, *The Edge of Glory*, London: Triangle, SPCK, 1985.

Adams, M M and R M, Ed, *The Problem of Evil*, Oxford: OUP, 1990.

Allchin, A M, *Participation in God: A Forgotten Strand in Anglican Tradition*, London: DLT, 1988.

Almond, B and Hill, D, *Applied Philosophy: Morals and Metaphysics in Contemporary Debate*, London: Routledge, 1991.

Ambler, R, 'Befriending the Earth: A Theological Challenge', London: *Friends Quarterly*, Jan 1990, pp. 7-17.

Ambler, R, *Global Theology: The Meaning of Faith in the Present World Crisis*, London: SCM, 1990.

Anderson, B W, *The Living World of the Old Testament*, London: Longmans, 1967.

Anderson, B W, Ed, *Creation in the Old Testament*, London: SPCK, 1984.

Aristotle, *Ethics*, trans J A K Thomson, London: Penguin, 1953.

Armstrong, D M, *What Is a Law of Nature?*, Cambridge: CUP, 1983.

Atkinson, D, *The Values of Science*, Nottingham: Grove, 1980.

Attfield, R, *The Ethics of Environmental Concern*, London: University of Georgia Press, Second Edition 1991.

Augustine , *City of God: trans. H. Bettenson*, London: Penguin, 1972.

Ayer, A J, *Language, Truth and Logic*, London: Penguin, 1990.

Bacon, F, *Novum Organum: Trans & Ed. P Urbach & J Gibson*, Chicago: Open Court, 1994.

Badham, P, 'Death-Bed Visions and the Christian Hope', *Theology*, July 1980, pp. 270-275.

Bainton, R H, *Here I Stand: A Life of Martin Luther*, New York: Mentor, 1950.

Banton, M, *Race Relations*, London: Tavistock Publications, 1964.

Barr, J, *Biblical Faith and Natural Theology*, Oxford: Clarendon, 1993.

Barr, J, *The Garden of Eden and the Hope of Immortality*, London: SCM, 1992.

Bauman, Z, *Postmodern Ethics*, Oxford: Blackwell, 1993.

Berger , P L and Luckmann, T, *The Social Construction of Reality*, London: Penguin, 1971.

Bettenson, H, *Documents of the Christian Church*, Oxford: OUP, 1963.

Bhaskar, R, *Reclaiming Reality: A Critical Introduction to Contemporary Philosophy*, London: Verso, 1989.

Birch, C, *Liberating Life: Contemporary Approaches to Ecological Theology*, New York: Orbis, 1990.

Black, J, *The Dominion of Man: The Search for Ecological Responsibility*, Edinburgh: EUP, 1970.

Bonner, G, *St. Augustine of Hippo*, Norwich: Canterbury Press, 1986.

Bornkamm, G, *Jesus of Nazareth*, London: Hodder & Stoughton, 1960.

Boyce, M, *Zoroastrians: Their Religious Beliefs and Practices*, London: RKP, 1979.

Boyd, R, Gasper, P & Trout, J D, Eds, R, *The Philosophy of Science*, Massachusetts: MIT, 1992.

Bradley, I, *God is Green: Christianity and the Environment*, London: DLT, 1990.

Brandt, R B, *Morality, Utilitarianism and Rights*, Cambridge: CUP, 1992.

Brink, D O, *Moral Realism and the Foundations of Ethics*, Cambridge: CUP, 1989.

Brown, P, *Augustine of Hippo: A Biography*, London: Faber and Faber, 1967.

Brown, L R, Ed, *State of the World 1994*, London: Earthscan, 1994.

Burrows A J M and Newbury, P, *Into the 21st Century: A Handbook for a Sustainable Future*, London: Adamantine, 1991.

Bury, J B, *The Idea of Progress: An Inquiry Into its Growth and Origin*, New York: Dover, 1932.

Capra, F, *The Turning Point: Science, Society and the Rising Culture*, London: Pelican, Flamingo, 1983.

Chadwick, H, *The Early Church*, London: Pelican, 1967.

Chadwick, O, *The Reformation*, London: Pelican, Penguin, 1964.

Chadwick, O, *The Victorian Church*, London: SCM, 1970.

Charlesworth, J H, *Jesus Within Judaism*, London: SPCK, 1990.

Chilton, B and McDonald, J I H, *Jesus and the Ethics of the Kingdom*, London: SPCK, 1987.

Chilton, B, *The Temple of Jesus: His Sacrificial Programme Within a Cultural History of Sacrifice*, Pennsylvania: Pennsylvania State University, 1992.

Chilton, B, Ed, *The Kingdom of God*, London: SPCK, 1984.

Church of England, Board for Social Responsibility, *Our Responsibility for the Living Environment*, London: CHP, 1986.

Church of Scotland, Society, Religion and Technology Project, *While the Earth Endures: A Report on the Theological and Ethical Considerations of Responsible Land Use*, Edinburgh: Quorum Press, 1986.

Cobb, J B and Griffin, D R, *Process Theology: an introductory exposition*, Belfast: Christian Journals Ltd, 1977.

Collins, J J, *The Apocalyptic Imagination*, New York: Crossroad, 1984.

Copleston, F, *History of Philosophy Volume 1*, London: Burns Oates, 1947.

Copleston, F, *History of Philosophy Volume 8: Bentham to Russell*, London: Burns & Oates, 1966.

Cosslett, T, Ed, *Science and Religion in the Nineteenth Century*, Cambridge: CUP, 1984.

Cottingham, J, *The Rationalists*, Oxford: OUP, 1988.

Cragg, G R, *The Church and the Age of Reason 1648-1789*, London: Pelican, Penguin, 1972.

Darwin, C, *The Origin of Species*, London: Penguin, 1984.

Davies, P, *The Mind of God: Science and the Search for Ultimate Meaning*, London: Penguin, 1992.

Davis, S T, *Encountering Evil*, Edinburgh: T & T Clark, 1981.

Descartes, R, *Discourse on Method and the Meditations: trans F E Sutcliffe*, London: Penguin, 1968.

Dobson, A, *Green Political Thought*, London: Routledge, 1995.

Dodd, C H, *The Parables of the Kingdom*, Glasgow: Collins, 1961.

Dowell, G, *Enjoying the World: The Rediscovery of Thomas Traherne*, London: Mowbray, 1990.

Dunn, J, *Unity and Diversity in the New Testament: An Inquiry into the Character* of *Earliest Christianity*, London: SCM, Second Edition 1990.

Dunn, J, Urmson, J O and Ayer, A J, *The British Empiricists*, Oxford: OUP, 1992.

Eliade, M, *A History of Religious Ideas, Volume 1: From the Stone Age to the Eleusinian Mysteries*, Chicago: University of Chicago Press, 1978.

Elliot, R, *Environmental Ethics*, Oxford: OUP, 1995.

Evans, G R, et al, *The Science of Theology*, Basingstoke: Marshall Pickering, 1986.

Evans, G R, *Augustine on Evil*, Cambridge: CUP, 1982.

Evans, G R, *Philosophy and Theology in the Middle Ages*, London: Routledge, 1993.

Ferré, Frederick, *Hellfire and Lightning Rods: Liberating Science, Technology and Religion*, Maryknoll, New York: Orbis, 1993.

Feyerabend, P, *Against Method: Outline of an Anarchistic Theory of Knowledge*, London: NLB, 1975.

Fishkin, J S, *Beyond Subjective Morality: Ethical Reasoning and Political Philosophy*, Yale: Yale UP, 1984.

Flew, A and MacIntyre, A, *New Essays in Philosophical Theology*, London: SCM, 1955.

Fox, R L, *Pagans And Christians*, London: Viking, Penguin, 1986.

Fuller, R H, *The Foundations of New Testament Christology*, London: Fontana, Collins, 1965.

Gillispie, C C, *Genesis and Geology*, Harvard: Harper Torchbooks, Harvard, 1959.

Gimpel, J, *The Medieval Machine*, London: Futura, 1979.

Glacken, C J., *Traces on the Rhodian Shore: Nature and Culture in Western Thought from Ancient Times to the End of the Eighteenth Century*, Berkeley & Los Angeles: University of California Press, 1967.

Goldman, A H, *Moral Knowledge: The Problems of Philosophy, Their Past and Present*, London: Routledge, 1988.

Graham, G, *Philosophy of Mind: An Introduction*, Oxford: Blackwell, 1993.

Grant, R, *Gods and the One God: Christian Theology in the Graeco-Roman World*, London: SPCK, 1986.

Gregorios, P, *The Human Presence: An Orthodox View of Nature*, Madras: Christian Literature Society, 1980.

Hampshire, S, *Spinoza*, London: Pelican, 1962.

Hampshire, Ed, S, *Public and Private Morality*, Cambridge: CUP, 1978.

Hanfling, O, *Essential Readings in Logical Positivism*, Oxford: Blackwell, 1981.

Happold, F C, *Mysticism: A Study and An Anthology*, London: Pelican, 1988.

Hawking, S, *A Brief History of Time: From the Big Bang to Black Holes*, London: Bantam, 1988.

Hendry, G S, *Theology of Nature*, Philadelphia: Westminster Press, 1980.

Hick, J, *Evil and the God of Love*, London: Collins Fontana, 1974.

Honderich, T and Burnyeat, M, Ed, *Philosophy As It Is*, London: Pelican, 1979.

Honderich, T, *How Free Are You?: The Determinism Problem*, Oxford: OUP, 1993.

Honderich, T, Ed, *Morality and Objectivity*, London: RKP, 1985.

Hookway, C, *Scepticism*, London: Routledge, 1990.

Hudson, W D, *Modern Moral Philosophy*, London: Macmillan, Second Edition 1983.

Hume, D, *Enquiries Concerning Human Understanding and Concerning the*

Principles of Morals, Oxford: OUP, 11th impression 1990.

Hunsinger, G, *How to Read Karl Barth: The Shape of His Theology*, Oxford: OUP, 1991.

Irenaeus, *Against the Heresies: Ed. A Roberts*, Edinburgh: T & T Clark, 1869.

Jacquette, Dale, *Philosophy of Mind*, Englewood Cliffs, New Jersey: Prentice Hall, 1994.

Jaki, S L, *The Purpose of It All*, Edinburgh: Scottish Academic Press, 1990.

Jeremias, J, *Rediscovering the Parables*, London: SCM, 1966.

Jeremias, J, *The Sermon on the Mount*, London: Athlone, 1961.

Johnson, R A, Ed, *Natural Science and Religion*, Englewood Cliffs, New Jersey: Prentice Hall, 1990.

Jonas, H, *The Gnostic Religion: The Message of the Alien God and the Beginnings of Christianity*, London: Routledge, 2nd Edition 1992.

Kaiser, C, *Creation and the History of Science*, London: Marshall Pickering, 1991.

Kelly, J N D, *Early Christian Doctrines*, London: Adam and Charles Black, 4th Edition 1968.

Kemp, D D, *Global Environmental Issues: A Climatological Approach*, London: Routledge, 1990.

Kenny, A, *The Metaphysics of Mind*, Oxford: OUP, 1989.

Kent, J, *The End of the Line?: The Development of Christian Theology in the Last Two Centuries*, London: SCM, 1982.

Körner, S, *Kant*, London: Penguin, 1990.

Kotwahl, F and Boyd, J, *A Guide to the Zoroastrian Religion*, Chico, California: Scholars Press, 1982.

Lee, P J, *Against the Protestant Gnostics*, Oxford: OUP, 1987.

Leff, G, *Medieval Thought: from St Augustine to Ockham*, London: Penguin, 1958.

Lehrer, K, *Theory of Knowledge*, London: Routledge, 1990.

Linzey, A, *Animal Theology*, London: SCM, 1994.

Locke, J, *An Essay Concerning Human Understanding. Ed A. D. Woozley.*, London: Collins, 1964.

MacIntyre, A, *After Virtue: A Study in Moral Theory*, London: Duckworth, Second Edition 1985.

MacIntyre, A, *Whose Justice? Which Rationality?*, Indiana: Notre Dame Press, 1988.

MacIntyre, A, *Three Rival Versions of Moral Enquiry*, London: Duckworth, 1990.

Mackie, J L, *Ethics: Inventing Right and Wrong*, London: Penguin, 1977.

Macquarrie, J, *Principles of Christian Theology*, London: SCM, 1966.

Mantzaridis, G I, *The Deification of Man: St Gregory Palamas and the Orthodox Tradition*, New York: St. Vladimir's Seminary Press, 1984.

Markus, R, *The End of Ancient Christianity*, Cambridge: CUP, 1991.

Mason, P, *Race Relations*, London: OUP, 1970.

Matthews Ed., M R, *The Scientific Background to Modern Philosophy: Selected Readings*, Cambridge: Hackett, 1989.

Merchant, C, *The Death of Nature: Women, Ecology and the Scientific Revolution*, San Francisco: HarperCollins, 1980.

Miller, R, *Arguments Against Secular Culture*, London: SCM, 1995.

Milne, J, *Man and Creation in the Light of Christian Platonism*, London: Friends of the Centre, 1992.

Minns, D, *Irenaeus*, London: Geoffrey Chapman, 1994.

Moberly, W, *Ethics of Punishment*, London: Faber & Faber, 1968.

Moltmann, J, *God in Creation: An Ecological Doctrine of Creation*, London: SCM, 1985.

Monro, D H, Ed, *A Guide to the British Moralists*, London: Collins, 1972.

Montefiore, H, Ed, *Man and Nature*, London: Collins, 1975.

Moule, C F D, *Man and Nature in the Old Testament*, Philadelphia: Facet, Fortress, 1967.

Murphy, J G, *Kant: The Philosophy of Right*, London: Macmillan, 1970.

Murphy, N, *Theology in the Age of Scientific Reasoning*, Ithaca & London: Cornell University Press, 1990.

Murray, R, *The Cosmic Covenant*, London: Sheed & Ward, 1992.

Nagel, Thomas, *The View From Nowhere*, Oxford: OUP, 1986.

Nebelsick, H, *Theology and Science in Mutual Modification*, Belfast: Christian Journals Ltd., 1981.

Niebuhr, H R, *Christ and Culture*, New York: Harper, 1956.

Nisbet, R, *History of the Idea of Progress*, London: Heinemann, 1980.

Northcott, M, *The Environment and Christian Ethics*, Cambridge: CUP, 1996.

O'Brien, J and Major, W, *In the Beginning: Creation Myths from Ancient Mesopotamia, Israel and Greece*, Chico, California: Scholars Press, 1982.

O'Hear, A, *An Introduction to the Philosophy of Science*, Oxford: Clarendon, 1989.

Oates, J, *Babylon*, London: Thames & Hudson, 1979.

Osborn, E, *The Emergence of Christian Theology*, Cambridge: CUP, 1993.

Pagels, E, *The Gnostic Gospels*, London: Weidenfeld & Nicolson, 1979.

Pagels, E, *Adam, Eve and the Serpent*, London: Penguin, 1990.

Papineau, D, *Reality and Representation*, Oxford: Blackwell, 1987.

Passmore, J, *Man's Responsibility for Nature*, London: Duckworth, 1974.

Peacocke, A R, *Creation and the World of Science*, Oxford: Clarendon, 1979.

Perkins, P, *Gnosticism and the New Testament*, Minneapolis: Fortress, 1993.

Perkins, P, *The Gnostic Dialogue: The Early Church and the Crisis of Gnosticism*, New York: Paulist, 1980.

Perrin, N, *The Kingdom of God in the Teaching of Jesus*, London: SCM, 1963.

Pétrement, S, *A Separate God*, 1995.

Phoebus Publishing Company & Octopus Books, , *Encyclopedia of World Mythology*, London: BPC Publishing Ltd, 1975.

Pickering, K T and Owen, L A, *An Introduction to Global Environmental Issues*, London & New York: Routledge, 1994.

Pippin, R B, *Modernism as a Philosophical Problem*, Oxford: Blackwell, 1991.

Plato, *Timaeus: trans. H D P Lee*, London: Penguin, 1971.

Polanyi, M, *Personal Knowledge: Towards a Post-Critical Philosophy*, London: RKP, 1958.

Polkinghorne, J, *One World: The Encounter of Science and Theology*, London: SPCK, 1986.

Polkinghorne, J, *Reason and Reality: The Relationship Between Science and Theology*, London: SPCK, 1991.

Polkinghorne, J, *Science and Creation: The Search for Understanding*, London: SPCK, 1988.

Polkinghorne, J, *Science and Providence: God's Interaction with the World*, London: SPCK, 1989.

Raz, J, *The Morality of Freedom*, Oxford: Clarendon, 1986.

Ringgren, H, *Israelite Religion*, London: SPCK, 1966.

Ringgren, H, *Religions of the Ancient Near East*, London: SPCK, 1976.

Robinson, J M, Ed, *The Nag Hammadi Library*, New York: E J Brill, 3rd Edition 1988.

Rogerson, J, *Genesis 1-11*, Sheffield: JSOT, 1994.

Rorty, R, *Philosophy and the Mirror of Nature*, Princeton: Princeton University Press, 1979.

Rudolph, K, *Gnosis*, Edinburgh: T & T Clark, 1983.

Russell, D S, *The Method and Message of Jewish Apocalyptic*, London: SPCK, 1971.

Rust, E C, *Nature and Man in Biblical Thought*, London: Lutterworth, 1953.

Sandars, N K, trans, *The Epic of Gilgamesh*, London: Penguin, 1964.

Sanders, E P, *Jesus and Judaism*, London: SCM, 1985.

Santmire, P, *The Travail of Nature: The Ambiguous Ecological Promise of Christian Theology*, Philadelphia: Fortress, 1985.

Saw, R L, *Leibniz*, London: Pelican, 1954.

Schilling, H K, *The New Consciousness in Science And Religion*, London: SCM, 1973.

Schlipp, P A, Ed, *The Philosophy of Karl Popper*, La Salle, Illinois: Northwestern University & Southern Illinois University, 1974.

Schumacher, E L, *A Guide for the Perplexed*, London: Abacus, 1977.

Sheldrake, R, *The Rebirth of Nature: The Greening of Science and God*, London: Rider, 1990.

Sherrard, P, *Human Image, World Image: The Death and Resurrection of Sacred Cosmology*, Ipswich: Golgonooza, 1992.

Sherrard, P, *The Rape of Man And Nature: An Enquiry into the Origins & Consequences of Modern Science*, Ipswich: Golgonooza, 1987.

Skinner, B F, *Beyond Freedom and Dignity*, London: Penguin, 1971.

Smith, M, *Palestinian Parties and Politics That Shaped the Old Testament*, London: SCM, 1971.

Southern, R W, *Western Society And The Church in the Middle Ages*, London: Penguin, 1970.

Stevenson, C L, *Ethics and Language*, Yale: Yale University Press, 1944.

Swinburne, R, *The Evolution of the Soul*, Oxford: Clarendon, 1986.

Taylor, C, *Sources of the Self: The Making of the Modern Identity*, Cambridge: CUP, 1989.

Thiessen, G, *The Miracle Stories of the Early Christian Tradition*, Edinburgh: T & T Clark, 1983.

Thomas, K, *Man and the Natural World: Changing Attitudes in England 1500-1800*, London: Penguin, 1983.

Thomas, K, *Religion and the Decline of Magic*, London: Penguin, Peregrine, 1971.

Trigg, J W, *Origen: The Bible and Philosophy in the Third-Century Church*, London: SCM, 1983.

Trigg, R, *Reality at Risk: A Defence of Realism in Philosophy and the Sciences*, Sussex: Harvester, 1980.

Tsirpanlis, C N, *Introduction to Eastern Patristic Thought And Orthodox Theology*, Collegeville, Minnesota: Liturgical Press, 1991.

Vermes, G, *Jesus and the World of Judaism*, London: SCM, 1983.

Vermes, G, *Jesus the Jew*, London: SCM, 1983.

Vesey, G, Ed, *The Philosophy in Christianity*, Cambridge: CUP, 1989.

Vidler, A R, *The Church in an Age of Revolution*, London: Penguin, 1961.

von Campenhausen, H, *The Formation of the Christian Bible*, London: A & C Black, 1972.

Von Rad, G, *Old Testament Theology*, London: SCM, 1975.

Waldron, J, Ed, *Theories of Rights*, Oxford: OUP, 1984.

Walker, B, *Gnosticism: Its History and Influence*, Wellingborough: Aquarian, 1983.

Ward, B, *Only One Earth: The Care and Maintenance of a Small Planet*, London: Penguin, 1972.

Ward, B, *Progress for a Small Planet*, London: Penguin, 1979.

Ward, K, *Rational Theology And the Creativity of God*, Oxford: Blackwell, 1982.

Weber, L, et al, *Theology of the Land*, Collegeville, Minnesota: Liturgical Press, 1987.

Westermann, C, *Creation*, London: SPCK, 1974.

Westermann, C, *Genesis 1-11*, London: SPCK, 1984.

Whiteley, D E H, *The Theology of St. Paul*, Oxford: Blackwell, 1972.

Wilkinson, L, Ed, *Earthkeeping: Christian Stewardship of Natural Resources*, Grand Rapids, Michigan: Eerdmans, 1980.

Wright, C, *Realism, Meaning and Truth*, Oxford: Blackwell, 1987.

Young, N, *Creator, Creation and Faith*, London: Collins, 1976.

Index